PREEMPLOYMENT HONESTY TESTING

AMERICAN SOCIETY FOR INDUSTRIAL SECURITY
1625 PRINCE STREET
ALEXANDRIA, VA 22314
(703) 519-6200

PREEMPLOYMENT HONESTY TESTING

Current Research and Future Directions

Edited by
JOHN W. JONES

Q

QUORUM BOOKS
NEW YORK • WESTPORT, CONNECTICUT • LONDON

Library of Congress Cataloging-in-Publication Data

Preemployment honesty testing : current research and future directions
/ edited by John W. Jones.
   p. cm.
  Includes index.
  ISBN 0–89930–620–9 (alk. paper)
  1. Employee selection. 2. Honesty—Testing. 3. Employment tests.
I. Jones, John W. (John Walter), 1953–
HF5549.5.S38P74   1991
658.3'1125—dc20   90–45145

British Library Cataloguing in Publication Data is available.

Library of Congress Catalog Card Number: 90–45145
ISBN: 0–89930–620–9

First published in 1991

Quorum Books, 88 Post Road West, Westport, CT 06881
An imprint of Greenwood Publishing Group, Inc.

Printed in the United States of America

The paper used in this book complies with the
Permanent Paper Standard issued by the National
Information Standards Organization (Z39.48–1984).

10 9 8 7 6 5 4 3 2 1

Copyright Acknowledgment

Grateful acknowledgment is given for permission to reprint the articles
that appear as chapters 2, 8, 11, and 18 from the *Journal of Business and
Psychology*, 1990, 1989, 1988, and 1990, respectively. Reprinted with the
permission of Human Sciences Press, Inc.

Contents

Figures

Tables

Preface

This book presents some of the most current research on preemployment honesty tests, psychological inventories designed to predict employee theft and other counterproductivity (e.g., illicit drug use, vandalism, accidents). The use of paper-and-pencil honesty tests, also referred to as integrity tests, to select a dependable work force spans more than 40 years. Comprehensive reviews of integrity testing practices are available (O'Bannon, Goldinger & Appleby, 1989; Sackett, Burris & Callahan, 1989). This book reviews some of the major trends in integrity testing practices.

More research that clearly documents the incidents of employee theft and other counterproductivity is being conducted. For example, although the exact amount of employee theft needs to be confirmed through basic applied research, both security researchers and human resource professionals widely accept the existence of costly amounts of worker theft. Table 1 summarizes some of the major base-rate research, which clearly documents the business necessity of preemployment honesty tests.

Companies interested in purchasing preemployment honesty tests seek to control more than just employee theft. The trend is toward the use of multidimensional integrity test batteries over single-purpose honesty tests. Single-purpose tests measure only job applicants' propensity for theft of company cash, merchandise, property, and information. Multidimensional integrity test batteries typically contain an honesty scale but also test scales that help companies control

Table 1
Prevalence of Employee Theft

Hollinger and Clark (1983) surveyed thousands of employees and found
that on average, the percentage of retail, hospital, and manufacturing
employees admitting to theft was 42%, 32%, and 26%, respectively.

Slora (1989) surveyed hundreds of fast food and supermarket employees
and found that 60% of fast food employees and 43% of supermarket workers
admitted to stealing company cash and property.

Carey (1989) reported an increase in internal bank fraud and
embezzlement from approximately $165 million in 1981 to approximately
$534 million in 1987.

Arthur Young, Inc. (1988) documented a 5% increase in the retail
industry's shrinkage rates from 1982 to 1987, representing approximately
$1.8 billion in losses due to the increase alone.

illicit drug use, reduce accidents, control damage and waste, and lower turnover
rates.

More industry-specific test batteries are being published and marketed to a
wide variety of industries, including banking, service stations, drug stores, and
police and military organizations. These batteries include an honesty scale and
also a number of different test scales specific to the targeted industry. For
example, test batteries for service station employees contain customer service
scales and applied math scales since service station employees must courteously
serve a high volume of customers while accurately handling cash and change.
Industry-specific tests also feature industry norms so that job applicants' scores
can be compared to the most representative comparison group.

Reputable integrity test publishers are best distinguished from less reputable
publishers by the quality and quantity of research they conduct on their selection
tests. The trend is toward more sophisticated and demanding research designs.
Test publishers are starting to use more predictive validity studies to show how
test scores accurately predict future counterproductivity. Multiyear time-series
analyses are starting to document that important business criteria (e.g., shrinkage
losses, turnover rates, accident costs) are significantly reduced after the successful

implementation of an integrity testing program. Control group designs are revealing that companies using integrity tests have fewer losses attributed to employee counterproductivity than companies not using integrity tests. Finally, special return-on-investment forecasts are being offered so that companies interested in using integrity tests can get a fairly accurate estimate of how much money the testing program will save their company.

Integrity tests have been scrutinized by different legal bodies. One state—Massachusetts—has severely limited employers' rights to hire employees at lowest risk to steal on the job, and it has also increased employers' risk of encountering negligent hiring claims due to theft and other forms of employee deviance (e.g., violence, illicit drug use, arson). As American companies experience increased inventory shrinkage, higher insurance losses, and fiercer competition in the marketplace, they will need more assertively to demand from their legislatures the right to use integrity test batteries to hire the most qualified group of employees.

The most reputable publishers of integrity tests are staffed with Ph.D.-level psychologists who are members of the American Psychological Association. As psychologists, they have a responsibility to market only professionally developed and validated employment tests. The marketplace is also becoming more sophisticated about integrity tests. Most companies are willing to purchase only tests developed by Ph.D.-level psychologists or comparable measurement specialists. The psychologists are required to show how their integrity test complies with generally accepted professional and legal standards. Ideally, integrity tests that lack sufficient research and documentation will not be used by any company until sufficient levels of research and field testing have been conducted.

TEXT ORGANIZATION

This book contains four major parts. Part I offers four introductory chapters. The first chapter reviews the history of honesty testing over 40 years. Chapter 2 summarizes empirical research that documents the base rate of employee theft and other counterproductivity. The third chapter describes how companies attempt to control employee theft with personnel selection programs. Special attention is given to preemployment integrity tests. Finally, chapter 4 reviews research showing that the use of honesty tests for personnel selection yields a meaningful return on investment.

The second part contains six chapters on current research trends. Chapter 5 provides a comprehensive overview on the psychometric properties of a leading integrity test and summarizes research establishing the reliability, validity, and fairness of a leading honesty test. Chapter 6 reviews the theoretical foundation for overt honesty tests. Chapter 7 summarizes validity generalization research and concludes, based on a meta-analysis of over 20 honesty test validation studies, that preemployment honesty tests yield useful levels of validity. Chapter

8 describes the accuracy of honesty tests and offers suggestions on how to reduce misclassification errors.

Chapter 9 examines job applicants' reactions to taking a preemployment honesty test. The authors conclude that the majority of applicants are not offended by testing, primarily because they readily perceive the business necessity of screening job applicants for theft proneness. Finally, chapter 10 examines the organizational climate of honesty. It suggests that organizations with high levels of turnover, poor profitability, and image problems are staffed with substantially more dishonest employees compared to organizations not experiencing these types of problems.

Part III contains five chapters dealing with future directions in preemployment integrity testing. Chapter 11 describes a personnel selection test designed to predict employee productivity. Chapters 12, 13, and 14 describe personnel tests used to reduce employee drug use, violence, and accidents, respectively. Chapter 15 describes how a personnel selection test that includes a tenure scale can be used to reduce turnover.

The fourth part contains three chapters that can assist companies interested in implementing an integrity testing program. Chapter 16 provides instructions for integrating an integrity test into a company's overall personnel selection process. Chapter 17 shows companies how to use integrity tests for personnel selection without infringing on job applicants' privacy rights.

Finally, chapter 18 summarizes recently developed guidelines for preemployment integrity tests—the Association of Personnel Test Publishers's *Model Guidelines for Preemployment Integrity Testing Programs* (APTP, 1990), which help to ensure that both integrity test publishers and test users alike adhere to effective, ethical, and legal testing practices. These guidelines help test users to select, administer, score, interpret, and store integrity tests. They also show test users how to optimally protect job applicants' privacy rights.

SUMMARY

American companies need to implement state-of-the-art loss control programs to control employee theft and other counterproductive practices. Employers will always use personnel selection procedures, and to date, a professionally developed integrity test is the most job-relevant, valid, fair, and effective procedure for hiring a high-quality work force. While critics of integrity testing exist, the integrity testing industry is continually striving to offer the highest-quality testing programs that effectively control theft-related losses. This book represents an overview of some of the major research findings that will affect integrity test use in the 1990s and beyond.

REFERENCES

Arthur Young, Inc. (1988). *An ounce of prevention: The tenth annual survey of security and loss prevention in the retail industry*. 1988–1989 Edition. New York: Arthur Young, Inc.

Association of Personnel Test Publishers. (APTP) (1990). *The Model Guidelines for Preemployment Integrity Testing Programs*. Washington, DC.

Carey, J. J. (1989). *Fraud Awareness in Banking*. Paper presented at the 12th Annual Bank Auditor's Conference, The Bank Administration Institute, Diplomat Hotel, Fort Lauderdale, March 6–10.

Hollinger, R., & Clark, J. (1983). *Theft by Employees*. Lexington, MA: Lexington Books.

O'Bannon, R. M., Goldinger, L. A., & Appleby, G. S. (1989). *Honesty and Integrity Testing: A Practical Guide*. Atlanta: Applied Information Resources.

Sackett, P. R., Burris, L. R., & Callahan, C. (1989). Integrity testing for personnel selection: An update. *Personnel Psychology*, 42, 491–529.

Slora, K. (1989). An empirical approach to determining employee deviance base rates. *Journal of Business and Psychology*, 4, 199–219.

I

INTRODUCTION

A History of Honesty Testing

Philip Ash

Society has always attempted to identify dishonest individuals who threaten or commit defalcations against the public order or private interests. Erisistratus (200 B.C.) took pulses to detect deception; in Europe and America, trial by combat or ordeal was common (Inbau & Reid, 1953). Scientific studies to identify the criminal minded began in 1895 with Lombroso's (1895, 1911) use of a plethysmograph for continuously monitoring blood pressure during the questioning of suspects, anticipating the development of the modern polygraph. Hugo Munsterberg, a pioneer in industrial psychology in the United States (Munsterberg, 1913), developed two approaches to the measurement of veracity and honesty (Munsterberg, 1908; Peyser, 1984; Landy, 1988). The first used four physiological measures and the second three "association latency" tests. He also used the term *lie detector* to describe his instruments and tests.

Honesty research by psychologists was given pause by the Hartshorne and May (1928) study of character, which concluded that honesty was probably not a unified and inherent trait. The study of criminal behavior became a major preoccupation of sociologists. The rising discipline of criminology was captured in the 1920s by sociology (Andrews & Wormith, 1989), and the individual as the unit of study (personality dimensions and individual differences) practically disappeared. Instead the leading criminological theories focused on social disorganization and structural issues such as poverty, oppression, and discrimination.

Later reanalysis of the Hartshorne and May data (Burton, 1963), however, substantially controverted their earlier conclusions with respect to individual differences in criminal behavior. With a few exceptions, psychological research on the diagnosis and prediction of dishonesty or counterproductive behavior did not resume until World War II. The topic is not mentioned in DuBois's (1970) history of psychological testing. Even from 1945 until the late 1960s, employee theft was not perceived as a major problem. Employee theft losses and crime rates then began to escalate rapidly. Employee theft alone increased from $1 billion a year in 1968 (Jaspan, 1968) to as much as $40 billion in the 1980s (Jones, 1981). Recent anonymous questionnaire surveys of employees in retail establishments, manufacturing concerns, hospitals (Hollinger & Clark, 1981), and fast food chains (Pristo, 1987) revealed that substantial proportions of employees admit to the theft of money and merchandise: fast food chains, 28 percent; retail establishments, 41.8 percent; manufacturing concerns, 26.2 percent; and hospitals, 32.2 percent. Jones and Joy (1988b) summarized 10 empirical studies comprised of a total of more than 130,000 subjects and found that the unweighted mean base rate for theft was 32 percent (SD = 16 percent). These losses led to a booming and much-needed testing subfield: honesty and integrity testing.

Four principal methods have been pursued to detect proclivity for dishonesty: polygraph and other physiological or electronic screening; biographical data analysis; special keys for standard personality tests and specially developed "disguised-purpose" or "personality-based," "honesty," "integrity," or "organizational delinquency" tests; and clear-purpose honesty tests, which typically pose specific questions about attitudes toward and admission of clearly delinquent behavior.

This chapter traces the development, proliferation, and, in one case, the apparent imminent demise, of honesty assessment measures. Current evaluations of the psychometric adequacy of these measures are given elsewhere (Buros, 1978; Mitchell, 1985; Sackett & Harris, 1985; O'Bannon et al., 1989; Sackett, Burris & Callahan, 1989.

THE POLYGRAPH

Hugo Munsterberg used four physiological measures to detect veracity and dishonesty: breathing rate, blood pressure, breathing depth, and heart rate (Munsterberg, 1908; Landy, 1988). Although his work was widely criticized in the press, he contributed significantly to the popularization of the concept of a lie detector.

Following Lombroso's (1911) lead, Marston (1917, 1921, 1924) employed the medical sphygmomanometer to record blood pressure continuously during questioning. He applied his technique to assess the truthfulness of a man indicted for murder, concluded the man was innocent, and tried to so testify. But the trial judge refused to accept his testimony, and the defendant's appeal was rejected by the U.S. Court of Appeals (*Frye v. United States*, 1923) on the grounds that the polygraph had not yet been found a valid procedure by the scientific community. Years later another man confessed to the crime, but the *Frye* precedent is still cited, although some courts have accepted polygraph evidence in criminal cases under specific limitations (Ansley, 1975; Reid & Inbau, 1977).

Development of the polygraph continued through the work of Larson (1921, 1922), Keeler (1930), and Reid (Inbau & Reid, 1953). By 1945, the polygraph provided measures of blood pressure, pulse, respiration, electrogalvanic response, and muscle activity, and several standardized administration techniques were developed (Reid & Inbau, 1977). Although originally designed to determine truthfulness or deception about past, usually criminal, activities, it began to be used widely for preemployment screening in an effort to assess proneness to future theft behavior. Before passage of the Employee Polygraph Protection Act (1988), preemployment accounted for probably 75 to 80 percent of all polygraph tests administered; estimates range up to 4 million preemployment tests a year (Lykken, 1981). (See Appendix 1 at the end of this chapter.)

Reaction against the preemployment polygraph soon began, however, stimulated to a large extent by union opposition and the opposition of the American Civil Liberties Union. California and Delaware passed laws limiting it in 1953 (California, 1953; Delaware, 1953); by 1987, 27 states, plus the District of Columbia, prohibited the use of the polygraph for employment selection (Bright & Hollon, 1985). The American Psychological Association (APA, 1986) passed a resolution opposing employee screening by polygraph unless it was validated in compliance with APA standards. The U.S. House of Representatives and the U.S. Senate passed bills to prohibit most preemployment polygraph screening nationally (U.S. House of Representatives, 1987), and in 1988 the Congress passed and the president signed the Polygraph Protection Act, effective December 17, 1988. This act substantially prohibits the use of the polygraph in preemployment screening in the private sector, defers to state laws, which are more stringent than the federal law, and excepts from its provisions the use of the polygraph for screening applicants to sensitive positions in the private sector and applicants for law enforcement, security, intelligence, and military positions in the public sector. The Joint Explanatory Statement (1988) that accompanied the legislation specifically exempted from the coverage of the act chemical testing to determine the presence of controlled substances or alcohol and "written or oral tests (commonly referred to as 'honesty' or 'paper and pencil' tests)." The term *lie detector* is otherwise broadly defined, to include "a polygraph, deceptograph, voice stress analyzer, psychological stress evaluator, or any other similar device (whether mechanical or electrical) that is used . . . for the purpose of rendering a diagnostic opinion regarding the honesty or dishonesty of the individual."

In 1989, pursuant to the Joint Explanatory Statement, the Congressional Office of Technology Assessment, in cooperation with the APA, initiated a broad review of paper-and-pencil honesty testing.

BIOGRAPHICAL DATA

Sir Francis Galton (1902) was probably the first to suggest that "the future of each man is mainly a direct consequence of the past. . . . It is, therefore, of high importance when planning for the future to keep the past under frequent review." Objective scoring of biographical data for selection purposes began in the insurance industry in 1894 and expanded rapidly, particularly in the military during World War II (Owens, 1976). The effect of biodata for the prediction of a wide variety of human performance measures has been shown by a number of studies (Asher, 1972; Owens, 1976; Reilly & Chao, 1982). Until recently, however, psychologists have not used biographical data to predict delinquency or proneness of theft or other criminal behavior.

The major work using biodata was done by Sheldon and Eleanor Glueck, Harvard University criminologists. Beginning in 1924, over a span of over 40 years they produced at least 10 books and innumerable studies employing scored and weighted biodata items to predict delinquency, readiness for parole, and other related issues (Glueck & Glueck, 1934, 1950, 1967, 1968). Their work included longitudinal studies over periods as long as 30 years. It should be noted that their concentration on personality and life history data was largely outside the mainstream of sociological thought. (See Appendix 2.)

The first employment selection attempt to predict dishonesty using biodata was Rosenbaum's (1976) study for a grocery chain. Haymaker (1986) reported on a similar in-house biodata form for predicting employee integrity and turnover in another grocery chain. McDaniel (1988) studied the validity of background investigations to predict suitability of candidates for positions of trust in sensitive occupations (law enforcement, nuclear power, and military and civilian positions requiring government-issued security clearances). While McDaniel draws a number of important distinctions between biographical data inventories and background investigations (e.g., the former are usually self-report, paper-and-pencil instruments, draw on a wide range of history items, are empirically scored, and solicit positive as well as negative information, while the latter involve collection by investigators, focus on history items indicative of security risk, are evaluated judgmentally, and look primarily to undesirable behaviors) like biodata inventories, applicant history is the basic predictor. McDaniel, however, used a self-report questionnaire as a surrogate of field-collected data. He found negligible to no validity of the background data scales for predicting employment suitability. A major problem with the use of biodata for preemployment selection is the severe constraints imposed by state laws and regulations on the permissibility of asking a wide range of questions relating to equal employment opportunity considerations (Ash, 1987, 1989).

DISGUISED-PURPOSE PERSONALITY-TYPE TESTS

A clear-purpose test is one whose purpose is clear or transparent to the test taker. A disguised-purpose test is one whose purpose or results are not clear to (or are disguised from) the examinee (Guion, 1965, 354). (See Appendix 3.) The most notable example is the Rorschach; few people uninitiated in the test's literature have much of an idea about the inferences that may be drawn from images they report they see in colored inkblots. Keys, however, have been developed to differentiate between the delinquent or criminally prone and the nondelinquent for a large number of both objectively scored and clinically interpreted personality and related tests.

Munsterberg (1908; Landy, 1988), experimenting with the use of association latency tests to detect veracity or dishonesty, developed three procedures: a list of target words, some related to a specific criminal incident and some not, for which he measured time; an automatograph, a slinglike device to obtain clues from handwriting; and a paper tracing task.

The most notable example of an early disguised-purpose test was the Porteus Mazes, originally developed as a culture-free maze-tracking intelligence test (Porteus, 1968). Porteus observed, however, that the quality of response (careful or careless, planful or impulsive) would yield a quality score that differentiated between delinquents and nondelinquents (Porteus, 1945, 1968). Although his findings were confirmed by a number of American investigators (Fooks & Thomas, 1957; Karpeles, 1932; Poull & Peters, 1929), only limited business and industrial use seems to have been made of them.

Among broad-spectrum personality tests used to diagnose or predict proneness to delinquency are the Rorschach (1921), the Minnesota Multiphasic Personality Inventory (Hathaway & McKinley, 1967), and the California Personality Inventory (1975).

Studies were conducted of the Rorschach Inkblot Test in India and Japan to predict criminality and delinquency (Ishamura, 1966; Majumbar & Roy, 1951; Mukherjee, 1965). The Rorschach is used for similar screening in the United States, particularly by police agencies (Murphy, 1972). Usually proneness to defalcatory behavior is only one of the dimensions of police unsuitability that is tapped.

The Minnesota Multiphasic Personality Inventory (MMPI) has been used extensively on the basis of the original scales and by way of special keys to diagnose or predict delinquency, honesty, integrity, and related characteristics, in the work situation as well as in other contexts. Hathaway and Monochesi's (1953) volume summarizing studies analyzing or predicting delinquency is the most widely used published test for police selection (Murphy, 1972; Ash, Slora & Britton, 1990). Characteristic of this use are a series of papers by Hargrove and Hiatt (1986) and Hiatt and Hargrove (1986a, 1986b) describing application to law enforcement officer selection.

The California Personality Inventory has also been used as a measure of delinquency (Gough, 1965; Gough & Peterson, 1952), leading to an offshoot scale, the Personnel Reaction Blank (Gough, 1971, 1972). It is designed to measure a construct labeled "wayward impulse," interpreted in the work milieu as lack of dependability, conscientiousness, acceptance of convention, and related subtraits.

Finally, there are three new personality-type tests. The Hogan Reliability Index (Hogan & Hogan, 1986, 1987) is designed to measure "organizational delinquency." The Employment Inventory (Paajanen, 1986) is designed to measure "productive and counterproductive" behaviors (including theft, rule violations, and drug use). Both tests were largely derived from the Personnel Reaction Blank. The Employee Productivity Index measures employee productivity, with subscales for organizational adjustment, dependability, interpersonal cooperation, drug avoidance, and safety (London House, 1985, 1988).

Personality-type tests purport to tap multiple dimensions of character (although a few of the clear-purpose tests purport to measure honesty only); predictor-theft criteria correlations tend to be lower for the personality-type tests than for the clear-purpose tests (Frost & Rafilson, 1989). The relative conformity of clear-purpose as compared with disguised-purpose tests to legal requirements and their relative acceptability to applicants are matters of current debate (e.g., Ash, 1989; Jones & Joy, 1988a). A large volume of research, however, does support the conclusion that neither of these types of tests results in discrimination or adverse impact against women or protected minorities (e.g., Ash, 1970, 1972; Joy, 1986; Sackett & Harris, 1985; Terris, 1979a; Terris & Jones, 1980).

CLEAR-PURPOSE HONESTY TESTS

Personnel psychologists have believed that direct personal questions about delinquent behavior invariably lead to "faking good" and lying and therefore yield little useful information about an applicant (e.g., Guion, 1965). Most early personnel research in the area therefore depended on inferences from responses to seemingly innocuous questions, and keys were developed by contrasting the response patterns of, say, delinquents with nondelinquents. That strategy, or a similar one, has been followed for all of the personality-type tests described.

Apparently the first test to pioneer experimentation with direct questions ("How often did you steal things?" "How many friends use drugs?" "Do you feel that you are ... honest?") was developed by Gilbert Lee Betts to screen inductees for military service. Called the Biographical Case History (Betts, 1947b), it was published for civilian use in 1947 (Laird, 1950; Laird & Laird, 1951). A revised version, the Life Experience Inventory (Betts & Cassel, 1957; Cassel & Betts, 1956), based on extended contrasted-group research (first-time criminals, recidivists, "honest" people) yielded significant validities. The test was withdrawn from circulation in 1958–1959, however, because the authors were concerned about possible lawsuits alleging invasion of privacy (Ash & Maurice, 1988).

The next test of this genre was the Reid Report, based on the pioneering work of John E. Reid in polygraph examining (Reid, 1951). Most of the questions were explicit ("How honest are you?" "How much money have you taken ... from employers?" "Did you ever think of stealing from places where you have worked?"). Psychometric research on the test's reliability and validity was not undertaken until 1968 (Ash 1970, 1971, 1972, 1974). In the first three studies, the criterion used was a polygraph test evaluation; in the fourth, responses of incarcerated convicts were compared with those of employment applicants. Reid originally used the scale only in his office, prior to administering a polygraph examination. When he made it available for clients to use on their own premises, he followed the polygraph-service model: the questionnaire is completed by the applicant on the client's premises, item response data or the test forms are conveyed to Reid by mail or telephone (and also, currently, by computer), and Reid scores and interprets the test and reports its results and a "hire–do not hire" recommendation to the client. The essence of this process is that the scoring key is proprietary and therefore not divulged to the client companies. This model has been followed almost uniformly in the honesty testing field.

Shortly after publication of the Reid Report, market demand increased rapidly, and many tests similar to the report were published and are still coming on the market (O'Bannon et al., 1989). The early ones, like the Reid Report, were validated against the polygraph. The most notable, and now the most widely distributed, of the genre is the London House Personnel Selection Inventory (London House, 1975, 1986). Currently available in 12 forms, tests in the series measure honesty (all forms), drug avoidance, nonviolence, employee/customer relations, emotional stability, safety, work values, supervision, and response validity (all forms). Supported by a broad and continuing research program (e.g., Alvord, 1985; Jones, 1980; London House, 1987; Moretti, 1986; Terris, 1985), the scales have been validated in predictive, concurrent, and quasi-experimental designs involving a wide variety of real-life delinquent behavior measures. (See Appendix 4.)

ETHICAL ISSUES

Most of the allegations of ethical problems with personality testing were articulated in the 1950s and early 1960s (Whyte, 1957; Baritz, 1960; Gross, 1962): personality testing tends to prevent progress by entrenching the mundate and prosaic, by encouraging uniformity, by producing a race of liars, and, most important, by violation of the examinee's privacy and personal integrity (Guion, 1965, pp. 372–379). Gross (1962) was the most vociferous critic: "The *mere attempt* to predict the behavior of individual men is a violation of personal dignity . . . and is therefore intrinsically immoral" (p. 280). These criticisms had some effect on honesty testing. Betts and Cassell (1957) withdrew their integrity test, the Life Experience Inventory, from the market out of concern for possible suits charging invasion of privacy (Ash & Maurice, 1988). Guion reviewed and substantially answered the Whyte-Baritz-Gross criticisms. On the critical issue of invasion of personal privacy, Guion (1965) wrote:

Nearly every interpersonal encounter involves at least a casual evaluation of personality. . . . Qualifications are not limited to skills or aptitudes; they may also include affective or motivational variables. General activity level or the sense of responsibility that pulls a man out of his easy chair and off to work are major qualifications for many jobs; they should be assessed and assessed competently. This is hardly an unwarranted "invasion" of privacy! . . . This author feels that it is clear invasion of privacy to ask an applicant to reveal details of thought or emotion that are not relevant to performance on the job for which he is considered [but] the whole concept of prediction from personality tests has been criticized on moral grounds: this author sees no validity in this criticism. All employment procedures—interviews, application forms, reference checks—imply a prediction of future performance based largely on assessments of personality. If prediction through personality testing is immoral *per se*, then all employment procedures are immoral; all such procedures imply a prediction that is often wrong. (pp. 375–376).

Two decades later, Sackett and Harris (1985, p. 271) offered essentially the same response for honesty tests: "It can be argued that, given an employer's legitimate interest in hiring employees who will not steal, inquiries about honesty are unethical only if the test is invalid, and . . . selection procedures with modest validities are the best that psychology has been able to devise; thus, selection errors are made with any test."

DISCUSSION

Many psychologists have looked askance at clear-purpose honesty tests. Misperceptions of the history and development of these tests tend to persist. For example, John Bales (1988), writing in the APA *Monitor*, quotes the APA Committee on Psychological Tests and Assessment as being "seriously concerned" about the use of these tests because "there is simply not enough known" about them, that they have used the polygraph as a criterion measure, and the research has been largely in-house.

As this review and the literature indicate, there is in fact a large body of published research on these tests, most of it by credentialed psychologists consulting with the test publishers but also a substantial number of studies by independent investigators in academia or in companies not related to the publishers, including at least a few leading industrial psychologists. The majority of studies between 1970 and 1975 used the polygraph as a criterion. Since then almost all studies have used real-life, on-the-job measures of counterproductive behavior: apprehension for theft, contrasted groups (convicts or employees apprehended for theft versus innocent employees), shrinkage, termination of defalcations, predictive validity studies in which applicants are hired without respect to test scores and followed up to identify those who commit defalcations, and so on. As the historical record indicates, furthermore, honesty testing is not a recent development. Its origins go back to Greek civilization, its psychometric formulation to the first decade of the twentieth century, and the evolution of clear-purpose tests to the World War II period. It is important, furthermore, to note the relative volume of published research on clear-purpose honesty tests with that of the widely used personality-type tests. For the former, the body of published research includes about 150 items. For tests like the Rorschach, the MMPI, and the CPI, it is difficult to find nearly as many relating to the use of the test for predicting honesty.

After two decades of preemployment polygraph testing, which has drawn to an end, paper-and-pencil (and recently telephone, audiotape, or computer-assisted) preemployment measures are becoming dominant in an ever-expanding market. Competition between clear-purpose and disguised-purpose (personality-type) tests began only in the last few years. The substantially greater research base of the leading clear-purpose tests as compared with disguised-purpose personality tests and biodata inventories and their generally higher reported validities against relevant criteria of dishonesty and other counterproductive behaviors (cf. Frost & Rafilson, 1988) suggest that their leadership in the field will be retained.

APPENDIX 1. POLYGRAPH HISTORY

1895   Lombroso (1895, 1911) uses a plethysmograph to obtain continuous recordings of pulse and blood pressure during questioning.

1908   Munsterberg (1908) popularizes the term *lie detector* and uses blood pressure, breathing rate, breathing depth, and heart rate to detect veracity or dishonesty.

1917   Marston (1917, 1921, 1924) uses a medical sphygonomanometer to monitor blood pressure continuously during questioning.

1921   Larson (1921, 1922) develops an instrument for recording blood pressure, pulse, and respiration.

1930   Keeler (1930) develops a polygraph that records blood pressure, pulse, respiration, and galvanic skin response.

1945   Reid (Reid & Inbau, 1977) adds a muscle activity recording channel to the Keeler polygraph and develops the most widely used method of questioning, the Reid Control Question Technique.

1945   Beginning of widespread use of polygraph for preemployment screening. By 1979, estimates of preemployment polygraph screening ranged from 1 million to 4 million applicants annually (Lykken, 1981).

1953   California (1953) and Delaware (1953) pass laws prohibiting employers from "demanding or requiring" (California) or "requiring, requesting, or suggesting" (Delaware) applicants to take a preemployment polygraph. By 1987, 27 states plus the District of Columbia limit or prohibit preemployment polygraph use (Bright and Hollon, 1985).

1986   The Council of Representatives of the American Psychological Association (APA, 1986) passes a resolution claiming the polygraph is unreliable for employee screening and asking for control of polygraph screening by compliance with APA Standards for Psychological and Educational Tests and Measures (1985).

1987   The U.S. House of Representatives Committee on Education and Labor reports favorably on House Resolution 1212, the Employee Polygraph Protection Act, which would prohibit most preemployment polygraph screening of job applicants

(U.S. House of Representatives, 1987). The bill was signed by the president; the act was effective December 27, 1988.

APPENDIX 2. BIOGRAPHICAL DATA FOR HONESTY ASSESSMENT

1934   Glueck, S., & Glueck, E. (1934) *One thousand juvenile delinquents*, the pioneer Glueck & Glueck study. The Gluecks produced over 10 books on their delinquency prediction schedules.

1950   Glueck, S., & Glueck, E. (1950). *Unraveling juvenile delinquency.*

1955   Kvaraceus, W. C. (1955). Prediction studies of delinquent behavior. The beginning of a series of the predictive efficiency of biodata for anticipating delinquency.

1961   Kvaraceus, W. C. (1961). Forecasting delinquency: A three-year experiment.

1967   Glueck, S., & Glueck, E. (1967). *Predicting delinquency and crime.*

1968   Glueck, S., & Glueck, E. (1968). *Delinquents and non-delinquents in perspective.*

1976   Study of biodata form for a grocery chain (Rosenbaum, 1976). The results were very modest.

1986   Supermarket General, a grocery chain, developed a biodata form for assessing employee integrity and turnover. Most of the criterion biodata correlations were low (Haymaker, 1986).

1988   A study of biographical constructs derived from a paper-and-pencil self-report surrogate for background investigations had little or no validity for predicting military-related delinquency (McDaniel, 1988).

APPENDIX 3. DISGUISED-PURPOSE TESTS FOR HONESTY ASSESSMENT

1908   Munsterberg (1908) develops three latency of response tests to measure dishonesty and veracity.

1915–1965   Samuel Porteus (1917, 1945, 1968) develops a "culture-free" maze-tracking intelligence test, which he finds is also predictive of juvenile delinquency and criminality. A number of American investigators validate his findings (e.g., Karpeles, 1932; Fooks & Thomas, 1957).

1952, 1966   Studies of the Rorschach Inkblot Test in India and Japan suggest it may be predictive of criminality (Majumbar & Roy, 1952; Mukherjee, 1965; Ishamura, 1966).

1952   Gough and Peterson begin research demonstrating that one of the scales of the California Personality Inventory is predictive of delinquent behavior. Their research leads to the development of the Personnel Reaction Blank (1965).

1953   The Minnesota Multiphasic Personality Inventory is demonstrated to have use in the analysis and prediction of delinquency (Hathaway & Monochesi, 1953).

1985–1988   A personality-type test measuring overall productivity, with scales for dependability, interpersonal cooperation, drug avoidance, and safety, the Employment Productivity Index (EPI), is published (London House, 1985). The Human Resource Inventory, an expanded version published by London House in 1988, contains measures of organizational adjustment and work performance.

1986   Two personality-type tests, derivative to some extent from the Personnel Reaction Blank, are published: the Employment Inventory (Paajanen, 1986) and the Reliability Index (Hogan & Hogan, 1986, 1987).

APPENDIX 4. CLEAR-PURPOSE HONESTY TESTS

Paper-and-Pencil Tests

1942   G. L. Betts develops the Biographical Case History (Betts, 1947a, 1947b) originally to screen men who were in disciplinary barracks and rehabilitation centers to prevent induction of men who were deemed unsatisfactory for military service.

1947   A civilian version of the Biographical Case History is published (Cassel & Betts, 1956; Laird, 1950; Laird & Laird, 1951).

1951   The *Reid Report* (1951), based on the work of John E. Reid in polygraph examining, is published.

1956   A revision of the Biographical Case History, the Life Experience Inventory, is marketed (Cassel & Betts, 1956; Betts & Cassel, 1957).

1964   The Stanton Survey (Klump, 1980; Reed, 1982).

1970   The Trustworthiness Attitude Survey (Cormack & Strand, 1970).

1971   The Pre-employment Opinion Survey (P.O.S. Corporation, undated).

1974   Published research reports on the *Reid Report* appear (Ash, 1970, 1971, 1972, 1974).

1975   The Personnel Selection Inventory. Scales to measure nonviolence, drug abuse, safety, and other related dimensions are added, supported by a large and continuing research program. About 62 published and in-house papers are summarized in the *Personnel Selection Inventory Information Guide* (London House, 1987).

1975   The Milby Profile (Bradley, 1980, 1981).

1977   ACM Attitude Evaluation (Magiera, 1977).

1978   Phase II Pre-Employment Analysis Questionnaire (Phase II Profile, 1982a, 1982b).

1979   Company Morale Questionnaire (Psychometric Behavioral Group, 1979).

1980   Wilkerson Pre-Employment Audit (Wilkerson, 1980; Morey, 1981).

1982   Accutrac Evaluation System (Durbrow, 1982).

1983   Personal Outlook Inventory (Selection Research Publishing, 1983).

1984   *AIMS Review* (A.I.M.S. Review, 1984).

1985   Security, Aptitude, Fitness Evaluation (SAFE) (Taccarino, 1983).

1986   Employee Reliability Inventory (Bay State Psychological Associates, 1986). True Tests (Miner, undated).

Computer-Assisted, Audiotape, or Telephone Formats

1984   *Compu-Scan* (audiotape) (Compu-Scan, 1984).

DES/Greentree Systems (computer-assisted interview) (Mitchell, 1984).

1986   CIC Integrity interview (telephone) (Barke, 1987).

> *Note:* This appendix lists representative tests published in 1942 or later. O'Bannon et al. (1989) describe 43 tests and indicate that there are at least 3 more for which data were not available. The list prior to 1980 is believed to be complete.

REFERENCES

AIMS Review (1984). Chicago: A.I.M.S. Review, Inc.

Alvord, G. (1985). Validation of the Personnel Selection Inventory as a screening test for bus operators. *Journal of Security Administration*, 8(11), 37–47.

American Psychological Association (1986). APA Council of Representatives Policy Position on Polygraph Testing, January/February Session. *American Psychologist*, 41(6), 659–660.

American Psychological Association, American Educational Research Association, & National Council on Measurement in Education (1985). *Standards for educational and psychological testing*. Washington, DC: American Psychological Association.

Andrews, D. A., & Wormith, J. S. (1989). Personality and crime: Knowledge destruction and construction in criminology. *Justice Quarterly*, 6(3), 289–309.

Ansley, N. (ed.) (1975). *Legal admissibility of the polygraph*. Springfield, IL: Charles C. Thomas.

Ash, P. (1970). The validation of an instrument to predict the likelihood of employee theft. *Proceedings of the 79th Annual Convention of the American Psychological Association*, 579–580. Washington, DC: The Association.

Ash, P. (1971). Screening employment applicants for attitudes toward theft. *Journal of Applied Psychology*, 55(2), 161–164.

Ash, P. (1972). Attitudes of work applicants toward theft. *Proceedings of the Seventeenth International Congress of Applied Psychology*, 985–988. Liège, Belgium.

Ash, P. (1974). Convicted felons' attitudes toward theft. *Criminal Justice and Behavior*, 1(1), 21–29.

Ash, P. (1987). *The legality of pre-employment inquiries*. Park Ridge, IL: London House.

Ash, P. (1989). The legality of pre-employment inquiries. Master tutorial presented at the 1989 Spring Meeting of the Society for Industrial Organizational Psychology, Boston, April.

Ash, P., & Maurice, S. J. (1988). Rediscovering the first clear-purpose honesty test. *Journal of Business and Psychology*, 2(4), 378–381.

Ash, P., Slora, K., & Britton, C. (1990). Police agency officer selection procedures. *Journal of Police Science and Administration*, 17(4) (in press).

Asher, J. J. (1972). The biographical item: Can it be improved? *Personnel Psychology*, 25, 251–269.

Bales, J. (1988). Integrity tests: Honest results? *APA Monitor*, 19(6), 1–4.

Baritz, L. (1960). *The servants of power*. Middletown, CT: Wesleyan University Press.

Barke, C. R. (1987). *Professional manual for the integrity interview*. Indianapolis: CIC Enterprises.

Betts, G. L. (1947a). The detection of incipient army criminals. *Science*, August 1.

Betts, G. L. (1947b). *Biographical case history*. Minneapolis: Educational Test Bureau.
Betts, G. L., & Cassel, R. N. (1957). *The Life Experience Inventory*. Cincinnati: C. A. Gregory Company.
Bradley, P. (1980). *The Milby System: Validation Study 1980-S*. Minneapolis: Milby Systems.
Bradley, P. (1981). *The Milby System: Adverse Impact Study 1981-M*. Minneapolis: Milby Systems.
Bright, T. L., & Hollon, C. J. (1985). State regulation of polygraph tests at the workplace. *Personnel*, Feb., 50–56.
Buros, O. K. (1978). *The Eighth Mental Measurements Yearbook*. Highland Park, NJ: Gryphon Press.
Burton, R. V. (1963). The generality of honesty reconsidered. *Psychological Review*, 70, 481–499.
California Labor Code (1953). Para 432.2.
Cassel, R. N., & Betts, G. L. (1956). The development and validation of a life experience inventory for the identification of "delinquency prone" youth. *American Psychologist*, 11, 336.
Compu-Scan (1984). Spanish Fort, IN: Compu-Scan.
Cormack, R. W., & Strand, A. L. (1970). *T.A. survey*. Oakbrook, IL: Government Personnel Consultants.
Delaware Code (1953). Title 19, Para 704.
DuBois, P. S. (1970). *A history of psychological testing*. Boston: Allyn & Bacon.
Durbrow, B. R. (1982). *ACCUTRAC Evaluation System*. Cincinnati: Barbrisons Management Systems.
Employee Polygraph Protection Act of 1988 (1988). Public Law 100–347.
Employee Reliability Inventory (1986). Boston: Bay State Psychological Associates.
Fooks, G., & Thomas, R. R. (1957). Differential qualitative performance of delinquents on the Porteus Maze. *Journal of Consulting Psychology*, 21, 351–353.
Frost, A. G., & Rafilson, F. M. (1989). Overt integrity tests versus personality-based measures of delinquency: An empirical comparison. *Journal of Business Psychology*, 3(3), 269–277.
Frye v. United States (1923). 293 Fed. 1013 (D.C. Cir.).
Galton, F. (1902). *Life history album* (2d ed.). New York: Macmillan.
Glueck, S., & Glueck, E. (1934). *One thousand juvenile delinquents*. Cambridge: Harvard University Press.
Glueck, S., & Glueck, E. (1950). *Unraveling juvenile delinquency*. New York: Commonwealth Fund.
Glueck, S., & Glueck, E. (1967). *Predicting delinquency and crime*. Cambridge: Harvard University Press.
Glueck, S., & Glueck, A. (1968). *Delinquents and non-delinquents in perspective*. Cambridge: Harvard University Press.
Gough, H. G. (1965). Cross-cultural validation of a measure of asocial behavior. *Psychological Reports*, 17, 379–387.
Gough, H. G. (1971). The assessment of wayward impulse by means of the Personnel Reaction Blank. *Personnel Psychology*, 24, 659–677.
Gough, H. G. (1972). *Manual for the Personnel Reaction Blank*. Palo Alto, CA: Consulting Psychologists Press.

Gough, H. G. (1975). *Manual for the California Personality Inventory*. Palo Alto, CA: Consulting Psychologists Press.

Gough, H. G., & Peterson, D. R. (1952). The identification and measurement of pre-dispositioning factors in crime and delinquency. *Journal of Consulting Psychology*, 16, 207–212.

Gross, M. L. (1962). *The brain watchers*. New York: Random House.

Guion, R. M. (1965). *Personnel testing*. New York: McGraw-Hill.

Hargrove, G. E., & Hiatt, D. (1988). F+4+9+ CN: An MMPI measure of aggression in law enforcement officers and applicants. *Journal of Police Science & Admn*, 16(4), 268–273.

Hartshorne, H., & May, M. A. (1928). *Studies in the nature of character*, Vol. I: *Studies in deceit*. New York: Macmillan.

Hathaway, S. R., & McKinley, J. C. (1967). *Manual for the Minnesota Multiphasic Personality Inventory*. New York: Psychological Corporation.

Hathaway, S. R., Monochesi, E. D. (eds.) (1953). *Analyzing and predicting delinquency with the MMPI*. Minneapolis: University of Minnesota Press.

Haymaker, J. (1986). Biodata as a predictor of employee integrity and turnover. Paper presented at the 94th Annual Convention of the American Psychological Association, Washington, DC, August 25.

Hiatt, D., & Hargrove, G. E. (1986). MMPI profiles of problem police officers. (Unpublished manuscript).

Hiatt, D., & Hargrove, G. E. (1988). Predicting job performance problems with psychological screening. *Journal of Police Science and Administration*, 16(2), 122–125.

Hogan, J., & Hogan R. (1986). *Hogan Personnel Selection Series manual*. Minneapolis: National Computer Systems.

Hogan, J., & Hogan R. (1987). How to measure employee reliability. Paper presented at the 95th Annual Convention of the American Psychological Association, New York, August.

Hollinger, R., & Clark, J. (1983). *Theft by employees*. Lexington, MA: Lexington Books.

Ishamura, J. (1966). Ten year follow-up study on the early prediction of juvenile delinquency by means of the Rorschach test. *Japanese Psychological Research*, 8, 151–160.

Inbau, F. E., & Reid, J. E. (1953). *Lie detection and criminal investigation*. Baltimore: Williams and Wilkins.

Jaspan, N. (1968). White collar thefts at $5 million a day. *National Underwriter*, 72, 16.

Joint explanatory statement: Employee Polygraph Act of 1988 (1988). U.S. Congress, Report 100–659. Washington, D.C., May 26.

Jones, J. W. (1980). Attitudinal correlates of employees' deviance: Theft, alcohol use, and nonprescribed drug use. *Psychological Reports*, 47, 71–77.

Jones, J. W. (1981). Attitudinal correlates of employee theft of drugs and hospital supplies among nursing personnel. *Journal of Nursing Research*, 30(6), 359–361.

Jones, J. W., & Joy, D. (1988a). Empirical investigation of job applicants' reactions to taking a pre-employment honesty test. Technical Report. Park Ridge, IL: London House Press.

Jones, J. W., & Joy, D. (1988b). Employee deviance base rates: A summary of empirical research. Technical Report. Park Ridge, IL: London House Press.

Jones, J. W., & Terris, W. (1981). Predictive validation of a dishonesty test that measures theft-proneness. Paper presented at the 18th Interamerican Congress of Psychology, Santa Domingo, Dominican Republic, June 21–26.

Joy, D. S. (1986). The use of the Personnel Selection Inventory to reduce employee theft: A review. Technical Report 51. Park Ridge, IL: London House.

Karpeles, L. M. (1932). A further investigation of the Porteus Maze as a discriminative measure in delinquency. *Journal of Applied Psychology*, 16, 426–437.

Keeler, L. (1930). A method for detecting deception. *American Journal of Police Science*, 1(1), 38–41.

Klump, C. (1980). *The Stanton Survey manual: Description and validation*. Chicago: The Stanton Corporation.

Kvaraceus, W. C. (1953). *KD Proneness Scale and Check List*. New York: Harcourt, Brace & World.

Kvaraceus, W. C. (1966). *Dynamics of delinquency*. Columbus, OH: Charles E. Merrill.

Laird, D. A. (1950). Psychology and the crooked employee. *Management Review* (April), 1–6.

Laird, D. A., & Laird, E. C. (1951). *Sizing up people*. New York: McGraw-Hill.

Landy F. (1988). The early years of I/O: Hugo Munsterberg and the polygraph. *Industrial Psychologist*, 25(4), 54–55.

Larson, J. A. (1921). Modification of the Marston deception test. *Journal of Criminal Law and Criminology*, 12(3), 390–399.

Larson, J. A. (1922). The cardio-pneumo-psychogram and its use in the study of emotions, with practical significance. *Journal of Experimental Psychology*, 5(5), 323–329.

Lombroso, C. (1895). *L'homme criminal*, 2d ed. Vol. 1. Paris: F. Alcan.

Lombroso, C. (1911). *Crime: Its causes and remedies*. Translated by H. P. Horton. Boston: Little, Brown.

London House (1975). *The Personnel Selection Inventory*. Park Ridge, IL: London House.

London House (1985). *Employee Productivity Index*. Park Ridge, IL: London House.

London House (1987). *Personnel Selection Inventory Information Guide*. Park Ridge, IL: London House.

London House (1988). *Human Resource Inventory*. Park Ridge, IL: London House.

Lykken, D. T. (1981). *A tremor in the blood*. New York: McGraw-Hill.

McDaniel, M. A. (1988). Biographical constructs for predicting employee suitability. Paper presented at the 96th Annual Convention of the American Psychological Association, Atlanta, August.

Magiera, A. C. (1977). *ACM Attitude Evaluation*. Merrillville, IN: Alex C. Magiera Associates, Inc.

Majumbar, A. K., & Roy, A. B. (1952). Latent personality content of juvenile delinquents. *Journal of Psychological Research* (Madras, India), 6(1), 4–8.

Marston, W. M. (1917). Systolic blood pressure symptoms of deception. *Journal of Experimental Psychology*, 2(2), 117–163.

Marston, W. M. (1921). Psychological possibilities, in the deception tests. *Journal of Criminal Law and Criminology*, 11(4), 551–570.

Marston, W. M. (1924). Studies in testimony. *Journal of Criminal Law and Criminology*, 15(1), 5–31.

Miner, J. R. (undated). *The development of the Intergram Truetest*. Atlanta: Intergram.

Mitchell, B. (1984). *DES-Greentree Systems*. Richardson, TX: DES-Greentree.

Mitchell, J. V., Jr. (ed.) (1985). *The Ninth Mental Measurements Yearbook.* Lincoln, NE: Buros Institute of Mental Measurements.

Morey, L. (1981). *Statistical properties of the Wilkerson Pre-employment Audit.* Tulsa, OK: Wilkerson and Associates.

Moretti, D. M. (1986). The prediction of employee counterproductivity through attitude assessment. *Journal of Business and Psychology,* 1(2), 134–147.

Mukherjee, K. (1965). Personality of criminals: A Rorschach study. *Council of Social and Psychological Research Bulletin,* no. 5, 15–18.

Munsterberg, H. (1908). *On the witness stand: Essays on psychology and crime.* New York: McLure.

Murphy, J. (1972). Current practices in the use of psychological testing by police agencies. *Journal of Criminal Law and Police Science,* 63, 570–576.

O'Bannon, R. M., Goldinger, L. A., & Appleby, G. S. (1989). *Honesty and integrity testing: A practical guide.* Atlanta: Applied Information Resources.

Owens, W. A. (1976). Background data. In M. D. Dunnette (ed.), *Handbook of industrial and organizational psychology.* Chicago: Rand-McNally.

Paajanen, G. E. (1986). Development and validation of the PDI Employment Inventory. Paper presented at the 94th Annual Convention of the American Psychological Association, Washington, DC, August.

Peyser, C. S. (1984). Munsterberg, Hugo (1863–1916). In R. Corsini (ed.), *Encyclopedia of psychology,* vol. 2, 410–411. New York: Wiley.

Phase II Profile (1982a). *Adverse impact studies.* Peoria, IL: Lousig-Nont and Associates.

Phase II Profile (1982b). *Statistical Validation Studies.* Peoria, IL: Lousig-Nont and Associates.

Porteus, S. D. (1917). Mental tests with delinquents and Australian aboriginal children. *Psychological Review,* 24, 32–42.

Porteus, S. D. (1945). Q-scores, temperament, and delinquency. *Journal of Social Psychology,* 21, 81–103.

Porteus, S. D. (1968). *Porteus' Maze test: Fifty years' application.* Palo Alto, CA: Pacific Books.

P.O.S. Corporation (undated). *Pre-employment Opinion Survey.* Chicago: Corporation.

Poull, L. E., & Peters, R. P. (1929). The Porteus Maze tests as a discriminative measure in delinquency. *Journal of Applied Psychology,* 13, 145–151.

Pristo, T. (1987). *Employee theft study.* Park Ridge, IL: London House.

Psychometric Behavioral Group (1979). *Company morale questionnaire.* Dallas: Author.

Reed, H. (1982). *The Stanton Survey: Description and validation manual.* Chicago: Stanton Corporation.

Reid, J. E., & Inbau, F. E. (1977). *Truth and deception.* 2d ed. Baltimore: Williams and Wilkins.

Reid Report (1951). Chicago: John E. Reid Associates.

Reilly, R. R., & Chao, G. T. (1982). Validity and fairness of some alternative employee selection procedures. *Personnel Psychology,* 35, 1–62.

Rorschach, H. (1921). *Rorschach Psychodiagnostic Plates.* Various editions by several publishers: Grune & Stratton, Psychological Corporation, World Book Company.

Rosenbaum, R. W. (1976). Predictability of employee theft using weighted application blanks. *Journal of Applied Psychology,* 61, 94–98.

Sackett, P. R. (1987). What's new in the integrity testing area since the 1984 Sackett and Harris review? Paper presented at the Society for Industrial/Organizational Workshop, Atlanta, April 2.

Sackett, P. R., Burris, L., & Callahan, C. (1989). Integrity testing for personnel selection: An update. *Personnel Psychology*, 42, 491–529.

Sackett, P. R., & Harris, M. M. (1985). Honesty testing for personnel selection: A review and critique. In H. J. Bernardin & D. A. Bownas (eds.), *Personality assessment in organizations*. New York: Praeger Publishers.

Selection Research Publishing (1983). *Development and validation of the Personal Outlook Inventory*. Chicago: The author.

Taccarino, J. (1983). *Security, Aptitude, Fitness Evaluation (SAFE)*. Chicago: SAFE, Inc.

Terris, W. (1979). Attitudinal correlates of theft, violence, and drug use. Paper presented at the 17th Interamerican Congress of Psychology, Lima, Peru.

Terris, W. (1985). Attitudinal correlates of employee integrity. *Journal of Police and Criminal Psychology*, 1, 60–68.

Terris, W., & Jones, J. W. (1980). Attitudinal and personality correlates of theft among supermarket employees. *Journal of Security Administration*, 3(2), 65–78.

Tescor Survey (1983). Tualatin, OR: American Tescor.

U.S. House of Representatives (1987). H.R. 1212, Employee Polygraph Protection Act. H.R. Committee on Education and Labor.

Whyte, W. H., Jr. (1957). *The organization man*. New York: Doubleday.

Wilkerson, O. K. (1980). *The Wilkerson Pre-employment Audit*. Tulsa, OK: Wilkerson and Associates.

2

An Empirical Approach to Determining Employee Deviance Base Rates

KAREN B. SLORA

The purpose of this chapter is to describe a method for determining the base rates of acts of employee deviance. Employee deviance may reflect acts of either employee theft—the unauthorized taking of cash, merchandise, or property—or production deviance—counterproductive activities that serve to slow the rate or quality of output (e.g., intentionally doing slow or sloppy work, using drugs on the job). Both types of deviance can be costly to employers in terms of losses in profits, inventory, morale, and image.

It is important to determine the true extent of these acts of employee deviance for several reasons. Establishment of base rates may be used to document the seriousness of employee deviance in terms of finding and implementing practical solutions to it. Base rates are also used in setting norm-referenced cutoff scores in preemployment integrity tests (Ash, 1989; Jones, 1989). Thus, these integrity tests should ideally screen out applicants who would be likely to steal or engage in counterproductive activities on the job.

The measurement of the frequency of acts of employee deviance, however, has been problematic. Commonly used measures (e.g., shrinkage, employee apprehensions) are not applicable to production deviance, such as slow work or other counterproductive work practices, or may not accurately reflect the true incidence of employee theft practices; for example, measures of inventory shrinkage may reflect losses due to accounting errors or mismanagement, as well as theft. The number of employees apprehended for theft accounts only for those who are caught. It is difficult to know the number who go undetected. Preem-

Gratitude is extended to Dr. William Terris for his helpful contributions, and to Michael Boye, M.A., for his assistance in the data analyses and report preparations. The assistance of Dr. Jane Halpert and the DePaul University Center for Industrial and Organizational Psychology is gratefully acknowledged.

ployment polygraph admissions may result in underreporting of theft and production deviance because the questions rarely survey the wide range of deviant
behaviors. Nevertheless, researchers using such approaches have obtained base
rates of employee theft ranging from 12 to 50 percent (e.g., Ash, 1976; Jones
& Joy, 1988; Tatham, 1974). Estimates of production deviance have not been
obtained using these approaches.

What is needed is a means of determining employee deviance base rates that
includes both employee theft and production deviance and otherwise undetected
acts of employee deviance. A promising approach is the anonymous theft survey
method, used by Hollinger and Clark (1983), to obtain estimates of various acts
of employee deviance across several industries. Employees in surveyed industries
completed questionnaires about their deviance activities. Depending on the industry, a 65 to 75 percent response rate was obtained. Hollinger and Clark found
average employee theft rates of 28 percent for manufacturing, 33 percent for
hospitals, and 35 percent for retail. For production deviance, they obtained
average estimates of 65 percent, 69 percent, and 82 percent, respectively for
these same industries.

The preliminary studies described next used an anonymous survey approach
to determine employee deviance base rates for two industries to determine the
extent and amount of employee deviance and to identify the types of theft and
counterproductive practices engaged in by employees.

STUDY 1: FAST FOOD SURVEY

METHOD

Subjects

Employees from two national fast food organizations, located mainly in the
Midwest and the West, participated in the survey.

One employee from each fast food unit was randomly selected using a stratified
random sampling approach; the strata were the major job categories for each
company. Only one employee was selected to decrease employee suspicion of
company involvement in the study. This also minimized the chance of employees
talking among coworkers about the survey and increased the likelihood that
selected employees would respond in an open, frank, and truthful manner.

A combined total of 872 participants were selected from both companies. For
company A, the total sample consisted of approximately 20 percent store or
assistant managers, and the remainder were production employees (including
shift leaders). For company B, the total sample consisted of approximately 40
percent production employees and 20 percent each of shift leaders, assistant
managers, and store managers.

Participants were unaware that the survey was being conducted by London House for the fast food companies. The survey process was designed so that it would appear to participants that they were involved in an anonymous study conducted by DePaul University.

Survey Questionnaire

The survey consisted of a number of questions designed to provide information about employee characteristics, theft practices, and other relevant areas. Three questions asked employees' opinions about the fairness of their employer's treatment of employees and beliefs about the acceptability of counterproductive work practices. Demographic information (e.g., current job title, age, marital status) was obtained to describe employees. Other items asked for frequency admissions (e.g., very often, often, occasionally, seldom, never) of various types of on-the-job theft or counterproductive behaviors (e.g., taken merchandise, faked ill, argued with customers) and for dollar estimates of the amount of money and merchandise the survey respondent and the "average eemployee" takes without permission. A general comments section allowed respondents to elaborate or comment on any other thoughts or experiences about employee theft or the survey.

Each survey was assigned a unique arbitrary code number to identify duplicate survey returns (e.g., a single respondent returns two surveys) and to link returned survey responses with other information (e.g., store shortages, turnover). The codes were placed on the back of each survey using either a pin-pricking technique or invisible ink. The implemented coding procedure, which was coordinated with DePaul University, was used so that no researcher could link employees with their survey responses, thus ensuring the anonymity of responses. This coding method proved acceptable to the subjects, companies, and researchers participating in such a sensitive base rate study.

Survey Mailing

A four-stage process was used to distribute the surveys and to increase the probability of a high return rate. The surveys were mailed in winter 1987 for company A and spring 1988 for company B.

Stage 1: A letter was sent to the employees selected to participate in the survey informing them they had been selected to participate in a general study regarding employee theft and that they would shortly be receiving a questionnaire. The letter emphasized that the study was being conducted by an academic institution and that all responses would remain entirely anonymous and confidential.

Stage 2: One week later, a packet of survey materials was sent to each participant containing a cover letter that reiterated the purpose and confidentiality of the survey as well as instructions for completion of the survey, a copy of the survey, a postage-paid return envelope, and a dollar bill, the last enclosed as an incentive for completing the questionnaire.

Stage 3: A first follow-up letter, the survey, and a postage-paid return envelope were sent to participants who had not yet returned a survey.

Stage 4: A second follow-up letter, the survey, and a postage-paid envelope were sent to the survey participants who still had not returned a survey. Follow-up letters were designed to encourage participant response and reemphasized the purpose and confidentiality of the study.

RESULTS

The four-stage survey process yielded a 48 percent response rate. Of 872 survey participants, 75 letters or surveys were returned as undeliverable; 384 surveys were completed and returned of the 797 surveys delivered.

Returned surveys were not used in the statistical analyses if the respondent indicated he or she was not currently working primarily in the fast food industry. Using this criterion, 43 surveys were dropped from the analyses. Thus, 341 surveys were analyzed.

To ensure that employees who responded to the survey were not substantially different from those who did not respond, comparisons were made for each company and for the total sample between respondents and nonrespondents on a number of store and demographic variables provided by the participating companies: overrings, mysterious disappearances (shortages), store location, store size, number of store robberies, job title, length of tenure, gender, and age. There were no significant differences (as shown by t-tests and chi squares) between those who returned surveys and those who did not return surveys for the total sample or for either company.

Demographics

About 55 percent of the fast food respondents were crew members, 19 percent assistant managers, and 26 percent store or district managers. Most of the respondents (over 70 percent) had been employed more than one year. About 45 percent of the respondents worked more than 40 hours per week. About 67 percent reported working evenings or nights or varied shifts. Fifty-six percent of the sample was younger than 24 years. There were more females than males (57 percent and 43 percent, respectively). About 43 percent of respondents had some college. Thirty percent of respondents indicated two or more employers during the past year. Thus, a substantial percentage of the respondents worked more than 40 hours, were female, were younger than 24 years, or were college educated.

Types of Deviant Behaviors

Item Admissions. Simple frequency analyses revealed substantial theft admissions for many of the items covered in the survey (Table 2.1). Seventy-eight

Table 2.1
Admissions for Fast Food Respondents

Item #	Subject	% Admitting	Very Often	Often	Occasionally	Seldom	Never
Theft:							
1.	Taken merchandise/equipment	22	1	3	5	14	78
8.	Taken supplies for personal use	23	1	1	5	17	77
17.	Eaten food without paying	54	8	9	13	25	46
18.	Taken money without permission	6	1	–	1	5	94
19.	Overcharged/shortchanged on purpose	4	1	1	1	3	96
20.	Changed company records	5	1	1	2	3	95
22.	Refunds for things not purchased	6	1	1	1	4	94
26.	Taken property from co-workers	1	1	–	–	1	99
30.	Falsified company documents	3	–	–	1	3	97
Theft Support:							
7.	Employee discount used for friends	30	1	1	11	18	70
21.	Sold merchandise to friends at reduced price	18	1	1	4	12	82
27.	Helped person take company property	5	1	–	1	4	95
28.	Saw co-workers steal company cash or property	34	2	2	12	18	66
31.	Did not report theft by others	13	1	1	3	9	87
Time Theft:							
13.	Come to work late	71	3	4	19	45	29
14.	Left work early without permission	15	–	–	4	12	85
15.	Absent with no excuse	21	1	1	4	16	79
23.	Faking illness and calling in sick	29	1	1	6	22	71
Counterproductivity							
2.	Damaged property while horsing around	11	1	–	1	11	89
4.	Wasted company materials on purpose	8	1	1	1	7	92
A.	Consumed drugs or alcohol on job	8	1	–	1	6	92
B.	Argued with customers, co-workers or supervisors	78	3	6	29	41	22
C.	Fought with customers, co-workers or supervisors	14	–	1	2	11	86
24.	Did slow, sloppy work on purpose	22	1	2	4	17	78
E.	Came to work hungover from drugs or alcohol	23	1	1	7	15	77

Table 2.1 (continued)

Item #	Subject	% Admitting	Very Often	Often	Occasionally	Seldom	Never
Other Items:							
3.	Did not report wasted company materials	36	1		8	25	64
16.	Used company car without permission	5	–	–	1	5	95
25.	Faked injury for workmans compensation	1	1	–	–	1	99

N = 341

NOTE : 1. Some items may not sum to 100 percent due to rounding.
2. Items A, B, C, D, and E are combined items to allow comparability across surveys.
3. Very often = 3 or more times a week
Often = 1 - 2 times a week
Occasionally = 1 - 2 times in one month
Seldom = Only once in 6 months
Never = Not even once

percent of the respondents admitted to arguing with customers, coworkers, or supervisors; 71 percent admitted to coming to work late; and 54 percent admitted to eating food without paying. Other notable admission percentages include 36 percent admitting to not reporting wasted company materials; 34 percent admitting to seeing coworkers steal company property; 30 percent indicating using their employee discount for friends; 29 percent admitting to faking illness and calling in sick; 23 percent admitting to taking supplies for personal use; 23 percent admitting coming to work hung over from drugs or alcohol; 22 percent admitting doing slow, sloppy work on purpose; and 21 percent admitting to being absent without an excuse.

Factors. Items were logically grouped into five a priori factors: (1) Cash/ Property Theft—stealing company property, merchandise (including food) or money; (2) Theft Support—helping others steal; (3) Time Theft—wasteful use of company time; (4) Counterproductivity—work behaviors associated with poor performance; and (5) Other—other dishonest activities. (Refer to Table 2.1 for items grouped with their factors.) A respondent who admitted to any of the acts grouped under a factor was categorized as admitting to that factor.

Table 2.2 lists the percentages of respondents who admitted to any type of theft on the factors. It shows that 84 percent of the respondents admitted to performing behaviors under the Poor Job Performance factor (e.g., arguing or fighting with others, alcohol or drug use) and 78 percent admitted to some type of Time Theft (e.g., tardiness, unexcused absences). Sixty-two percent admitted to some type of Cash/Property Theft (e.g., taking merchandise, eating food); however, excluding the eating of food, 35 percent of respondents admitted to some type of Cash/Property Theft. Fifty-two percent admitted to Theft Support

Table 2.2
Admissions for Theft Factors for Fast Food Employees

Factor	% Admitting*
1. Cash/Property Theft	62%
2. Theft Support	53%
3. Time Theft	78%
4. Counterproductivity	84%
5. Other	35%
Total	96%

*Percent of respondents who admitted to the acts associated with the factor at least once in six months (i.e., responses of seldom, occasionally, often, or very often).

(e.g., not reporting theft, seeing others steal). Almost all respondents (96 percent) admitted to some employee deviance.

Dollar Amounts. Survey participants were asked to estimate the value of stolen merchandise or cash for a typical week. Table 2.3 displays the approximate dollar amounts fast food employees admitted taking in a typical week without permission, and the respondents' estimates of how much money or merchandise the "average employee" takes in a typical week from the employer without permission. Items were combined to provide estimates of the total value of money and merchandise taken.

To summarize the results presented in Table 2.3, 7 percent of respondents indicated they themselves take from $10 to $50 per week. However, 52 percent of respondents indicated that the "average employee" takes cash and merchandise valued from $10 to $100 per week. Respondents seem to perceive that the "average employee" takes substantially more property and cash than the respondents themselves do.

DISCUSSION

The results are based on the survey responses of 341 employees from two fast food companies. It is difficult to know how representative these two companies are of the entire fast food industry, particularly since the surveys were conducted at the companies' requests. As a result, the findings in this preliminary study cannot be extrapolated to the fast food industry as a whole. Nevertheless, they can be considered suggestive of the extent of the employee deviance in this industry.

Results indicated that the anonymous survey approach can yield substantial admissions of employee theft and counterproductivity. Many of the fast food employees admitted to theft and counterproductive behaviors. A majority of respondents admitted to arguing with others and tardiness, behaviors not typically

Table 2.3
Total Dollar Amount of Weekly Theft Admissions for Fast Food Respondents

	0	.50	$1	$2	$5	$10	$25	$50	$100	$500	Over $500
34. Merchandise Average Employee Takes	14%	4%	5%	13%	24%	19%	9%	7%	5%	1%	-
35. Merchandise You Take	73%	4%	5%	8%	6%	3%	1%	1%	1%	-	-
36. Money Average Employee Takes	38%	4%	7%	8%	15%	11%	10%	4%	2%	1%	-
37. Money You Take	94%	1%	1%	2%	1%	1%	-	-	-	1%	-
Merchandise and Money Average Employee Takes (34 and 36)	11%	3%	4%	13%	17%	24%	10%	10%	8%	1%	1%
Merchandise and Money You Take (35 and 37)	72%	4%	5%	8%	5%	4%	1%	1%	1%	1%	-

N = 341

measured in standard measures of employee deviance. Also, over half admitted to eating food without paying for it. This may reflect the strong opportunity for this type of theft in fast food restaurants.

The employees perceived substantial amounts of theft in their workplaces. In fact, they seemed to perceive that the "average employee" takes substantially more cash and property than they themselves do. The actual amount taken probably falls between these extremes; employees may underestimate the value of their own theft and overestimate the value of others' theft. The implication is that this perceived prevalence may be related to the perceived acceptability of theft within fast food establishments. The finding that a third of respondents saw others steal company cash or property and that over half admitted to some type of theft support behavior suggests that theft is somewhat tolerated by employees, management, or both. Reasons for the prevalence of theft support are suggested in a study that used the same fast food data set (Slora, 1988). In that study, beliefs about management fairness and attitudes were related to specific theft and counterproductive practices. That is, employees may steal because they feel that management "owes them" or because they believe that others at times engage in such "unacceptable" practices.

STUDY 2: SUPERMARKET SURVEY _____

METHOD

Subjects

Supermarket companies were recruited to participate in this study with the cooperation of a major trade association, the Food Marketing Institute. The seven participating companies were instructed to select randomly one employee from each supermarket store, excluding employees who were store managers, department heads, or warehouse employees or had less than two months' tenure. As in study 1, only one employee was selected from each store. The participating companies were provided with written instructions on how to select the survey participants randomly. When needed, a list of random numbers was also provided to the companies. Thus, a combined total of 504 supermarket employees was randomly selected by the companies to receive surveys. The survey participants were from the Northeast, Midwest, Southwest, and South.

Survey Questionnaire

The survey questionnaire was almost identical to the survey used in study 1. The only changes were in the coding of some of the demographic variables (e.g., respondents indicated the exact date of birth rather than only year). The items of employee deviance frequency admissions and dollar estimates were the same as in study 1.

Coding of the surveys, however, was used only to allow for comparisons and analyses across and within companies. The appropriate company codes were placed on the back of each survey using invisible ink. Individual employees were not distinctively coded. The coding procedures ensured that no researcher could link employees with their survey responses, thus ensuring the anonymity of employees' survey responses.

Survey Mailing

The same four-stage survey process used in study 1 was used to mail the surveys to the participants. The survey was implemented in the late fall of 1988 through early winter 1989.

RESULTS

The four-stage survey process yielded a 59 percent rate for the supermarket employees. Of 504 surveys mailed to participants, 19 letters or surveys were returned as undeliverable, and 296 were completed and returned of 485 total surveys sent and delivered. Fifteen of these 296 surveys were determined to be duplicate survey returns; that is, the same person returned two completed surveys. (Surveys that shared the same company number, birthdate, and demographic information were judged to be from the same person.) Thus, employees from 281 stores completed and returned usable surveys. (It was not possible to compare respondents to nonrespondents because the participating companies did not provide store or demographic information for the selected survey participants due to concerns over confidentiality.)

Surveys were not included in the analyses if the respondent indicated he or she was not currently working primarily in the supermarket industry or was employed in a store security capacity. Moreover, all of one company's respondents were in the security field; further examination showed these employees had not been randomly selected using the instructions provided by the researchers for participation in the survey. Thus 234 surveys from the supermarket employees of six companies were used for the subsequent data analyses.

Demographics

About 36 percent of the 234 supermarket respondents were front-end workers (cashiers and baggers), and 18 percent had supervisory titles (e.g., bakery manager, assistant grocery manager). Most of the respondents (over 63 percent) had been employed more than one year. About 56 percent of the respondents worked under 40 hours per week. About 60 percent of the respondents reported working evenings and nights or varied shifts. Seventy-one percent of the sample was 30 years old or younger. There were more females than males (53 percent and 47 percent, respectively). About 85 percent had completed high school. Twenty-six percent of respondents indicated two or more employers during the past year. Thus, a sizable percentage of the respondents were high school graduates, worked less than 40 hours, were female, or were 30 years old or younger.

Types of Deviant Behaviors

Item Admissions. Simple frequency analyses showed substantial admissions on several survey items (Table 2.4). The most frequent admissions of employee theft and production deviance among the 234 supermarket respondents were: coming to work late (70 percent), arguing with coworkers or supervisors (61 percent), and arguing with customers (37 percent). Other notable admission percentages include eating food without paying (35 percent), not reporting wasted company materials (30 percent), faking illness and calling in sick (26 percent), and doing slow or sloppy work on purpose (23 percent). Also, 18 percent admitted coming to work hung over from alcohol, 18 percent admitted to causing damage while "horsing around," 17 percent admitted to being absent without an excuse, and 17 percent admitted to not reporting theft by others.

Table 2.4
Admissions for Supermarket Respondents

Item #	Subject	% Admitting	Very Often	Often	Occasionally	Seldom	Never
Theft:							
1.	Taken merchandise/equipment	18%	1%	1%	3%	13%	82%
8.	Taken supplies for personal use	15%	1%	1%	2%	12%	85%
17.	Eaten food without paying	35%	3%	5%	8%	20%	65%
18.	Taken money without permission	1%	–	–	1%	1%	99%
19.	Overcharged/shortchanged on purpose	3%	–	–	1%	2%	98%
20.	Changed company records	1%	–	–	–	1%	99%
22.	Gave/received refunds for things not purchased	2%	–	–	1%	1%	98%
26.	Taken property from co-workers	1%	–	–	–	1%	99%
30.	Falsified company documents	1%	–	–	–	1%	99%
Theft Support:							
7.	Used employee discount for friends	11%	–	2%	3%	6%	89%
21.	Sold merchandise to friends at reduced price	9%	–	1%	2%	6%	91%
27.	Helped person take company property	4%	–	–	1%	3%	96%
28.	Saw co-workers steal company cash	4%	–	1%	1%	3%	96%
29.	Saw co-workers steal company property/merchandise	31%	1%	2%	10%	17%	69%
31.	Did not report theft by others	17%	1%	3%	4%	10%	83%
Time Theft:							
13.	Came to work late	70%	1%	6%	21%	42%	30%
14.	Left work early without permission	14%	–	–	3%	11%	86%
15.	Absent with no legitimate excuse	17%	–	–	1%	16%	83%
23.	Faking illness and calling in sick	26%	–	–	6%	20%	74%

Table 2.4 (continued)

Item #	Subject	% Admitting	Very Often	Often	Occasionally	Seldom	Never
Counterproductivity							
2.	Damaged property while horsing around	18%	–	1%	3%	14%	82%
4.	Wasted company materials on purpose	5%	–	–	1%	4%	95%
5.	Consumed drugs on job	2%	1%	–	–	1%	98%
6.	Consumed alcohol on job	3%	–	–	1%	3%	97%
9.	Argued with customers	37%	1%	1%	4%	31%	63%
10.	Argued with co-workers or supervisors	61%	1%	4%	20%	36%	39%
11.	Fought with customers	4%	–	1%	2%	2%	96%
12.	Fought with co-workers or supervisors	7%	–	1%	1%	6%	93%
24.	Did slow, sloppy work on purpose	23%	–	1%	2%	20%	77%
32.	Came to work hungover from alcohol	18%	–	1%	4%	14%	82%
33.	Came to work hungover from drugs	2%	1%	–	1%	1%	98%
Other Items:							
3.	Did not report wasted company materials	30%	1%	1%	7%	21%	70%
16.	Used company car without permission	1%	–	–	–	1%	99%
25.	Faked injury for workmans compensation	–	–	–	–	–	100%

N = 234

NOTE : 1. Some items may not sum to 100 percent due to rounding.

3. Very often = 3 or more times a week
   Often = 1 - 2 times a week
   Occasionally = 1 - 2 times in one month
   Seldom = Only once in 6 months
   Never = Not even once

Table 2.5
Admissions for Theft Factors for Supermarket Employees

Factor	% Admitting*
1. Cash/Property Theft	43%
2. Theft Support	39%
3. Time Theft	77%
4. Counterproductivity	75%
5. Other	29%
Total	94%

*Percent of respondents who admitted to the acts associated with the factor at least once in six months (i.e., responses of seldom, occasionally, often, or very often).

These figures refer to the aggregate percentages across all supermarket stores and companies of this sample and should be interpreted as reflecting the industry as a whole, not as necessarily being representative of a single company. The percentages range across companies: 19 to 43 percent admit to eating food without paying, 16 to 38 percent admit to seeing coworkers steal company property, 59 to 80 percent admit to coming to work late, 16 to 38 percent admit to faking illness and calling in sick, 29 to 47 percent admit to arguing with customers, 51 to 68 percent admit to arguing with coworkers or supervisors, and 23 to 36 percent admit to not reporting wasted company materials. The percentages should be interpreted with caution, however, since the company sizes ranged from 24 to 134 stores.

Factors. Items were grouped into five a priori factors as in study 1. A respondent who admitted to any of the acts grouped under a given factor was categorized as admitting to that factor.

Table 2.5 lists the percentage of respondents who admitted to any type of deviance on the factors. To summarize the table, 75 percent of respondents admitted to performing behaviors under the Counterproductivity factor (e.g., arguing or fighting with others, on-the-job alcohol or drug use), and 77 percent admitted to some type of Time Theft (e.g., tardiness, unexcused absences). Forty-three percent admitted to some type of Cash/Property Theft (e.g., taking merchandise, eating food); however, excluding the eating of food, 27 percent of respondents admitted to some type of Cash/Property Theft. Thirty-nine percent admitted to Theft Support (e.g., not reporting theft, seeing others steal). Almost all respondents (94 percent) admitted to some employee deviance. Percentages admitting to these factors within the companies ranged from 29 to 53 percent for the Cash/Property Theft factor, 24 to 53 percent for the Theft Support factor, 67 to 82 percent for the Time Theft factor, 71 to 77 percent for the Counterproductivity factor, and 20 to 37 percent for the "Other" factor.

Table 2.6
Total Dollar Amount of Weekly Theft Admissions for Supermarket Respondents

	0	.50	$1	$2	$5	$10	$25	$50	$100	$200	$500	Over $500
34. Merchandise Average Employee Takes	28%	7%	8%	12%	15%	10%	6%	6%	4%	2%	-	-
35. Merchandise You Take	82%	5%	4%	4%	3%	2%	1%	1%	-	-	-	-
36. Money Average Employee Takes	58%	3%	6%	7%	9%	6%	6%	3%	2%	1%	-	-
37. Money You Take	98%	1%	-	-	1%	-	-	-	-	-	-	-
Merchandise and Money Average Employee Takes (34 and 36)	27%	6%	7%	14%	11%	14%	6%	6%	7%	3%	-	-
Merchandise and Money You Take (35 and 37)	80%	6%	4%	4%	3%	2%	1%	1%	-	-	-	-

Notes: 1. N = 234 except for Item 34: N = 225, Item 35: N = 233, Item 36: N = 255

2. Missing values were treated as 0 for summations.

Dollar Amounts. Survey participants were asked to estimate the value of stolen merchandise or cash for a typical week. Table 2.6 displays breakdowns in terms of the approximate dollar amounts supermarket employees admitted themselves or that they saw "average employees" taking in a typical week without permission. Items were combined to provide estimates of the total value of money and merchandise taken.

Three percent of respondents indicated they themselves take from $10 to $50 per week ($50 was the maximum amount of total weekly theft admitted). However, 35 percent of respondents indicated that the "average employee" takes a total value from $10 to $300 per week. The range across companies of the dollar amount respondents admitted themselves taking weekly was $.08 to $1.43. The range across companies' respondents indicated the "average employee" taking weekly was $7.20 to $39.94. Respondents seem to perceive that the "average employee" takes substantially more property and cash than the respondents themselves do.

Other calculations were made on the basis of the dollar amount of theft admissions to estimate the total cost of these theft practices to organizations.

Table 2.7
Average Annual Supermarket Employee Theft Estimates

Method of Estimation	Single Employee	150 Employee Store	25 Store Chain	50 Store Chain	100 Store Chain
Amount of Actual Respondent Admissions	$44.72	$6,708	$167,700	$335,400	$670,800
Amount Perceived Taken By "Average Employee"	$1,209	$181,350	$4,533,750	$9,067,500	$18,135,000

These are summarized in Table 2.7. The average amount of cash and merchandise taken by a single respondent annually is estimated at $44.72 (based on a reported mean weekly amount of $0.86). The estimate of the annual cost of theft per store, based on 150 employees per store, is $6,708. Thus, a company of 25 supermarket stores may have $167,700 in estimated total losses due to employee theft, a company of 50 supermarket stores may have $335,400 in estimated total losses due to employee theft, and a company of 100 supermarket stores may have $670,800 of estimated total losses due to employee theft.

If perceptions by the respondents of the average employee are used, the average amount of cash and merchandise taken annually by a single average employee is $1,209 (based on a reported mean weekly amount of $23.25). The estimated annual cost per store, given 150 employees per store, is $181,350. Thus, a company with 25 supermarket stores may have estimated total losses of $4,533,750 due to employee theft, a company with 50 supermarket stores may have estimated total losses of $9,067,500 due to employee theft, and a company of 100 supermarket stores may have estimated total losses of $18,135,000 due to employee theft.

DISCUSSION

Substantial admissions of employee deviance were obtained from 234 supermarket employees of six companies. Forty-three percent admitted to some type of cash or property theft and 39 percent to some type of theft support behavior. Also, about one out of five (18 percent) admitted coming to work hung over from alcohol or to causing damage while horsing around. Thus, employees admitted to a variety of theft and production deviance activities.

It appears that these supermarket employees perceive employee theft to be prevalent in their stores. Almost a third saw coworkers steal company property or merchandise. Perceptions of the amount taken by the average employee were substantially higher than respondents' estimates of their own value of stolen goods. This may reflect the perceived prevalence of theft in supermarkets, as well as the acceptability of theft practices among workers. Findings from these supermarket data reported elsewhere show that beliefs about company fairness and employees' acceptance of theft are related to specific theft and counterproductive behaviors (Slora & Boye, 1989).

The findings obtained from the survey of supermarket employees are suggestive of the prevalence of employee deviance in the supermarket industry as a whole. The incidence of these practices varies across companies. The reported ranges across companies for the survey items and factors support this contention.

Possibly the reported supermarket industry percentages based on the sample used in this study may be underestimates of percentages typical of the supermarket industry as a whole. It is likely that the companies that agreed to participate were highly interested in employee theft problems. Such companies are more likely to be security conscious and to implement stringent store security measures. Also, two of the six companies in the analyzed sample have used some sort of preemployment integrity screening. The proportion in the sample using integrity tests reflects the findings of a survey conducted by the Food Marketing Institute (1989) of its membership; they found that 30.2 percent of supermarkets used preemployment integrity tests. In the analyzed supermarket survey sample, it is likely that fewer applicants were hired who would later steal on the job in these two companies. This contention is supported by a quasi-experimental analysis of these data (Jones & Slora, 1989) showing that the test-using companies had significantly lower employee theft monetary loss estimates.

GENERAL DISCUSSION

An anonymous survey approach yielded substantial admissions from both fast food and supermarket employees. The findings across the studies were similar: a substantial portion of respondents admitted to some type of cash or property theft and to theft support activities. In both studies, about three-quarters of respondents admitted to various counterproductive work practices. Also, respondents perceived employee theft to be prevalent in their workplaces.

Differences in the findings between the industries may be attributed in part to differences in the opportunities for stealing. For example, over half of the fast food employees admitted to eating food without paying for it; for supermarket employees a little over a third admitted to eating food. This is not surprising given that much food in the supermarkets is already packaged and usually not being processed or cooked as in fast food restaurants.

It should be noted, however, that these samples are not directly comparable due to the different number of companies in the samples, the differing geographic locations, and the time lag of about a year between the two surveys. Thus, any differences must be interpreted with caution. Further research is suggested on larger nationwide samples to allow for more direct comparisons between industries.

Advantages of Surveys

These findings from the fast food and supermarket industries suggest that an anonymous survey approach may be useful as a means of determining base rates of employee deviance. The substantial response rates and frequency of admissions show that employees are willing to report their deviant activities on a self-report measure. Given the self-report nature of such a measure and its possibly incriminating nature, it is surprising the numbers of employees who do admit to such acts of deviance. It is possible the actual incidences of employee deviance are much higher. Also, employees admitted to a variety of deviant work behaviors, indicating they were open to answering queries on a range of behaviors.

Another useful feature of such a survey approach is that it can measure otherwise undetected acts of employee deviance. For example, production deviance is difficult to measure; commonly used estimates rely on supervisory ratings and personnel records of counterproductivity. The findings of these surveys of fast food and supermarket employees showed substantial numbers admitting to arguing, doing slow or sloppy work on purpose, and other counterproductive behavior. In addition, the survey approach yielded estimates of employee theft substantially higher than most other methods. For example, a trade association survey found an average of only three instances of employee theft per supermarket store (Food Marketing Institute, 1989), substantially lower than the findings here would suggest.

The surveys may have produced the acceptable response rates because of their anonymous nature and because of the two follow-up surveys. Subjects were guaranteed anonymity and confidentiality, and survey materials appeared to be from a major university. The follow-ups may have underscored to subjects the importance of these surveys. Future research should explore the importance of anonymity in ensuring an adequate response rate.

This survey method, like any other, is not perfect. The logistics of ensuring anonymity while tracking responses in a four-stage survey process can be complex and costly. Also, it is difficult to know if the respondents differed in some relevant way from nonrespondents. It is suggested that, wherever possible, some comparisons be made to ensure the comparability of groups by drawing on a sample base where some store or demographic characteristics are known of nonrespondents.

Implications

Such a survey approach offers promise as a means of determining base rates of employee deviance, as well as establishing research constructs. The determination of employee deviance base rates is important not only to security professionals but also to psychologists who must determine the usefulness of selection tests. Some psychologists (e.g., Murphy, 1987) have suggested that some psychological tests have limited utility when base rates are low; this argument has been applied to the utility of preemployment integrity tests (Manhardt, 1989; Murphy, 1989). However, this argument is moot if the base rate is substantial and reflects the selection ratio (Ash, 1989; Murphy, 1989). The surveys described here found substantial employee deviance base rates for two industries. The finding of substantial base rates of employee theft and counterproductivity suggests that valid and reliable integrity tests that use norm-referenced cutoff scores (cf. Jones, 1989) are useful for the purpose of selecting applicants less likely to engage in dishonest activities on the job. In addition, the establishment of employee deviance base rates and the identification of specific behaviors allow for the application of practical solutions to the costly problems of employee deviance.

REFERENCES

Ash, P. (1976). The assessment of honesty in employment. *South African Journal of Psychology*, 6, 68–79.

Ash, P. (1989). Establishing cutoff scores for preemployment honesty tests: Professional, psychometric, ethical and legal considerations. Unpublished manuscript.

Food Marketing Institute (1989). *The food marketing industry speaks, 1989: Loss prevention issues study highlights*. Washington, D.C.: The Institute.

Hollinger, R., & Clark, J. (1983). *Theft by employees*. Lexington, MA: Lexington Books.

Jones, J. W. (1989). The use of norm-referenced cutoff scores with preemployment honesty tests. Unpublished research note. Park Ridge, IL: London House.

Jones, J. W., & Joy, D. S. (1988). Employee deviance base rates: A summary of empirical research. Unpublished research note. Park Ridge, IL: London House.

Jones, J. W., & Slora, K. B. (1989). Theft reduction through personnel selection: A control group design in the supermarket industry. Technical Report 30. Park Ridge, IL: London House.

Manhardt, P. J. (1989). Base rates and tests of deception. Has 1/0 psychology shot itself in the foot? *Industrial-Organizational Psychologist*, 26(2), 48–50.

Murphy, K. R. (1987). Detecting infrequent deception. *Journal of Applied Psychology*, 72, 611–614.

Murphy, K. R. (1989). Maybe we should shoot ourselves in the foot: Reply to Manhardt. *Industrial-Organizational Psychologist*, 26(3), 45–46.

Slora, K. B. (1988). Employee theft in the fast food industry: Preliminary base rate information. Technical Report 1. Park Ridge, IL: London House.

Slora, K. B., & Boye, M. W. (1989). Employee theft in the supermarket industry: Final report of findings. Technical Report 2. Park Ridge, IL: London House.

Tatham, R. (1974). Employees' views on theft in retailing. *Journal of Retailing*, 49–55.

3

Selection Alternatives to the Preemployment Polygraph

JOHN W. JONES AND WILLIAM TERRIS

The main purpose of preemployment polygraph examinations was to screen job applicants with a propensity for employee theft, a crime which is widespread, difficult to detect, and the most costly crime against business (American Management Association, 1977). When Hollinger and Clark (1983) surveyed thousands of employees to establish the base rate of employee theft, they found that 42 percent of retail sector employees, 32 percent of hospital employees, and 26 percent of manufacturing personnel admitted to this crime. Slora (1988) conducted an anonymous survey among fast food employees and found that 62 percent admitted to theft of company property or cash, and 78 percent admitted to time theft (e.g., faking illness and calling in sick, leaving work early without permission). These findings are consistent with Hefter's (1986) claim that one in three employees steals at work. Moreover, Meinsma's (1985) research suggests that anywhere from 10 percent to 30 percent of all business bankruptcies can be attributable in part to employee theft problems. These researchers are beginning to quantify both the total frequency and cost of employee theft. The existence of significant theft in the workplace is widely accepted by security researchers and professionals.

Businesses have used two general approaches to reduce theft losses. The first, to alter the work environment so as to preclude the possibility of theft, is primarily aimed at shoplifters. It includes the use of undercover security officers, closed-circuit televisions, and special sensor tags on each inventory article. Although these systems may be effective in reducing theft by shoplifters, employee thieves often circumvent them.

A second approach has been to concentrate on the preemployment screening process to minimize the selection of job applicants likely to engage in theft-related behaviors. This approach is aimed at employee theft. Preemployment screening appears to be one of the methods of choice for retail organizations in their efforts to control employee theft as a source of inventory shrinkage and profit drain (Sackett & Harris, 1984). Theft rates are lower in organizations that conduct careful and extensive preemployment screening (Baumer & Rosenbaum, 1984).

Among the most popular selection methods used to determine the integrity of prospective employees has been the preemployment polygraph exam. In 1988, however, the federal Employee Polygraph Protection Act was passed, requiring employers to find alternative methods of testing job applicants.

THE EMPLOYEE POLYGRAPH PROTECTION ACT OF 1988

The Employee Polygraph Protection Act, which became effective December 27, 1988 (Frierson, 1988; House of Representatives, 1988), outlaws most business uses of polygraphs, especially preemployment polygraph exams used to screen out job applicants with a history of theft. In fact, the act outlaws any type of physiologically based "lie detectors," including polygraphs, deceptographs, and voice stress analyzers. Businesses may be assessed a civil penalty of not more than $10,000 if they violate this provision. Moreover, employers may be liable to prospective employees affected by such a violation. Equitable relief to the applicant of both an offer of employment and the payment of lost wages and benefits can be deemed appropriate by the courts.

Polygraphs were outlawed for three major reasons. First, there was a lack of scientifically acceptable research that showed that job applicants' polygraph results were accurate predictors of their past or future theft. That is, the preemployment polygraph exam was never thoroughly and scientifically validated with job applicants. It should be noted that although there is little evidence that the preemployment polygraph actually works, neither is there any research evidence that it does not work. There simply is very little scientific research.

Second, the accuracy, fairness, and consistency of the polygraph exam appeared to be a function of the skill of the examiner. For example, more reliable admissions were obtained by licensed, highly trained examiners as opposed to less skilled examiners. The polygraph industry never established and enforced a universal standard of competence that had to be met by all polygraphers; consequently, examples of abuse were common.

Finally, the preemployment polygraph examination has been criticized as being unpleasant and stressful to applicants. Although polygraphers were often skilled at interrogation and getting theft admissions from applicants, this process tended to provoke strong negative feelings from applicants (e.g., Lykken, 1981).

Employee theft is still a very serious and costly problem for businesses to grapple with. In many jobs, employees know that they can easily steal cash or valuable merchandise or equipment without any serious possibility of being caught. Hence, the federal ban on preemployment polygraph exams will lead employers to seek other methods to determine the honesty of job applicants.

The purpose of this chapter is to describe various screening alternatives to the preemployment polygraph, especially preemployment honesty tests. These psychological inventories are easy to administer and have scientific studies documenting their ability to screen out applicants who are likely to engage in on-the-job theft. Advantages and disadvantages of each selection procedure are summarized in Table 3.1.

THEFT REDUCTION THROUGH PERSONNEL SELECTION

Preemployment Polygraph Examinations

There are a few exceptions to the Polygraph Protection Act. The act does allow governmental units—federal, state, or local—to continue the use of polygraphs except as limited by state laws. Some companies with nuclear power–related contracts with the Department of Energy may also be allowed to use the polygraph. And, businesses will be allowed to use polygraphs for selection in two situations: the hiring of certain private security firm employees and the hiring of persons with access to specified drugs (Schedule I, II, III, or IV drugs as defined in the Federal Control Substances Act).

The purpose of a preemployment polygraph examination is to uncover all undetected dishonest acts committed by a job applicant during a certain period of time. The underlying theory is that past behavior predicts future behavior. The preemployment examination typically covers many different areas of dishonest behavior. For instance, in a typical preemployment examination, the examiner will try to uncover the following information:

1. prior convictions,
2. prior undetected thefts of money from the job,
3. prior undetected thefts of property and merchandise from the job,
4. various types of undetected theft off the job,
5. illegal drug use,
6. selling of illegal drugs, and
7. other information requested by the employer.

The preemployment polygraph examination yields two types of information: admissions and signs of deception. Thus, the applicant will make or not make an admission to any question and either show or not show signs of deception.

Table 3.1
Main Screening Methods Used to Reduce Employee Theft

Screening Method	Convenience Issues	Main Problems	Main Advantages
Preemployment polygraph	Requires additional time if exam is off site	Illegal for most business uses	May discourage dishonest applicants from even applying
		May offend job applicants	Often results in actual admissions from applicants
		Validity is questioned	
		Difficulty in obtaining well-trained examiners	
Selection interview	Usually part of hiring procedure	No evidence of validity	Inexpensive (already part of hiring procedures)
		Difficult to determine truthfulness in discussing theft and counter-productivity	Structured integrity interviews show promise
Reference checks	Often time-consuming	Little evidence of validity	May increase truthfulness of applicants
		Most misconduct is undetected	Verifies information provided on application form and resume
		Company reluctant to give negative information	
Credit checks	Quick but somewhat costly	Relevance to theft not clear	Obtains information relevant to financial need and fiscal responsibility
		May not meet EEOC guidelines	
Honesty tests	Can easily be made part of the usual screening procedure	Test scores can be misinterpreted	More validity data than other selection methods
		Not all honesty tests are thoroughly validated	Inexpensive
			Typically not offensive
			No adverse impact (meets EEOC guidelines)
			May discourage dishonest applicants from even applying

Admissions have an obvious type of face validity. The applicant who admits taking $200 in merchandise from a previous employer had probably taken that much at the very least. The validity (accuracy) of the polygrapher's interpretation of deception is much more controversial (e.g., Sackett & Decker, 1979).

Employment Interviews

The traditional interview is an important part of almost every company's personnel selection procedures. Consequently, there have been many studies investigating the various types of validity of the employment interview (Schmitt, 1976); unfortunately there has been no published research investigating the effectiveness of the employment interview as a method to predict and reduce employee theft. The general validity of the interview apparently depends on the interviewer's having accurate and complete information about the job and worker requirements (Landy, 1976). Interviewers, however, are not likely to have accurate or complete information regarding valid predictors of employee theft since relatively little is known about this subject. They are likely to rely on certain stereotypes when making a judgment regarding honesty (e.g., firm handshake, shifty eyes, type and style of clothes). Finally, the employment interview is likely to cause problems in the areas related to equal employment opportunities (Arvey, 1979). Traditional employment interviews need to be validated against theft criteria before they can be seen as viable alternatives to preemployment polygraph exams.

Wilson (1988) is pioneering a new approach to employment interviewing, structured integrity interviewing, which can be used to identify job applicants at risk for dishonest behavior in the workplace.

Structured integrity interview questions are based on a thorough analysis of the job and the opportunities to steal at work. The interviewers typically ask job applicants to describe their past job behavior, highly predictive of how a person will perform in a new job (Janz, 1982). Some structured questions are phrased to ask applicants how they would respond to hypothetical scenarios related to employee theft in the workplace. All structured questions are presented in the *Structured Interview Guide.* Answers to *each* question are rated on a five-point, behaviorally anchored rating scale to improve the overall accuracy of this selection procedure.

Wilson's structured integrity questions ask applicants to describe situations where they were particularly honest or dishonest at another job. In addition, she recommends a series of probing questions in case applicants are resistant to answering questions related to their levels of integrity and dependability truthfully and comprehensively. Interviewers are taught how to ask these types of sensitive questions in order to put applicants at ease when answering them. Structured integrity interviewing is one of the most promising new strategies in the field of personnel interviewing because of the much higher levels of validity than traditional, open-ended interviews (McDaniel, 1988).

Reference Checks

Perhaps the major purpose of the reference check is to verify information the applicants have supplied to the company. Applicants expecting reference checks are thought to be more truthful in the information they supply to the company. Usually reference checks are costly and time-consuming when one considers the amount of information produced. Perhaps this is the reason that most companies do not perform complete reference checks on most applicants. There is little, if any, direct evidence that the use of reference checks actually reduces employee theft (Terris, 1985).

While reference checks are probably desirable, they do have major limitations in terms of obtaining information relevant to employee theft. One problem is that employers are often reluctant to give negative information concerning past employees because of possible lawsuits. In fact, dishonest employees caught stealing sometimes make a deal with their employers: the employee agrees to resign and return the money or property in return for a good or at least a neutral reference. A more important problem is that in most companies, the employer is not aware of which employees are stealing. Another problem is that there is little evidence as to the validity or accuracy of data obtained from reference checks. Finally, job applicants can usually omit from the reference list the names of any companies where they are known to have stolen money or merchandise.

Criminal Background Checks

Criminal background checks and investigations can vary from little more than a reference check to a complete investigation of an individual's entire life. Usually the background check is limited to a check on a person's past criminal history. Arrest records, while probably valid, are seldom used to make a hiring decision because of possible legal ramifications. Several states ban employers outright from either asking about or using arrest information to make a hiring decision. While federal laws apparently do not absolutely forbid using arrest information, using arrest records to make hiring decisions would probably result in adverse impact against blacks and some other minority groups.

Convictions, on the other hand, can be considered when making a hiring decision, although one possible requirement is that only relevant or job-related criminal histories be considered. For example, an applicant with a prior conviction for theft could be denied employment where the opportunity for on-the-job theft is great (e.g., clerks in a jewelry store). It is not yet certain if a company can use irrelevant convictions. Actually the question of relevant versus irrelevant convictions is essentially an empirical one; research is needed to show whether a certain type of conviction is predictive of future employee theft.

There are a number of problems with criminal checks. First, legal and practical obstacles make it time-consuming and difficult to obtain criminal records. Any information obtained is likely to be incomplete or misleading. For example, most crimes are never detected, most detected crimes never lead to actual arrest, and apparently many arrests do not lead to a conviction. Furthermore, many convictions are based on plea bargaining or some other type of reduced sentencing. It should also be remembered that employee thieves are almost never caught or convicted.

Credit Checks

Some employers use credit checks to make a hiring decision. The rationale is that applicants with either a great need for money to pay bills or a history of irresponsible financial management are thought to be greater risks for positions of trust. Although there apparently is no empirical evidence to support this belief, it does seem likely that individuals who need a great deal of money might be more tempted to steal than those without a great need. Credit checks seem to have a high probability of producing adverse impact against racial minorities.

Employment Application Blanks

Weighted employment application blanks and similar biographical data have been found to be valid predictors of job success in many different occupations (England, 1971); nevertheless, only one study has been published related to employee theft (Rosenbaum, 1976). The main predictors in this study were essentially racial in nature, and the validity coefficients were low. Hence, current research suggests that this procedure does not accurately predict theft and in fact may lead to discrimination against racial minorities. Much more research is needed to determine the viability of the employment application blank as an alternative to preemployment polygraphs.

Psychological Assessment

Historically, attempts to predict criminal behavior with personality tests have not been successful (Schuessler & Cressey, 1950). Commonly used personality tests such as the Sixteen Personality Factor Questionnaire (16PF) (Cattel, Eber & Tatsuoka, 1970) and the Minnesota Multiphasic Personality Inventory (MMPI) (Dahlstrom & Welsh, 1960) have not been found to predict employee theft.

More recently, an extensive amount of research has been conducted with paper-and-pencil honesty tests, psychological tests designed to predict job applicants' proneness for theft and other forms of counterproductivity. Most honesty tests are designed to measure job applicants' attitudes toward, perceptions of, and opinions about theft. Validation research that complies with test development guidelines of the American Psychological Association has been published for a number of honesty tests (London House, 1980). Although all honesty tests differ from one another in important ways, all of the tests measure attitudes related to one or more of the following psychological constructs:

1. Tolerance of others who steal.
2. Projection about the extent of theft by others.
3. Acceptance of rationalizations for theft.
4. Antisocial beliefs and behaviors.
5. Admissions of theft-related activities.

Unlike general personality testing and other types of personnel screening procedures, there has been a great deal of validity research where honesty test scores have predicted theft behavior. Most of the current research with honesty tests has been conducted with the Personnel Selection Inventory (PSI) (McDaniel & Jones, 1988; Sackett & Harris, 1984). Terris (1979a) found that the PSI accurately predicted theft admissions made in preemployment polygraph examinations. Ash (1970, 1971, 1972, 1976) was able to obtain a similar pattern of results with another preemployment honesty test.

The validity of the PSI is not limited to polygraph admissions. It has also been found to predict supervisors' ratings of employees' dishonesty (Jones & Terris, 1983a), applicants who are likely to get caught stealing once hired (Jones & Terris, 1981), applicants who have a criminal history (Jones & Terris, 1985), and applicants who are likely to make theft admissions in an anonymous testing situation (Terris, 1979b; Jones, 1980, 1981).

Other longitudinal studies have shown that a group of convenience stores using the PSI experienced a 50 percent reduction in shrinkage over approximately 18 months (Terris & Jones, 1982). This impact-on-losses study was replicated in the home improvement center industry (Brown et al., 1987). Several other studies (Jones & Terris, 1984; Terris & Jones 1982) have shown that applicants and employees from high-theft stores score more poorly on honesty tests than do applicants and employees from low-theft stores.

Employee Theft Profile

The following psychological profile emerges from the empirical research on honesty tests. Employee thieves tend to:

1. Rate themselves lower in honesty and in other related areas of integrity (e.g., illicit drug abuse).
2. Believe or suspect that most employees steal.
3. Accept the many common rationalizations for theft.
4. Often fantasize about successful theft.
5. Obsessively think and ruminate about theft.
6. Make many more theft-related admissions.
7. Are more deviant in other areas of life (e.g., illegal drug use, violence, unsafe behavior).

Hence, employee thieves have a definite psychological profile that is different from honest employees. Paper-and-pencil honesty tests can accurately measure the various dimensions of this profile. Yet although honesty tests can predict employees' theft proneness, they must be fair to all minority groups and must be nonoffensive to applicants.

Adverse Impact Analysis. Personnel selection methods, including honesty tests, cannot adversely discriminate against any race or sex groups (EEOC, 1979). All of the honesty tests report a lack of adverse impact against protected groups (Terris, 1979a). Female applicants do as well as or better than males in all of the studies, and no racial differences have been found. Hence, honesty tests appear to be fair to all groups. Adverse impact studies should routinely be conducted for any selection method that a company chooses as a replacement for the preemployment polygraph.

Test Takers' Reactions. Unlike preemployment polygraphs, the majority of job applicants are not offended when they take a paper-and-pencil honesty test. Jones and Joy (1988) found that 82 percent of the applicants who took the PSI had no objections to the test. The few applicants who did object to it were reliably more likely to score below standards (in the dishonest direction). Similar results were found by Ryan and Sackett (1987). It appears that employment applicants with both tolerant attitudes toward theft and a history of dishonest activities are most likely to be defensive about and object to taking preemployment honesty tests.

Truthful Responses. Some people falsely assume that more intelligent job applicants might deduce the purpose of preemployment honesty tests and skew their answers to reflect falsely a more honest disposition. Yet Jones and Terris (1983b) established that job applicants' intelligence test scores are not related to their honesty scores. Smarter people did not score better on the honesty test.

Honesty tests typically contain a Distortion scale to determine if job applicants are being truthful and candid with their answers. Applicants are also discouraged from trying to "fake good," or distort their answers, on honesty tests since the instructions state that any attempts to provide inaccurate answers can be detected and could invalidate the test results. Because paper-and-pencil honesty tests appear to be valid, fair, and usable, they appear to be one of the more acceptable alternatives to the preemployment polygraph.

ALTERNATE EXPLANATIONS

An impressive amount of research data is accumulating that indicates that using psychological honesty tests for screening new hirees reduces employment theft. Jones and Terris (1985) conducted a postdictive validity study and found one honesty test to be over 90 percent accurate in predicting past criminal convictions of department store applicants. They also showed that applicants screened with an honesty test engaged in significantly less employee theft compared to applicants who were not screened. Brown et al. (1987) conducted a five-year study and showed that implementation of an honesty test reliably reduced two types of counteproductive employee behaviors: theft and narcotic drug use. Inventory shrinkage losses were also reduced by over $2.25 million during the course of the study.

Companies using psychological honesty tests generally believe that they are effective because they screen out theft-prone individuals and screen in honest, productive employees. There are, however, other possible explanations that could explain a reduction in theft. One is that the use of a valid selection procedure creates an organizational climate unfavorable to theft. Employees prone to steal may be less likely to consider the possibility of theft if their fellow employees obviously disapprove (Hollinger & Clark, 1983). Another possibility is that using an honesty test sends a message to all applicants and employees that the company cares about preventing theft and will do something about it. Perhaps this serves as a warning signal to all employees. This is the deterrent effect. A third possible explanation is that a selection system sensitizes the entire work force to these issues. Using a psychological test to screen out theft-prone applicants usually generates a great deal of discussion about theft in all levels of the organization. It is possible that values and opinions may be changed somewhat in the process. A fourth possible explanation is that the implementation of a personnel selection procedure creates system changes within the organization. For example, interviewers may begin to do a better job interviewing, perhaps security personnel will become more vigilant, and so on. From the point of view of the organization, the reasons that something works may be less important than the fact that it works. From the point of view of the personnel researcher, however, the reasons are important. Certainly when we understand why something works, we can also maximize the effectiveness of the procedure.

New Directions in Personnel Selection

Preemployment polygraph examinations typically provided companies with additional information besides applicants' likelihood to steal. They were also used to assess applicants' history of illicit drug use, their tendency to quit work over work-related conflicts, and their feigning worker compensation injuries when no true injury existed. Companies need information in these areas to control drug-related accidents, turnover costs, and escalating insurance premiums, respectively.

Many honesty tests, including the PSI, have been designed to provide companies with important supplemental information too. Table 3.2 highlights the different supplemental areas measured by the PSI. The Drug Avoidance scale can be used by companies that want to control drug-related crimes and accidents. The Customer Relations scale identifies applicants who will provide good-quality service to customers. The Safety scale is useful for businesses concerned about controlling escalating insurance costs. The Work Values and Supervision scales tell companies if applicants will be productive workers and follow their super-

Table 3.2
Additional Areas of Inquiry Measured by the PSI

Test Scales and Versions	PSI-1	PSI-3	PSI-3S	PSI-4	PSI-5	PSI-5S	PSI-7	PSI-7S	PSI-7ST	PSI-7RST
Detailed Personal History	X			X	X					
Honesty		X	X	X	X	X	X	X	X	
Drug Avoidance		X	X	X	X	X	X	X	X	X
Non-violence		X	X	X	X	X				
Customer Relations							X	X	X	X
Emotional Stability			X		X	X				
Safety						X		X	X	X
Work Values							X	X	X	X
Supervision							X	X	X	X
Tenure									X	X
Responsibility										X
Employability Index							X	X	X	X
Validity Scale — Distortion	X	X	X	X	X	X	X	X	X	X
Validity Scale — Accuracy	X	X	X	X	X	X	X	X	X	X

visors' orders, respectively. The Tenure scale informs management if an applicant is likely to quit a job prematurely, thus wasting training dollars and leaving
a company understaffed. The Responsibility scale identifies dependable and
conscientious applicants *without* assessing their attitudes toward theft. These
additional scales are accurate predictors of the job-related behaviors they purport
to predict. Supplemental scales can help companies better contain costs and
increase profits in areas other than just theft reduction.

CONCLUSION

There are no simple solutions to controlling employee theft and other forms
of counterproductivity; however, theft reduction through personnel selection
appears to be an effective strategy for protecting bottom-line profits. Research
is needed to determine the extent to which any personnel selection procedure is
a valid measurement of job applicants' propensity for on-the-job counterproductivity. Companies should consider the following issues before choosing any
selection strategy as an alternative to preemployment polygraph examinations:

1. Companies should only use adequately validated selection procedures. Ideally the
   validation strategy would include a series of studies in which the selection procedure
   is validated in many different ways against many different types of counterproductivity.
   Since each validation approach has different strengths and weaknesses, a multimethod
   validation approach is best.
2. An adverse impact analysis should be conducted for any selection procedure being
   considered, performed in accordance with the Equal Employment Opportunity Commission guidelines.
3. Nearly all the existing validation research has been conducted with psychological
   honesty tests. Companies should attempt to validate any personnel selection procedure
   that does not have sufficient validation research.

REFERENCES

American Management Association (1977). *Crimes against business project: Background and recommendations*. New York: American Management Association.
Arvey, R. (1979). Unfair discrimination in the employment interview: Legal and psy-
    chological aspects. *Psychological Bulletin, 86,* 736–765.
Ash, P. (1970). The validation of an instrument to predict the likelihood of employee
    theft. *Proceedings of the 78th Annual Convention of the American Psychological
    Association.* Washington, DC: APA.
Ash, P. (1971). Screening employment applicants for attitudes toward theft. *Journal of
    Applied Psychology, 55,* 161–164.
Ash, P. (1972). Attitudes of work applicants toward theft. *Proceedings of the Seventeenth
    International Congress of Applied Psychology.* Liège, Belgium.
Ash, P. (1976). The assessment of honesty in employment. *South African Journal of
    Psychology, 6,* 68–79.

Baumer, T. L., & Rosenbaum, D. P. (1984). *Combatting retail theft: Programs and strategies*. Boston: Butterworth.

Brown, T. S., Jones, J. W., Terris, W., & Steffy, B. D. (1987). The impact of pre-employment integrity testing on employee turnover and inventory shrinkage losses. *Journal of Business and Psychology*, 2, 136–149.

Cattel, R. B., Eber, H. W., & Tatsuoka, M. M. (1970). *Handbook for the Sixteen Personality Factor Questionnaire (16PF)*. Champaign, IL: Institute for Personality and Ability Testing.

Campbell, D., & Stanley, J. (1963). *Experimental and quasi-experimental designs for research*. Chicago: Rand McNally.

Dahlstrom, W. G., & Welsh, G. S. (1980). *An MMPI Handbook*. Minneapolis: University of Minnesota Press.

England, G. W. (1971). *Development and use of weighted application blanks*. Rev. ed. Minneapolis: University of Minnesota Industrial Relations Center.

Equal Employment Opportunity Commission (EEOC) (1979). Adoption of questions and answers to clarify and provide a common interpretation of the Uniform Guidelines on Employee Selection Procedures. *Federal Register*, 44, 11996–12009.

Frierson, J. G. (1988). The new federal polygraph law's impact on business. *Commerce*, Fall, 70–71.

Hefter, R. (1986). The crippling crime. *Security World*, 23, 36–38.

Hollinger, R., & Clark, J. (1983). *Theft by employees*. Lexington, MA: Lexington Books.

House of Representatives. Employee Polygraph Protection Act of 1988. 100th Congress, 2d. Session. Report 100–659.

Janz, T. (1982). Initial comparisons of patterned behavior description interviews versus unstructured interviews. *Journal of Applied Psychology*, 67, 577–580.

Jones, J. W. (1980). Attitudinal correlates of employees' deviance: Theft, alcohol use, and nonprescribed drug use. *Psychological Reports*, 47, 71–77.

Jones, J. W. (1981). Attitudinal correlates of employee theft of drugs and hospital supplies among nursing personnel. *Journal of Nursing Research*, 30(6), 351–359.

Jones, J. W., & Joy, D. (1988). Empirical investigation of job applicants' reactions to taking a preemployment honesty test. *Technical Report*. Park Ridge, IL: London House.

Jones, J. W., & Terris, W. (1981). Predictive validation of a dishonesty test that measures theft proneness. Paper presented at the 18th Inter-American Congress of Psychology, Santo Domingo, Dominican Republic, June 21–26.

Jones, J. W., & Terris, W. (1983a). Predicting employees' theft in home improvement centers. *Psychological Reports*, 52, 187–201.

Jones, J. W., & Terris, W. (1983b). Personality correlates of theft and drug abuse among job applicants. *Proceedings of the Third International Conference on the 16PF test*. Champaign, IL: IPAT Press.

Jones, J. W., & Terris, W. (1984). The organizational climate of honesty: empirical investigation. Technical Report 27. Park Ridge, IL: London House.

Jones, J. W., & Terris, W. (1985). Screening employment applicants for attitudes toward theft: Three quasi-experiments. *International Journal of Management*, 2, 62–72.

Landy, F. J. (1976). The validity of the interview in police officer selection. *Journal of Applied Psychology*, 61, 193–198.

London House (1980). *Personnel Selection Inventory (PSI)*. Park Ridge, IL: London House.

Lykken, D. T. (1981). *A tremor in the blood*. New York: McGraw-Hill.

McDaniel, M. A. (1988). Employment interviews: Structure, validity, and unanswered questions. Paper presented at the Third Annual Convention of the Society for Industrial and Organizational Psychology, April.

McDaniel, M. A., & Jones, J. W. (1988). Predicting employee theft: A quantitative review of a standardized measure of honesty. *Journal of Business and Psychology*, 2, 327–345.

Meinsma, G. (1985). Thou shalt not steal. *Security Management*, 29, 35–37.

Rosenbaum, R. W. (1976). Predictability of employee theft using weighted application blanks. *Journal of Applied Psychology*, 61, 94–98.

Ryan, A. M., & Sackett, P. R. (1987). Pre-employment honesty testing: Fakability, reactions of test takers, and company image. *Journal of Business and Psychology*, 1, 248–256.

Sackett, P., & Decker, P. (1979). Detection of deception in the employment context: A review and critical analysis. *Personnel Psychology*, 32, 487–506.

Sackett, P. R., & Harris, M. E. (1984). Honesty testing for personnel selection: A review and critique. *Personnel Psychology*, 37, 221–246.

Schmitt, N. (1976). Social and situational determinants of interview decisions: Implications for the employment interview. *Personnel Psychology*, 29, 79–101.

Schuessler, KI., & Cressey, D. (1950). Personality characteristics of criminals. *American Journal of Sociology*, 55, 476–484.

Slora, K. (1988). Employee theft in the fast food industry. Technical Report 2. Park Ridge, IL: London House.

Terris, W. (1979a). Attitudinal correlates of employee integrity: Theft-related admissions made in pre-employment polygraph examinations. *Journal of Security Administration*, 2, 30–39.

Terris, W. (1979b). Attitudinal correlates of theft, violence and drug use. Paper presented at the 17th Interamerican Congress of Psychology, Lima, Peru.

Terris, W. (1985). *Employee theft: Research, theory, and applications*. Park Ridge, IL: London House Press.

Terris, W., & Jones, J. W. (1982). Psychological factors related to employee theft in the convenience store industry. *Psychological Reports*, 51, 1219–1238.

Wilson, C. (1988). New developments in selection interviewing. Paper presented at the Training '88 Conference for Human Resource Professionals, New York, December 12–16.

4

Improving Corporate Profitability with Preemployment Integrity Tests

STEVEN H. WERNER, DENNIS S. JOY, AND JOHN W. JONES

It is widely acknowledged that internal employee theft is one of a number of factors contributing to inventory shrinkage, cash shortages, and, in some cases, business failure. Although accurate and reliable estimates of the typical amount of financial loss resulting from internal theft incurred by businesses are difficult to obtain, theft by employees, as well as other forms of workplace counter-productivity (e.g. on-the-job drug abuse, carelessness, violations of safe personnel practices), have had a significant impact on the profit-making structure of most major businesses today. This is an unacceptable fact given that U.S. corporations are struggling to regain a strong leadership role in the global economy. An estimate by the National Corrective Training Institute indicated the overall shrinkage losses for all segments of retailing were between $16 billion and $24 billion annually. Findings recently published by the Bureau of National Affairs have confirmed this earlier estimate: "A conservative estimate of the annual economic loss to U.S. business from employee theft ranges from $15 billion to $25 billion per year" (Shepard & Duston, 1988).

Hollinger and Clark (1983) determined that the average base rate of employee theft in the retail sector was 42 percent of workers. These findings are consistent with even more recent research conducted by Hefter (1986) that suggests that one in three employees steals at work. Research conducted by Slora (1988) indicates that theft in the fast food industry is significantly more prevalent than in other industries. Admittedly, no methods can accurately determine the share of total company loss due to internal theft, shoplifting, bookkeeping error, or other unidentified sources. However, it is also important to note that companies have both a right and a need to protect their assets from potentially dishonest and counteproductive employees.

In an attempt to counter the significant business costs of employee theft, personnel managers have demonstrated an increasing interest in screening out potentially dishonest applicants before they are hired and given the opportunity to steal (Sackett, Burris & Callahan, 1987; Sackett & Harris, 1984). Businesses have used a number of methods in their efforts to control and reduce employee theft. Many of these procedures have been incorporated into the personnel selection process. For example, employee background and reference checks, more stringent interviewing procedures, preemployment polygraph examinations, and paper-and-pencil integrity inventories have been used by employers in order to get a better picture of the applicant prior to making a hiring decision. This chapter focuses on the impact of the use of written integrity inventories, like the London House Personnel Selection Inventory (PSI) on corporate profitability.

The PSI (London House, 1980), one of the best-validated instruments of its type (Joy, 1988; McDaniel & Jones, 1988), was developed by psychologists to predict an individual's potential for theft of company property, merchandise, and money, as well as other counterproductive behaviors that would detract from overall corporate profit. The PSI assesses an applicant's attitude and values regarding theft and other forms of counterproductive behavior. Extensive research in over 65 studies (Joy, 1988; Jones & Terris, 1981; McDaniel & Jones, 1988; Terris, 1985) has indicated that the PSI is a reliable and valid instrument for use in identifying potential thieves among job applicants.

The PSI has been validated in a wide variety of commercial and nonprofit organizational settings, including department stores, convenience stores, home improvement centers, supermarkets, hotels, hospitals, and banks. In addition, it has been validated using a variety of experimental methods, including postdictive, concurrent, and predictive criterion-related validation strategies. A number of studies have been conducted using quasi-experimental designs such as time-series and nonequivalent control group methodologies. In almost every case, test scores have been significantly related to a number of theft-related indexes and behaviors, among them, theft admissions made during polygraph examinations, anonymous theft admissions, cash drawer shortages, terminations for theft, prior criminal arrest and conviction records, time theft, company shrinkage, rule violations, and poor productivity.

Extensive research with the PSI and other similar psychological tests has indicated that they are effective at screening out potential employee thieves. Although these experimental studies have demonstrated that preemployment integrity assessment programs increase both organizational productivity and profits, operating executives justifiably demand estimates of the expected benefits of their personnel selection programs. London House's research studies and interviews with companies that use the PSI indicate that significant increases in corporate profitability result when integrity assessment systems are incorporated into the personnel selection process.

USING AN INTEGRITY ASSESSMENT SYSTEM TO INCREASE PROFITS

A business organization that uses tests like the PSI can anticipate profit increases through reduced screening costs, crime rates and employee terminations for theft. Reductions in shrinkage, turnover, and insurance costs can be expected along with increased productivity.

The costs of adequately screening personnel with traditional methods, like preemployment interviewing, are rapidly becoming prohibitive. Comprehensive interviewing is time-consuming and often impractical or even unreasonable for the majority of entry-level jobs. In addition, with the recent outlawing of the expensive (and typically unreliable) preemployment polygraph examination, paper-and-pencil integrity screening makes sense given that a typical polygraph examination costs between $25 and $80 and the cost of a typical paper-and-pencil inventory ranges between $9 and $14 depending on the scoring method and quantity ordered.

Companies that use the PSI have reported lower employee crime rates and fewer employee terminations for theft. Since the PSI helps in screening in individuals who are less likely to steal from the workplace, companies can realize potentially higher profits for a number of reasons. First, costly theft surveillance equipment used to catch internal thieves becomes less necessary. Second, companies can invest less capital in large security forces since they do not have to devote extensive time to preventing or catching employee thieves. Third, companies can realize higher profits because the products they produce as well as the supplies they use to produce them are less likely to be stolen when the work force has been prescreened for integrity.

Company shrinkage rates reflect the value of all goods lost due to a variety of causes, one of which is internal theft. Research with the PSI has indicated that it is effective in reducing shrinkage rates. For example, a study conducted with a national department store chain with approximately 250 store units field-tested the PSI during 18 new store openings (Jones, 1988). The company measured that its annual shrinkage rate as a percentage of sales was 3.41 percent. This estimate represented losses totaling over $50 million. Certainly not all of this figure is directly attributable to internal theft, but after eight months, the average shrinkage rate of the 18 stores that used the PSI for selection purposes was reduced to 2.84—a 16.7 percent drop. If the company-wide shrinkage rate was lowered to just 2.84, the company would theoretically save over $8 million.

A study conducted with a 30-unit convenience store chain monitored shrinkage rates for a consecutive 42-month period (Terris & Jones, 1982). During the first 23 months, all stores had used polygraphs as a means of preemployment assessment (phase A). During the remaining nineteen months, the PSI was used in place of the polygraph (phase B). Results indicated that the average monthly shrinkage rate per store unit during phase A was $515; during phase B, this amount dropped to $249. The between-phase difference was statistically significant ($p < .001$) and represented a 51.7 percent reduction in monthly shrinkage and a monthly savings of nearly $8,000 to the chain.

Other companies have documented significant reductions in their shrinkage rates attributable to their use of PSI. A study conducted with another major department store chain (Joy & Jones, 1988) demonstrated that the PSI was effective at reducing employee theft and corporate shrinkage. As a criterion, the company monitored annual inventory shrinkage for two years prior to implementing the PSI to establish a baseline estimate of their average annual shrinkage. The estimate indicated that average annual shrinkage over this two-year period was 2.8 percent of sales. After using the PSI for one year, the company's annual shrinkage dropped to 1.9 percent of sales—a 33 percent reduction in average shrinkage over three years. At the beginning of the sixth year, the company discontinued the testing program when management changed; inventory shrinkage soared to 4.1 percent of sales. In effect, therefore, the study incorporated a reversal design in which the treatment (implementation of the PSI) was removed. This type of design allows one to draw even more reliable conclusions about the effect of the selection program on inventory shrinkage. (The company did not release annual sales figures due to the proprietary nature of this information.) The results of this study, presented in Figure 4.1, demonstrated that when an effective integrity assessment program like the PSI is removed from the job applicant screening procedure, inventory shrinkage rates tended to return to, and even surpass, original baseline shrinkage rates.

In another study (Jones & Terris, 1983), a chain of 77 home improvement centers implemented the PSI to reduce on-the-job theft and drug abuse. The PSI was not used from 1979 through 1981 (phase A); in 1982 and 1983 (phase B), over 4,000 job applicants were screened with the PSI. Employee terminations due to theft and drug abuse were significantly reduced in phase B ($p < .01$). Moreover, shrinkage rates as a percentage of sales dropped from approximately 4.0 percent during 1981 to less than 2.5 percent during 1983. Cost accounting methods indicated that shrinkage costs were reduced from $7.5 million in 1981 to $6.0 million in 1982 and finally to $5.25 million in 1983—a savings of $3.75 million over the two years of PSI usage.

Finally, in an extensive study designed to document the impact of a valid personnel selection instrument in the supermarket industry, Jones and Slora (1989) demonstrated the substantial differences in employee theft across supermarket locations by comparing units using published preemployment integrity tests to units not using such screening instruments. In this study, an anonymous theft criterion survey was sent to randomly selected employees from one of six nationally based supermarket chains. Two of these chains used preemployment integrity instruments; the remaining four did not. The results indicated that employees in the screening stores reported significantly less weekly theft of cash,

Figure 4.1
Relationship between PSI Usage and Shrinkage Rate as a Percentage of Sales

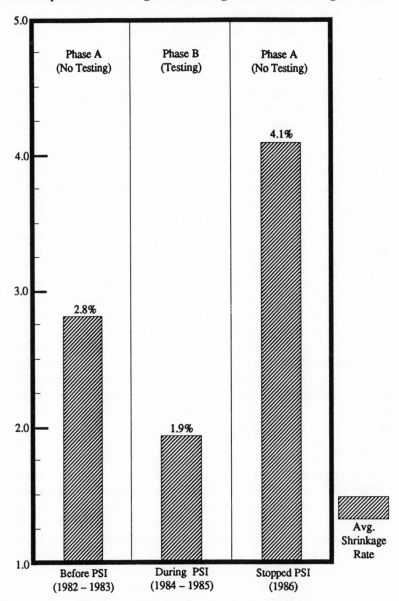

merchandise, and company property by coworkers than employees in the non-screening stores ($p < .05$). In addition, chain-wide estimates of annual employee theft indicated substantial increases in theft for stores that did not incorporate a valid integrity screening program as part of their selection procedure. Of the supermarkets surveyed, annual employee theft estimates from stores not using preemployment screening methods were often double those of stores using a valid preemployment screening program.

Research studies have also indicated that the PSI is effective in reducing turnover (e.g., Brown, Jones, Terris & Steffy, 1987; Jones & Terris, 1982). Turnover can have deleterious effects on work force productivity and morale. If honest employees stay with a company significantly longer than dishonest employees, companies can achieve increases in profits in two ways: by lowering the costs of personnel recruitment and training methods and by developing a more honest and cohesive work force that is less likely to steal from the workplace.

Insurance costs also fall with the use of the PSI (e.g., Jones & Steffy, 1987). When the PSI was implemented in a national restaurant chain, internal theft was reduced to such a degree that the insurance premiums required to protect the company against theft of property and merchandise decreased substantially. After a few years of screening, it was discovered that insurance costs were significantly lower in the establishments that used the PSI compared to those that did not use the PSI. The corporate director of security attributed the lower insurance costs to fewer acts of employee crime and dishonesty.

Research has also demonstrated a strong relationship between integrity and productivity (Joy, 1988; Terris & Jones, 1984). Obviously the effects of greater productivity can lead to increases in profits. One reason for this increased productivity is that honest employees are less likely to engage in time theft by extending their work breaks without authorization. This means that honest employees devote more time to work. Finally, research has shown that honest employees report less stress from their work and more job satisfaction and that these positive attitudes contribute to increased productivity in the workplace.

ALTERNATIVE METHODS OF MEASURING PROFITABILITY

The beneficial impact of any integrity assessment system needs to be measured and documented. Companies must weigh the potential costs of implementing such a system with the benefits that might be gained from its use. Over the last two decades, a variety of sources have documented the substantial losses due to employee theft and other forms of counterproductive behavior in organizations. While much has been written about the validity of the integrity assessment instrument as a method to reduce employee theft and counterproductivity, little has been done to show the cost-effectiveness of such instruments.

Moretti (1985) conducted an extensive study of over 250,000 job applicants screened with the PSI. The sample was representative of a host of industries: convenience stores, banks, department stores, drugstores, home improvement centers, and supermarkets. Data on self-admissions of theft over the past three years by these applicants were also collected. The results of several extremely conservative cost-effectiveness estimates indicated an average potential net savings above and beyond the cost of testing of $24.22 per applicant through the use of the PSI, with savings in individual industries ranging from $10.62 to $43.76 per applicant. In addition, the total dollar value of all theft admissions for applicants who were not recommended for hire on the PSI equaled $2.07 million in comparison to $98.00 for the PSI-recommended group.

In addition to the traditional financial accounting–based cost-benefit analysis, companies can also turn to utility analysis, a more statistically oriented approach. A utility analysis is intended to determine the potential increases in work force productivity that can be anticipated to result from the use of a job-related, reliable, and valid personnel screening procedure. Hence, utility analysis refers to the overall usefulness of a selection system. Given the inherent validity of the selection procedure and the expected range of performance of the typical "good" employee who meets the standards of the test, the incremental dollar value of this person's performance can be estimated with utility analysis. These estimates are made by incorporating such concepts as test validity, applicant selection ratios, and the standard deviation (or range) of employee performance for a particular position into a series of relatively complex, regression-derived formulas. In essence, utility analysis can provide an estimate of the quality of the individuals who would be selected using a valid personnel screening device.

A great deal of research has been conducted on the use of utility analysis (see Cascio & Ramos, 1986; Schmidt & Hoffman, 1973; Schmidt, Hunter, McKenzie & Muldrow, 1979 for reviews). Studies examining a variety of industries have indicated that utility analysis is a valid and effective method for estimating the institutional gain anticipated to result from the implementation of a personnel selection program.

A utility analysis recently conducted by Werner (1988) for a major fast food chain using the Schmidt and Rauschenberger formulas (1986) indicated a substantial average gain in productivity of $1,188 per employee per year when the PSI was incorporated into the selection procedure. Taken as a whole, the company intended to hire 500 employees per year for these positions. The anticipated gain in productivity due to the use of a validated integrity assessment instrument would have been over $594,000 per year for the total group of applicants. Once the costs incurred through testing were subtracted, the results indicated that by using the PSI as part of the selection procedure, at a cost of $9.50 per applicant, the estimated gain in productivity would be approximately $1,178 per employee per year and over $589,000 for the entire group of 500.

CONCLUSION

Integrity assessment programs are necessary to reduce employee theft and crime. Internal theft often goes undetected, and many companies are likely to rationalize the loss that they experience to bookkeeping errors and shoplifting. Because most internal theft is undetected, true estimates of the impact of this type of dishonest behavior are difficult, if not impossible, to obtain. However, proved methods do exist with which to reduce company losses due to internal crimes. Specifically developed and validated integrity assessment tools, like the PSI, are available to screen in desirable job applicants who are not prone to steal from the workplace.

REFERENCES

Brown, T. S., Jones, J. W., Terris, W., & Steffy, B. (1987). The impact of pre-employment integrity testing on employee turnover and inventory shrinkage rates. *Journal of Business and Psychology* 2(2).

Cascio, W. F., & Ramos, R. A. (1986). Development and application of a new method for assessing job performance in behavioral/economic terms. *Journal of Applied Psychology*, 71, 20–28.

Hefter, R. (1986). The crippling crime. *Security World*, 23, 36–38.

Hollinger, R. C., & Clark, J. P. (1983). Deterrence in the workplace: Perceived severity, perceived certainty and employee theft. *Social Forces*, 62, 398–418.

Jones, J. W. (1988). Impact of the Personnel Selection Inventory on department store shrinkage. Unpublished technical report. Park Ridge, IL: London House.

Jones, J. W., & Slora, K. B. (1989). Theft reduction through personnel selection: A control group design in the supermarket industry. Unpublished technical report. Park Ridge, IL: London House.

Jones, J. W., & Steffy, B. D. (1987). The impact of applied psychology on the reduction of insurance losses. Unpublished technical report. St. Paul, MN: St. Paul Companies.

Jones, J. W., & Terris, W. (1981). Predictive validation of a dishonesty test that measures theft proneness. Paper presented at the 18th Interamerican Congress of Psychology, Santo Domingo, Dominican Republic.

Jones, J. W., & Terris, W. (1982). The use of the Personnel Selection Inventory to predict turnover in a group of security guards: A pilot study. Unpublished technical report. Park Ridge, IL: London House.

Jones, J. W., & Terris, W. (1983). Predicting employees' theft in home improvement centers. *Psychological Reports*, 52, 187–201.

Joy, D. S. (1988). *Reliability and Validity of a Preemployment Honesty Test*. Unpublished technical report. Park Ridge, IL: London House.

Joy, D. S., & Jones, J. W. (1988). Relationship between the use of the Personnel Selection Inventory and company shrinkage rates. Unpublished technical report. Park Ridge, IL: London House.

London House (1980). Personnel Selection Inventory (PSI). Park Ridge, IL: London House.

McDaniel, M. A., & Jones, J. W. (1988). Predicting employee theft: A quantitative review of a standardized measure of honesty. *Journal of Business and Psychology*, 2, 327–345.

Moretti, D. M. (November 1985). The utility of integrity testing. Paper presented at the Annual National Conference of the Association of Human Resources Management and Organization Behavior, Boston.

Sackett, P. R., Burris, L., & Callahan, C. (1987). Integrity testing for personnel selection: An update. Unpublished manuscript.

Sackett, P. R., & Harris, M. M. (1984). Honesty testing for personnel selection: A review and critique. In J. H. Bernardin and D. A. Bownas (eds.), *Personality assessment in organizations*, 236–276. New York: Praeger Publishers.

Schmidt, F. L., & Hoffman, B. (1973). An empirical comparison of three methods of assessing the utility of a selection device. *Journal of Industrial and Organizational Psychology*, 1, 1–11.

Schmidt, F. L., Hunter, J. E., McKenzie, R. C., & Muldrow, T. W. (1979). Impact of valid selection procedures on workforce productivity. *Journal of Applied Psychology*, 62, 609–626.

Schmidt, F. L., & Rauschenberger, J. (1986). Utility analysis for practitioners: A workshop. Presented at the First Annual Conference of the Society for Industrial and Organizational Psychology, Chicago, April.

Security report: Retailers on the defensive (1983). *Chain Store Age Executive*, February.

Shepard, I. M., & Duston, R. (1988). *Thieves at work: An employer's guide to combating workplace dishonesty*. Washington, DC: Bureau of National Affairs.

Slora, K. B. (1988). The London House survey of employee theft in the fast food industry: Preliminary findings. Unpublished technical report. Park Ridge, IL: London House.

Terris, W. (1985). Attitudinal Correlates of Employee Integrity. *Journal of Police and Criminal Psychology*, 1(1), 60–68.

Terris, W., & Jones, J. W. (1982). Psychological factors related to employee's theft in the convenience store industry. *Psychological Reports*, 51, 1219–1238.

Terris, W., & Jones, J. W. (1984). Psychological correlates of employee theft in department stores. Unpublished technical report. Park Ridge, IL: London House.

Werner, S. H. (1988). Utility analysis estimates for the use of the Personnel Selection Inventory with a major fast food chain. Unpublished technical report. Park Ridge, IL: London House.

II

CURRENT RESEARCH

5

Basic Psychometric Properties of a Preemployment Honesty Test: Reliability, Validity, and Fairness

DENNIS S. JOY

The general purpose of the Personnel Selection Inventory (PSI) is to identify job applicants who are likely to exhibit counterproductive behaviors on the job that hinder, deter, or detract from normal job productivity or company profitability. The PSI Honesty scale was specifically designed to measure employment applicants' attitudes toward theft and the likelihood they would engage in theft on the job. It is one of the leading integrity tests in terms of both quality and quantity of scientific research (cf. O'Bannon et al., 1989; Sackett, Burris & Callahan, 1989).

The PSI is the result of over 15 years of research by psychologists, criminologists, and legal experts. This research shows that typical employee thieves have a certain cluster of attitudes, values, and beliefs about theft that clearly distinguish them from employees who do not engage in theft. Employees who steal tend to view themselves as average people in a basically dishonest world. These individuals project their own dishonesty and thus see theft as prevalent. This allows them to rationalize that everyone steals, so they feel they are acting according to accepted norms. The typical dishonest employee is also more tolerant of theft in others and holds less punitive attitudes about theft. Dishonest employees are more tempted to steal, ruminate more about theft-related activities, exhibit more interthief loyalty, and more readily accept common rationalizations for their theft. The PSI Honesty scale measures these attitudinal predispositions.

RELIABILITY

The PSI honesty Scale has consistently demonstrated high reliability coefficients. Three types of reliability have been reported for the scale: split-half, internal consistency (alpha), and temporal stability (test-retest).

Terris (1985) reports the split-half (Spearman-Brown) reliability of the PSI Honesty scale as r = .95. This estimate was computed on a sample of 470 job applicants for positions of trust having access to cash and merchandise. In this and other studies, the alpha reliability coefficient is typically also r = .95. To investigate the temporal stability of the Honesty scale, Rafilson (in press) administered the scale to 62 white-collar workers and one week later asked these same employees to complete the scale again. The test-retest reliability for this study was reported as r = .91. These studies, using samples from diverse settings, indicate the PSI Honesty scale to be highly reliable. These estimates indicate the scale items are highly intercorrelated and tap the same underlying construct. The measurement of this construct is stable over time.

Using the internal consistency reliability estimate of r = .95, the standard error of measurement can be computed. If one uses the standard deviation of the distribution of raw scale scores based on general test norms ($N = 10,000$; $\bar{X} = 47.61$; $SD = 9.00$), the standard error of measurement is 2.01. For normalized standard scores ($\bar{X} = 50$; SD = 20) the standard error of measurement is 4.47. Standard scores are reported to clients and used for decision-making purposes.

VALIDATION

In a discussion of validity, the Equal Employment Opportunity Commission in its Uniform Guidelines on Employee Selection (1979) states that a selection procedure is justified by documenting a statistical relationship between scores on the selection procedure and measures of relevant job performance. *Principles for the Validation and Use of Personnel Selection Procedures* (1980) defines validity as the degree to which inferences from scores on tests or assessments are justified or supported by evidence. The primary question to be answered in validation is the degree to which these inferences are appropriate. With the PSI, or any other honesty test, the key question is, To what degree does evidence support the inference that there is a relationship between test scores and theft? To date, over 80 validation studies have been conducted with the PSI series, including one meta-analysis (McDaniel & Jones, 1988). The majority of these studies have either been published in professional journals or presented at scientific conferences. Independent reviews of the PSI also appear in the *Ninth Edition of the Buros Mental Measurements Yearbook* (Sauser, 1985) and *Test Critiques* (Craig, 1985).

Validity studies in the area of employee theft can be difficult to conduct due to practical and methodological problems—many of them centering around the particular criterion selected for a study. Since most employee theft is never detected, a largely hidden phenomenon is being investigated. This makes predictive validity studies particularly difficult to conduct since reliable theft criteria (i.e., a subject being apprehended for theft) are hard to obtain. Another methodological problem can occur when the reliability or even validity of the theft criteria comes into question. This issue can be particularly troublesome when polygraph results are the only criterion used to validate an honesty test. Results of a polygraph can be unreliable since they may depend on the judgment or skills of the examiner, and there are virtually no uniform standards governing the training or quality of these examiners. In fact, many experts recommend that any comparison based on polygrapher judgments (such as chart readings or inferences of deception) should be rejected out of hand. A criterion that is seriously questioned in the scientific community has little validity as a sole evaluation criterion (Sackett & Harris, 1984; American Medical Association Council on Scientific Affairs, 1986).

Polygraph outcomes (e.g. pass-fail) as a criterion can also be irrelevant for purposes of validating an honesty test. An applicant may "fail" or be "not recommended" on a polygraph because of health or credit problems. These irrelevancies will underestimate the validity of the honesty test. On the other hand, actual theft admissions gained by highly skilled and licensed polygraphers are acceptable criteria. Even so, an honesty test should also be validated against other theft measures (e.g., anonymous admissions, criminal apprehensions, supervisors' ratings).

The implication of these problems is not that research on employee theft cannot be done but that a multimethod approach should be employed. Since any method may have certain weaknesses and limitations, it is particularly important to examine the accumulation of validation evidence across a variety of methods (cf. McDaniel & Jones, 1988), a general strategy recommended by Campbell and Stanley (1963). Using a number of different independent methods, measurement procedures, and criteria also provides convergent evidence of validity (Campbell & Fiske, 1959). This independence of methods is a common denominator among the major types of validity. Cronbach (1971) argues that validation of an instrument calls for an integration of many types of evidence. The varieties of different types of investigations are not alternatives; the investigations should supplement one another.

The following review of PSI research focuses on theft-related validity in the following categories: comparisons with polygraph theft admissions, anonymous admissions of theft (self-reports), contrasted groups, prediction of future theft, and quasi-experimental designs (e.g., time-series analysis). This sequence of research was chosen for its developmental qualities, moving from the earlier and weaker forms of evidence to later and stronger forms of evidence.

Comparisons with Polygraph Theft Admissions

The research reviewed here examines the relationship between attitudes toward deviant behavior, as measured by the PSI Honesty scale, and theft-related admissions made on polygraph examinations. In all studies, the PSI was administered prior to the polygraph, and polygraph examiners were unaware of any applicants' PSI scores.

Terris (1985) studied 470 job applicants for positions of trust involving access to money, merchandise, and other property. Applicants included people from all age, race, sex, educational, and occupational groups. Subjects were placed into one of six categories depending on their actual polygraph-induced theft admissions.

Category 1: No money or merchandise taken in the last three years.

Category 2: $1–$5 money, $1–$50 in merchandise, or $1–$5 in shoplifting.

Category 3: $6–$25 in money, $51–$100 in merchandise, or $6–$15 in shoplifting.

Category 4: $26–$75 money, $101–$150 in merchandise, or $16–$50 in shoplifting.

Category 5: $75 or more money, more than $150 in merchandise, or more than $50 shoplifting.

Category 6: A pattern of serious thefts (many instances of category 5 theft).

Results of the study showed a strong relationship between the Honesty scale scores and subsequent polygraph admissions of theft ($r = .56$, $p < .01$). This study has been replicated with bank applicants (Moretti, Jones & Terris, 1983; Moretti, 1984b), airport applicants (Moretti, 1983b), retail department store employees (Moretti, 1983a, 1984a), and managerial applicants (Terris & Jones, 1982b). The attitude scores were correlated with theft admissions and not polygraph-based ratings of deception. The reliability of measures of deception has been questioned; the reliability of actual admissions cannot be questioned.

The statistically significant relationships found in these studies support a basic proposition of honesty tests: that there is a relationship between one's attitudes and past theft. The fact that these relationships are not perfect indicates there are other factors, most likely situational, that influence theft. Applicants with dishonest attitudes may not have stolen from prior jobs, either because they have never worked before or they worked in a highly controlled environment where the opportunity for theft did not exist. Dishonest people such as this could pass a preemployment polygraph but still be at risk to steal from a future employer when both the need and the opportunity for theft are present.

Anonymous Self-Reports

Another strategy used to validate the PSI has been to correlate test results on the inventory with anonymous self-reported admissions of past theft. Using theft admissions reported anonymously helps to control the possible influence of social desirability affecting the criterion. In all studies reported here, admissions were obtained independently of the PSI. Subjects were asked to indicate the number of times they had been involved in a number of different crimes, and for theft, to estimate the dollar amounts of cash or merchandise they had taken.

A series of studies using this methodology has been conducted. Terris (1979a) studied the relationship between PSI Honesty scale scores and anonymous admissions of theft and criminal behaviors engaged in within the three previous years. The sample consisted of 146 currently or previously employed college students. The Honesty scale correlated with the dollar amount of admitted theft $(r = .63, p < .001)$. In a sample of 36 supermarket employees, Jones (1979) found significant correlations between Honesty scale scores and anonymous admissions of the total estimated dollar value of stolen merchandise $(r = .56, p < .01)$. Moretti (1980) found significant correlations between Honesty scale scores and anonymous admissions of on-the-job theft $(r = .56, p < .05)$, estimated dollar amounts of stolen merchandise and property $(r = .63, p < .01)$, and number of criminal behaviors $(r = .59, p < .01)$, among a sample of warehouse dock workers and supermarket employees. Jones (1980) obtained anonymous admissions of merchandise stolen from their employers by 39 employees from a relatively heterogeneous selection of companies. Honesty scale scores significantly correlated with the total estimated dollar amount of all merchandise stolen $(r = .41, p < .005)$.

Terris and Jones (1980) sampled employees from two separate retail food stores. The sample from one location $(N = 27)$ included mostly part-time employees (93 percent), and the sample from the second location $(N = 15)$ included mostly full-time employees (93 percent). In each location there was a significant correlation between the PSI Honesty scale scores and admissions of total employee theft $(r = .61, p < .01$ and $r = .81, p < .01)$. In other studies, Weichman and Bae (1983) administered the PSI and an anonymous self-report questionnaire to 70 college students. The group of students admitting to having been arrested scored significantly lower on the Honesty scale than did the group making no such admissions $(F = 11.08, p < .01)$.

Jones (1981a) analyzed the relationship between the PSI and anonymous admissions of theft among 34 nurses in a hospital trauma emergency room in four categories of theft. There were significant correlations between the Honesty scale scores and admissions of theft of general supplies (e.g., toilet paper, pens, towels, hand lotion) $(r = .45, p < .01)$, medical supplies (e.g., bandages, bandage tape, dressings) $(r = .38, p < .01)$, drugs/medication (e.g., aspirin, penicillin, insulin) $(r = .60, p < .01)$, and total theft $(r = .59, p < .01)$.

Jones (1981b) investigated the relationship between the PSI and endorsement of nuclear crime and admissions of past criminal behavior among college students $(N = 74)$. A significant correlation was found between the Honesty scale scores and theft admissions $(r = .51, p < .01)$.

In a sample of 77 high school students, Jones (1982) found that among several personality measures, the best predictor of total admitted theft was the PSI Honesty scale $(r = .51, p < .01)$. Moretti (1982) found a significant correlation $(r = .41, p < .01)$ between the honesty scores and admitted theft in a sample of 196 hospital and grocery store employees. Jones and Terris (1983a) found a significant correlation between the number of theft crimes admitted to by 104 convenience store applicants and the Honesty scale (r = .45, $p < .01$).

As in the polygraph studies, these findings support a basic relationship between attitudes toward theft and actual theft admissions. The consistent replication of findings in this section under anonymous conditions would also indicate that social desirability is not as significant a factor in honesty testing research as some critics might argue. However, a methodological weakness that remains with both polygraph and anonymous admissions is that the classification of honesty in both is based on self-report data. An independent classification of the subject's honesty, one not based on self-reports, would bolster the validity evidence of the test.

Contrasted Group Studies

Independent classification of a person's honesty can be accomplished using a contrasted group design. The logic of this validation approach requires that groups be established on the basis of independent theft or dishonesty measures or on the theoretical basis that the groups should score substantially different on an instrument designed to assess honesty (e.g., PSI). To the extent that these groups differ empirically on the Honesty scale provides support for the validity of the scale. For example, it would be expected on theoretical or logical grounds that a group of convicted and incarcerated felons (e.g., armed robbers) should score substantially worse on the Honesty scale than would a group of job applicants. If group membership is established on empirical grounds, then it would be expected that groups of employees working in stores experiencing substantial internal theft problems should have worse Honesty scale scores, on the average, than employees working in stores experiencing little internal theft.

As part of one research study, Jones and Terris (1981b) compared the average honesty scores of 116 incarcerated felons (e.g., thieves, murderers, drug dealers) with the average honesty scores of 200 job applicants. As expected, inmates scored significantly lower than applicants (t = 23.5, $p < .001$). In a separate analysis, scores of the same 116 felons were compared to honesty scores of another sample of 527 department store applicants. The sample of department store applicants was divided into two groups based on their PSI scores: those recommended for employment (scoring above normal recommended cutoffs, N = 177) and those not recommended for employment (scoring below normal recommended cutoffs, N = 350). Inmates scored, on average, significantly lower on the Honesty scale compared to both the recommended (t = 30.0, $p < .001$) and the not-recommended groups (t = 29.5, $p < .001$). Thus, not only do incarcerated felons score worse than applicants in general, but they also score worse than the not-recommended applicants.

In another study by Terris and Jones (1983), an intensive criminal history search was undertaken on 177 department store applicants who completed the

PSI. The background check, which was part of the company's selection process, identified 20 applicants with criminal records. While 56 percent of the applicants with no reported criminal record passed the PSI, only 10 percent of the applicants with a criminal record passed the PSI ($\chi^2(1) = 13.3$ $p < .01$). Results also showed that the applicants with a criminal history scored significantly lower on the Honesty scale than did applicants with no criminal history ($t = 5.8$, $p < .001$).

Jones and Terris (1983e) studied the organizational climate of honesty in 30 restaurants employing 521 workers. Executives from the restaurant chain selected 15 "problematic restaurants" and 15 "nonproblematic restaurants" for between-group comparisons. Estimates of the amount of internal theft and cash overages or shortages were the primary variables considered in the classification. All 521 employees representing all job classifications completed the PSI. The major findings showed that the average Honesty scale score was significantly lower among employees for the 15 problematic restaurants ($t (28) = 2.6$, $p < .02$) than among employees for the 15 nonproblematic restaurants.

Jones and Terris (1983b) also used a contrasted groups approach in the home improvement industry. Eighty-six employees from separate locations of a national home improvement center chain completed the PSI. Five locations were classified on the theft criterion in terms of either inventory records (the amount of lumber surplus or shortage) or the corporate security director's ratings of the number of times he had conducted an internal theft investigation at each center. Results showed that the home improvement centers with better honesty climate scores (i.e., the average Honesty scale score for each center) tended to have lumber surpluses, and the centers with poorer honesty climates tended to have lumber shortages ($r = .52, p < .025$). In addition, the centers with better honesty climates were rated by the security director as having the lowest number of cases of reported internal theft ($r = -.37$, $p < .025$). When individual honesty scores were used for employees within each location, a between-center analysis of variance for the five locations audited for lumber shortages was marginally significant ($F = 2.4$, $p < .06$). The center with the largest surplus scored significantly higher on honesty scores than the center with the largest inventory shortage on a Duncan Multiple-range Post Hoc Analysis ($p < .05$).

Studies using the preceding contrasted groups design represent a significant advance in the validation of the PSI. They go beyond self-report data and use independent classifications of subjects' honesty. These studies also expand the criteria used to validate the PSI and incorporate criteria of direct interest to users of the test (e.g., inventory shrinkage, cost shortages) into the validation process.

Prediction of Future Theft (Predictive Validity)

A major step in the validation of the PSI has included demonstrations of the ability of the PSI to predict future theft in the workplace. According to the Equal Employment Opportunity Commission's Uniform Guidelines on Employee Selection (1979), "Whatever method of validation is used, the basic logic is one of prediction; that is, the presumption that level of performance on the selection procedure will, on the average, be indicative of level of performance on the job after selection. Thus, a criterion related study, particularly a predictive one, is often regarded as the closest to such an ideal" (p. 248). According to the *Principles for the Validation and Use of Personnel Selection Procedures* (American Psychological Association, 1980), "This design answers the most common employment question; i.e., does the predictor indeed have forecasting value with respect to *later* job behaviors. As such, the predictive model addresses itself to the basic selection issue as it normally occurs in the employment context" (p. 6).

The general logic of the predictive validity design as it relates to the PSI requires applicants for positions of trust to be tested and then hired regardless of their test scores. Since the testing is typically done as the last stage in the selection process, all tested applicants have been deemed suitable for employment on other criteria. The relationship between test scores and relevant future theft criteria is then examined. In each study cited below, London House normal recommended cutoff scores were used to determine pass-fail status on the test. Store managers did not know applicants' test scores.

In a grocery store chain, 482 applicants at one location were administered the PSI. The overall passing rate was 52 percent. During the subsequent year, theft investigations terminated 20 employees who admitted to an excess of $8,000 in theft. Three of these employees had not been administered the PSI. Of the remaining 17, 94 percent (16 of 17) failed the PSI. The difference in the passing rates (proportions) of the theft-terminated group (6 percent) and the unterminated group (52 percent) is statistically significant ($p < .005$) (Brown & Joy, 1985).

A midwestern grocery chain selected one of its regional areas to evaluate the PSI. All 36 stores in this area administered the PSI to all applicants eligible for hiring over a one-year period. Approximately 3,800 applicants were tested, with an overall passing rate of 42 percent. At the end of one year, the chain provided data from the test area listing all employees terminated for theft ($N = 91$). The results from the chain again confirm the accuracy of the PSI in identifying the potential employee thief. Eighty-two percent (75 of 91) of the employees terminated for theft had failed the PSI. The difference in the passing rate (proportions) of the theft-terminated group (18 percent) and the unterminated group (42 percent) is statistically significant ($p < .05$) (Brown & Joy, 1985).

In a study conducted by Terris and Jones (1983), over 500 applicants for positions at a major department store chain were given the PSI. The results showed that employees subsequently dismissed for theft ($N = 32$) scored significantly lower on the Honesty scale ($p < .05$) than did the employees not caught stealing. If ordinary standards had been used, 78 percent of these employees caught stealing would have failed the PSI and been rejected as applicants. In Jones and Terris (1981a), 80 applicants for the position of Salvation Army kettler were given the PSI. (Kettlers are hired as temporary help to solicit donations during the Christmas season.) One result showed that the kettlers who failed the PSI brought back significantly less money to headquarters each day than kettlers who passed the PSI (F = 7.6, $p < .01$).

Also in Jones and Terris (1981a), 127 job applicants at a convenience store chain were given the PSI. Fifty-nine applicants were not recommended for employment based on these test results and 68 were recommended. Eleven of the not-recommended applicants, although scoring below standards, were nevertheless hired. Fifty of the recommended applicants were also hired. Store managers were asked to rate the 61 new employees on the following variables: (1) whether the employee in question had been caught stealing company cash or merchandise or been disciplined for mishandling cash and merchandise (e.g., cash drawer shortages; missing merchandise) and (2) whether the employee had been suspected of theft. Six of the 61 employees were either caught stealing cash or merchandise or were disciplined for mishandling company cash or merchandise. These employees who stole or mishandled company cash and/or merchandise scored significantly lower on the PSI Honesty scale than the 55 employees who had no such problems (t[59] = 2.1, $p < .05$). The majority of applicants who scored extremely low on the dishonesty scale were not hired; therefore only data from a small, restricted set of the not-recommended group could be included in the analysis. The observed relationship between dishonesty and employee theft most likely underestimates the true validity because of the restriction of range of the PSI test scores.

In a fast food restaurant chain (Terris & Jones, 1982b), 238 hourly applicants completed the PSI. One year later 90 of these applicants were still employed by the chain and were rated by their managers on several measures of theft and counterproductive behavior. Statistically significant Pearsonian correlations ($p < .05$ in all cases) showed that the subjects who scored poorly on the PSI engaged in more of the following counterproductive behaviors once hired than subjects who scored favorably on the PSI: mishandled company cash and merchandise; deleted an overring without approval; took company merchandise home without approval; took food without paying for it; ignored work orders; gave food away; argued with customers, coworkers, and supervisors; intentionally damaged company property or merchandise; took money from registers without authorization; and went home early without permission.

In the home improvement industry (Jones & Terris, 1983b), 86 employees from eight different centers were rated by their managers on various forms of theft and counterproductive behavior eight months after being hired. These employees had completed the PSI as applicants and were hired regardless of their scores. Results showed that employees scoring poorer on the Honesty scale were viewed by their managers as mishandling company cash or merchandise more often than employees scoring better on the Honesty scale (r = .21, $p < .05$). Moretti (1984b) found similar results in a retail department store environment. Four hundred ninety-eight employees were rated by supervisors three months after they had completed the PSI and were hired. Employees who scored poorer on the Honesty scale were viewed by their managers as coming up short of cash on the register more often ($r = .16$, $p < .05$).

The results of these studies show the value of the PSI as a predictor of future theft in the workplace. In the studies that examined the pass-fail status of detected thieves, the percentage of thieves failing the PSI ranged from 78 percent to 94 percent. This would indicate that an average of 80 to 85 percent of known thieves would be expected to score below standards on the PSI. This contention was also supported by an extensive review of the major honesty tests by Baumer and Rosenbaum (1984). These authors held that the most important approach to test validation involves predictive validity and that the PSI seemed to be an exception to their general conclusion that written honesty tests have not been shown to predict theft-related behavior among employees.

In another major predictive validation study, Jones, Joy, Werner, and Orban (1989) compared PSI Honesty scale scores of a group of 1,073 severely counterproductive employees from four different samples to the PSI Honesty scale scores of a comparison group of 100,000 job applicants randomly selected from a normative database. The counterproductive group was comprised of applicants from retail supermarkets ($N = 741$), public transportation ($N = 264$), hotel ($N = 55$), and service stations ($N = 13$). The individuals in the counterproductive group had all been tested as applicants, hired regardless of scores, and later terminated or reprimanded for gross misconduct (e.g., theft, rule violations, insubordination, drug use). Results indicated the counterproductive group scored significantly lower on the Honesty scale than did the comparison group ($t = 18.57$, $p < .001$). Additional analyses showed that all of the counterproductive subgroups scored significantly lower than the comparison group on the Honesty scale.

These predictive validity studies are very important to conduct strictly from a standpoint of test validation, even though they underestimate test validity due to a restriction of range in the criteria measure. From a practical point of view, however, they are very difficult to conduct since test scores are not used in the selection process. If a prospective client company has reason to believe the test is valid, it is usually unwilling to conduct such a study since it wants to make hiring decisions based on test scores and use the PSI as an intervention to reduce theft. For this type of client, demonstrations of the effectiveness of the PSI to reduce corporate losses attributable to theft are of considerable value.

Quasi-Experimental Designs

True (randomized) experiments would be ideal to test the effectiveness of the PSI as an intervention; however, in field settings there are often major practical, economical, and ethical obstacles. Less complete but sophisticated quasi-experimental designs can still provide useful data concerning the practical effectiveness (i.e., reductions in theft as measured on criteria of direct interest to corporate test users) and the scientific validity of the PSI.

The various quasi-experimental designs are thoroughly described in a classic work by Campbell and Stanley (1963) and by Cook and Campbell (1979). A time-series design is particularly well suited to evaluate the effectiveness of preemployment integrity testing. This sort of experiment is described in detail by Glass, Wilson, and Gottman (1975). In the context of the PSI, measures on a theft criterion of interest are taken over an extended period of time. The validity or effectiveness of the PSI is gauged by the extent to which changes in theft associated with the presence of the PSI occur in the expected direction. In the studies reviewed below, more detail and illustrations will be presented than in other sections because of the complexity and sophistication of the designs. In the time-series designs three measures of employee theft have been incorporated into the design: inventory shrinkage, employee terminations for theft, and rates of employees passing routine polygraph examinations.

STUDY 1: SHRINKAGE

Inventory shrinkage rates reflect the value of all goods missing through a variety of causes—shoplifting, vendors' theft, misplaced merchandise, book-keeping error, and theft by employees. Estimates of shrinkage due to employee theft, found in government, trade, security, insurance, and business publications, are as high as 70 percent (U.S. Department of Commerce, 1972).

In a time-series study conducted by Terris and Jones (1982a), an entire district of convenience stores from a nationwide chain participated. This district expanded from 20 to 30 stores during the course of the 42-month investigation. It had over $5 million in sales for the 1978–1979 fiscal year, over $7 million in sales for the 1979–1980 fiscal year, over $8 million in sales for the 1980–1981 fiscal year, and approximately $5 million in sales halfway through the 1981–1982 fiscal year. Every store in this study was subjected to a complete audit each month for a 42-month period. Phase A served as a baseline. It consisted of shrinkage rates for each of the 23 months from March 1978 to January 1980. All preemployment screening during phase A was done with polygraph examinations. During phase B the PSI replaced the polygraph in preemployment screening. This change started to take place during February 1980. Hence, phase B, a 19-month period, ranged from February 1980 through August 1981. No other change in company policy was reported to have occurred. Two measures of shrinkage were used in this study: the average monthly shrinkage rate per store unit and shrinkage rates per month as a percentage of total monthly sales ((losses/sales) × 100). This latter measure controlled for the increase in the number of store units, as well as increases in sales during the course of the study. Results of this study are presented in figure 5.1.

The average shrinkage rate per store unit in phase A was $515. The average monthly shrinkage rate per store unit during phase B was $249. The mean

Figure 5.1
Company Shrinkage in Terms of Dollar Losses and Percentage of Sales as a Function of Time and Screening Method

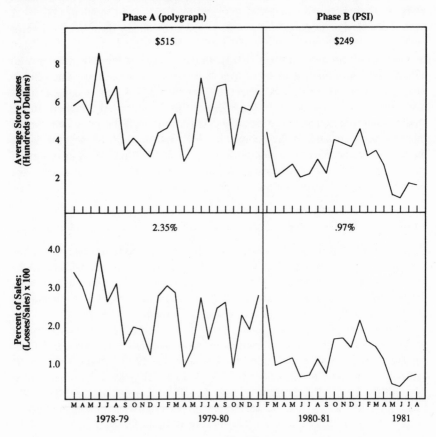

difference between phase A and phase B was statistically significant (t[40] = 6.1, $p < .001$). In addition, the average shrinkage rate as a percentage of sales was 2.35 percent during phase A. In phase B, shrinkage as a percentage of sales averaged .97 percent. The phase A percentage rates were significantly higher than the phase B rates (t [40] = 6.65, $p < .001$). These differences represent a 52 percent reduction in monthly shrinkage, an annual savings of almost $100,000 to the chain. Also, by using the PSI the chain achieved a reduction in shrinkage greater than had been previously realized with the polygraph.

STUDY 2: EMPLOYEE TERMINATIONS FOR THEFT _____

A second time-series analysis was conducted by Brown, Jones, Terris, and Steffy (1987) in a chain of home improvement centers. This study, conducted over a five-year period (1979–1983), assessed the ability of the PSI to reduce employee terminations for theft. Phase A, the baseline, consisted of 12 three-month quarters ranging from January 1979 through December 1981. Phase B consisted of 6 three-month quarters ranging from January 1982 through June 1983. During phase B the PSI was used for screening. The total number of theft terminations per quarter was the first variable analyzed. The second measure was the ratio of theft terminations over the total number of stores. This latter measure controlled for the variation in the number of store units. Results of this study are presented in Figure 5.2.

The average apprehension rate of 39.6 during phase A was significantly greater than the average apprehension rate of 25.3 during phase B (t = 2.7, $p < .05$). The average ratio score (number of theft terminations per quarter/number of stores open) of .57 during phase A was also significantly greater than the average ratio of .32 during phase B (t = 4.8, $p < .05$). Of note in Figure 5.2 is that in the pre-PSI phase, there was a significant increasing trend in theft terminations between time and termination ratio (r = .659, $p < .01$), and in the PSI phase, this trend was reversed to a significant decreasing trend between time and termination ratio (r = $-.835$, $p < .01$).

Shrinkage figures were available for three years of this study: the last year of the pretest period (1981) and both years of the posttest period (1982, 1983) (Figure 5.3). During 1981 shrinkage was $7.5 million (3.75 percent of sales). Shrinkage was reduced to $6.0 million (2.8 percent of sales) during 1982, and to $5.25 million (2.45 percent of sales) during 1983. This resulted in a savings of $3.75 million to the company.

STUDY 3: INCREASE IN NUMBER OF EMPLOYEES PASSING ROUTINE POLYGRAPH _____

Brown and Pardue (1985) demonstrated the effectiveness of the PSI in a drugstore chain by showing an increase in the number of employees passing yearly routine polygraph examinations during a three-year investigation. In January of the first year of the investigation, the chain introduced the PSI as part of its preemployment hiring process. Only applicants who passed this and all other phases of the screening process were hired. It was also the policy of the chain to administer annual routine polygraph examinations to its employees. During the three years of the study, the chain administered 1,256 routine polygraph exams. Employees were classified as passing the polygraph if there were no theft admissions. If admissions of theft were made during the examination, the employee was classified as failing the polygraph exam. Results of the study are shown in Table 5.1.

Figure 5.2
Termination Ratios per Store before and after Use of the PSI

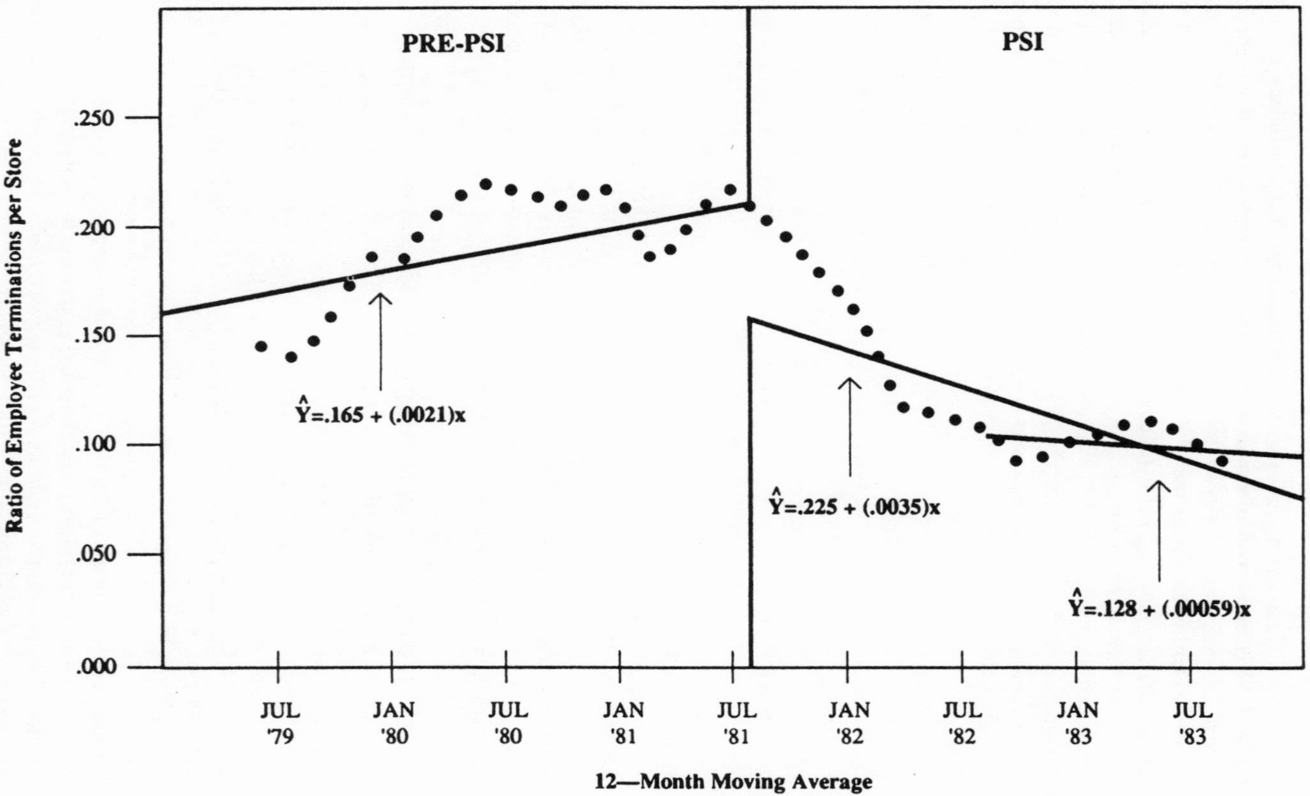

PRE-PSI

PSI

$\hat{Y}=.165 + (.0021)x$

$\hat{Y}=.225 + (.0035)x$

$\hat{Y}=.128 + (.00059)x$

Ratio of Employee Terminations per Store

.250
.200
.150
.100
.050
.000

JUL '79   JAN '80   JUL '80   JAN '81   JUL '81   JAN '82   JUL '82   JAN '83   JUL '83

12—Month Moving Average

Figure 5.3
Annual Shrinkage, 1981–1983

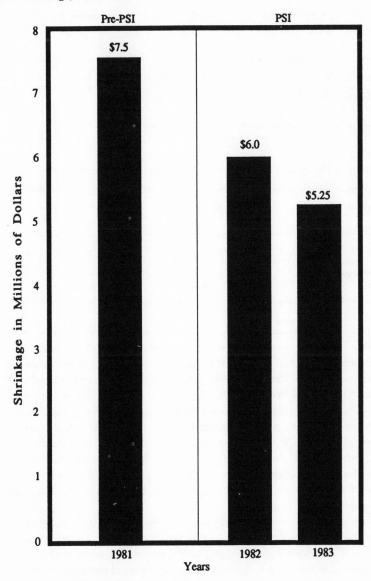

From 1981 through 1983 there was just over a 100 percent increase in the number of routine polygraph examinations administered. The percentage of employees who passed the examination increased from 42 percent to 64 percent over the period, with the largest increase during the final year. This represents a significant increase in the proportion of employees passing the polygraph

Table 5.1
Three-Year Summary of Those Passing and Failing Routine Polygraph

Polygraph Results	1981		1982		1983	
	%	n	**%**	n	**%**	n
Pass (No Admissions)	42	116	48	205	64	355
Fail (Admissions)	58	159	51	215	35	196
Inconclusive	0	0	1	3	1	7
Total		275		423		558

Table 5.2
Summary of Percentage Passing and Failing Routine Polygraph in 1983

Polygraph Results	Hired with PSI		Hired Without PSI		Total	
	%	n	**%**	n	**%**	n
Pass (No Admissions)	81	274	37	815	64	355
Fail (Admissions)	19	64	62	132	35	196
Inconclusive	0	0	1	7	1	7
Total		338		220		558

examination. Unfortunately, polygraph passing rates prior to 1981 were not available. One can assume that the 22 percent increase of employees passing the routine polygraph is due in part to the increased number of honest employees who are now part of the work force. This assumption was examined directly by a more detailed analysis of the 1983 data (Table 5.2). The employees who were given polygraphs in 1983 ($N = 558$) were divided into two groups: employees who were hired having passed the PSI ($N = 338$) and employees who never completed the PSI ($N = 338$) because they were hired before implementation of the program. Of the employees who were hired with the PSI, 81 percent passed the routine polygraph, whereas only 37 percent of those who were hired without the PSI passed their polygraph examination. Again this difference was significant ($z = 11.0$, $p < .001$).

Shrinkage figures were also available during this study (Figure 5.4). The annual rate at the end of the first year of testing was 3.4 percent of sales; at the end of the second year, this figure dropped to 3.2 percent of sales. A decline to 2.5 percent of sales was seen at the end of the third year of testing, and through the first two months of the fourth year, a further reduction to 1.7 percent of sales occurred. This represents a drop in shrinkage of 1.7 percent of sales over the course of the study, resulting in a savings of $1.25 million to the chain. Although pretest shrinkage data were not available, the results of this study support the effectiveness of the PSI by replicating the finding of a reduction while the testing program was in effect.

Figure 5.4
Annual Shrinkage, 1981–1984

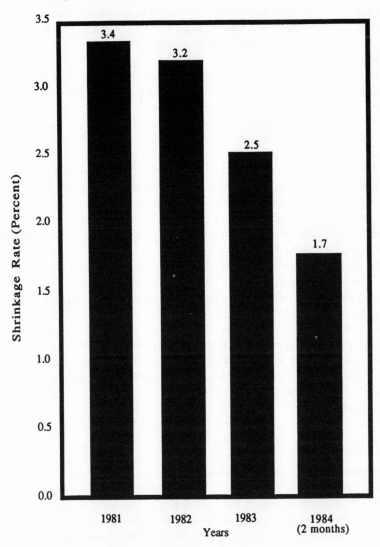

RELATED QUASI-EXPERIMENTAL STUDIES

Jones and Terris (1985) used a quasi-experimental design to evaluate the effectiveness of the PSI in a department store chain. Two groups of employees were compared on theft criterion measures: 120 current employees who had passed the PSI as applicants and 134 current employees who were never screened with the PSI. All 254 subjects anonymously completed a questionnaire of how often they stole company cash, merchandise, and property; gave unauthorized discounts to friends and relatives; ignored company rules and regulations; overcharged customers for personal gain; "borrowed" company property without authorization; and gave unauthorized discounts to customers. The main finding showed that the employees passing the PSI scored significantly better on the anonymous theft questionnaire than the unscreened employees (t = 3.7, $p <$ .01).

Joy (1985) studied the admitted theft of employees who were apprehended for actual theft in the workplace. Employees apprehended for theft in a home improvement center were divided into two groups: employees screened with the PSI ($N = 32$) and employees who were not screened with the PSI ($N = 199$). The average dollar amount of admitted theft of the apprehended employees screened with the PSI was significantly less than the average dollar amount of admitted theft of those apprehended employees not screened with the PSI (t = 3.13, $p <$ .001). In another setting using the same design, Joy (1985) found that the average admitted theft of a group of 49 department store employees apprehended for theft who passed the PSI was significantly less than the average admitted theft of a group of 270 unscreened employees also apprehended for theft (t = 3.12, $p <$ .001).

One additional quasi-experimental design study has recently been completed and is in the data analysis stage. Although statistical tests have yet to be performed, preliminary results are presented in Figure 5.5. A national department store chain with approximately 250 stores field-tested the PSI during 18 new store openings over eight months. For this time period, shrinkage was 2.84% of sales for the 18 stores using the PSI. This figure is substantially lower than the company-wide average of 3.41 percent of sales for the same period (Jones, 1988). If the company-wide shrinkage rate fell to just 2.84, the company would theoretically save over $8 million. This study is consistent with other time-series research (Joy & Jones, 1989).

TEST FAIRNESS

Any preemployment selection procedure must be fair to minority groups. The standard of fairness is Title VII of the Civil Rights Act of 1964 (as amended by the Equal Employment Opportunity Act of 1972). This body of federal legislation dealing with fair employment practice makes it unlawful for employers to refuse to hire or otherwise classify applicants in ways that would deprive or tend to deprive them employment opportunities because of race, color, religion, sex, or national origin. The assessment of test fairness invokes the four-fifths (or 80 percent) rule of thumb; that is, the passing rates on a selection procedure for various protected groups must be within 80 percent of the passing rates for the majority group.

A series of passing rate analyses were conducted for the PSI. Representative samples of applicants were obtained for a variety of industries (banks, convenience stores, restaurants, home improvement centers, supermarkets and drug-

Figure 5.5
Impact of the PSI on Shrinkage: A Comparison of Stores Using the PSI for Selection to Company-wide Figures

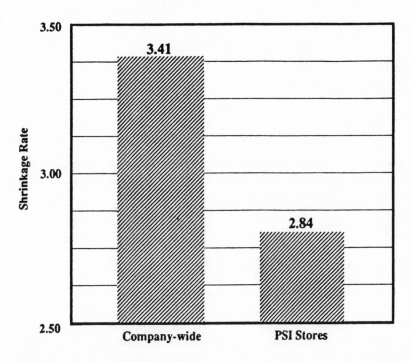

Table 5.3
Summary of Adverse Impact Analysis: Applicants Meeting PSI Standards as a Function of Sex Categories

Groups	Total N	N Meeting Standards	% Meeting Standards	EEOC Compliance Ratio
Male	21201	11962	56.4	-
Female	23000	15220	66.2	1.17
Total	44201	27182	61.5	

stores, hotels, manufacturing) and geographic locations. Using London House's standard recommended cutoff scores, the number and percentage of applicants passing the PSI in the various sex and race groups was determined (Tables 5.3 and 5.4).

Results of these analyses show the passing rates, as reflected in the compliance ratios (e.g., passing rate for a protected minority group/passing rate for the majority group), for racial minorities and females to be well within .80 of the passing rates for white and male applicants.

Table 5.4

Summary of Adverse Impact Analysis: Applicants Meeting PSI Standards as a Function of Race Categories

Groups	Total N	N Meeting Standards	% Meeting Standards	EEOC Compliance Ratio
White	32117	20111	62.6	–
Hispanic	2305	1443	62.6	1.00
Black	6777	4255	62.8	1.00
Others(a)	875	611	69.8	1.11
Total	42074	26420	62.8	

(a) Includes American Indian, Asian, and Pacific Islander.

These results support the fairness of the PSI. Selection rates resultant from PSI usage do not show any discriminatory adverse impact on the employment of minority sex or race groups.

CONCLUSION

The evidence from the reviewed studies provides substantial support for the reliability, validity, and fairness of the PSI. The manner in which the validity evidence has been collected has some major strengths. One is that the relationship between the PSI and independent measures of theft has been established using several different methods and criteria. The PSI has been shown to (1) exhibit a high degree of correspondence to results of independently conducted polygraph examinations, (2) be highly related to anonymous self-reports of theft behavior, (3) predict group membership of persons who should differ on honesty on either theoretical or empirical grounds, (4) predict future theft on the job with a high degree of accuracy, and (5) show substantial reductions in theft when implemented as a selection instrument.

A second strength of the validation research is that within each of the validation methods used, there is replication of findings with independent samples, an important condition for the believability of the findings.

A third strength of the PSI validation research is that statistically significant findings have been replicated in a wide variety of settings (e.g., department stores, drugstores, convenience stores, banks) using a variety of samples (e.g., retail sales clerks, management applicants, dockworkers, donation collectors). This sort of replication across settings and samples strengthens the external validity of the findings.

In addition to the reviewed psychometric properties of the PSI, research also shows it to contain other important properties. The PSI is readable at the seventh-grade educational level (Werner & Ash, 1988) and thus can be comprehended by the vast majority of applicants to positions for which it is used. Also, the PSI is perceived to be job related and inoffensive to over 90 percent of applicants who complete it (Jones & Joy, 1988). Finally the PSI meets relevant professional standards. It complies with the American Psychological Association's (APA) *Primary Standards for Educational and Psychological Testing* (Jones, 1989) and conforms to APA Division 14's *Principles for the Validation and Use of Personnel Selection Procedures* (Slora, 1989).

Companies that use selection tests like the PSI generally believe they are effective because they screen out the potential employee thief. Research supports this belief. Theft-prone applicants who score below standards on preemployment integrity tests have a set of attitudes toward theft that are reliably different from the attitudes of more honest applicants who score above standards. By screening out potentially theft-prone job applicants while selecting in highly productive and dependable applicants, companies improve the overall quality of their work force.

REFERENCES

American Medical Association Council on Scientific Affairs (1986). Council Report—Polygraph. *JAMA*, 256(9), 1172–1175.

American Psychological Association. Division of Industrial-Organizational Psychology (1980). *Principles for the validation and use of personnel selection procedures*. 2d ed. Berkeley, CA: APA.

Baumer, T. L., & Rosenbaum, D. P. (1984). *Combating Retail Theft*. Boston: Butterworth.

Brown, T. S., Jones, J. W., Terris, W., & Steffy, B. (1987). The impact of preemployment integrity testing on employee turnover and inventory shrinkage losses. *Journal of Business and Psychology*, 2(2).

Brown, T. S., & Joy, D. S. (1985). The predictive validity of the Personnel Selection Inventory in the grocery industry. Unpublished technical report. Park Ridge, IL: London House.

Brown, T., & Pardue, J. (1985). The effectiveness of the Personnel Selection Inventory in reducing drug store theft. *Psychological Reports*, 56, 875–881.

Campbell, D. T., & Fiske, D. W. (1959). Convergent and discriminant validation by the Multitrait-Multimethod Matrix. *Psychological Bulletin*, 56, 81–105.

Campbell, D. T., and Stanley, J. C. (1963). *Experimental and quasi-experimental designs for research*. Chicago: Rand McNally.

Cook, T. D., & Campbell, D. T. (1979). *Quasi-experimentation: Design and analysis issues for field settings*. Boston: Houghton Mifflin.

Craig, J. R. (1985). Personnel Selection Inventory. In Keyser, D. J., & Sweetland, R. C. (eds.), *Test Critiques*. Kansas City: Test Corporation of America.

Cronbach, L. J. (1971). Test validation. In R. L. Thorndike (ed.), *Educational measurement*. Washington, DC: American Council on Education.

Equal Employment Opportunity Commission (1979). Uniform Guidelines on Employee Selection Procedures. *Federal Register*, 44(43).

Glass, G. V., Wilson, V. L., & Gottman, J. M. (1975). *Design and analysis of time series experiments*. Boulder, CO: Associated University Press.

Jones, J. W. (1979). Employee deviance: Attitudinal correlates of theft and on-the-job alcohol abuse. Paper presented at the Fifth Annual Convention of the Society of Police and Criminal Psychology, Chicago.

Jones, J. W. (1980). Attitudinal correlates of employees' deviance: Theft, alcohol use, and nonprescribed drug abuse. *Psychological Reports*, 47, 71–77.

Jones, J. W. (1981a). Attitudinal correlates of employee theft of drugs and hospital supplies among nursing personnel. *Journal of Nursing Research*, 30(6), 349–351.

Jones, J. W. (1981b). *Personality profiles of endorsers of nuclear crime*. Paper presented at the 89th Annual Convention of the American Psychological Association, Division of Military Psychology, Los Angeles.

Jones, J. W. (1982). Correlates of police misconduct: Violence and alcohol use on the job. Technical Report 7. Park Ridge, IL: London House.

Jones, J. W. (1988). Impact of the Personnel Selection Inventory on department store shrinkage: Preliminary findings. Unpublished technical report. Park Ridge, IL: London House.

Jones, J. W. (1989). The Personnel Selection Inventory Honesty Scale: Compliance with APA's Primary Standards for Educational and Psychological Testing. Unpublished technical report. Park Ridge, IL: London House.

Jones, J. W., & Joy, D. S. (1988). Empirical investigation of job applicants' reactions to taking a preemployment honesty test. Paper presented at the 97th Annual Conference of the American Psychological Association, New Orleans.

Jones, J. W., Joy, D. S., Werner, S., & Orban, J. (1989). Construct validation of pre-employment honesty test: A between-group comparison with 101,073 job applicants. Technical Report 31. Park Ridge, IL: London House.

Jones, J. W., & Terris, W. (1981a). Predictive validation of a dishonesty test that measures theft proneness. Paper presented at the 18th Interamerican Congress of Psychology, Santo Domingo, Dominican Republic.

Jones, J. W., & Terris, W. (1981b). Convicted felons' attitudes toward theft, violence and illicit drug use. Paper presented at the Seventh Annual Convention of the Society of Police and Criminal Psychology, New Orleans.

Jones, J. W., & Terris, W. (1982a). Attitudes toward theft as predictors of employee theft among salesclerks. Paper presented at the 90th Annual Convention of the American Psychological Association, Washington, D.C.

Jones, J. W., & Terris, W. (1982b). The use of the Personnel Selection Inventory to predict turnover in a group of security guards: A pilot study. Technical Report 21. Park Ridge, IL: London House.

Jones, J. W., & Terris, W. (1982c). Personality profiles of endorsers of nuclear crime. *Personnel Selection and Training Bulletin*, 3(1), 31–41.

Jones, J. W., & Terris, W. (1983a). Personality correlates of theft and drug abuse among job applicants. *Proceedings of the Third International Conference on the 16PF Test*, 85–94.

Jones, J. W., & Terris, W. (1983b). Predicting employees' theft in home improvement centers. *Psychological Reports*, 52, 187–201.

Jones, J. W., & Terris, W. (1983c). Psychologically screening criminally deviant and potentially counterproductive job applicants: implications for nuclear security. *Journal of Security Administration*, 6(1), 17–30.

Jones, J. W., & Terris, W. (1983d). Screening nuclear security guard applicants for criminal potential. *American Nuclear Society Transactions*, 160–161.

Jones, J. W., & Terris, W. (1983e). The organizational climate of honesty: An empirical investigation in restaurants. Paper presented at the 55th Annual Conference of the Midwest Psychological Association, Chicago.

Jones, J. W., & Terris, W. (1985). Screening employment applicants for attitudes toward theft: Three quasi-experimental studies. *International Journal of Management*, 2 (3), 62–76.

Joy, D. S. (1985). The effect of the Personnel Selection Inventory on theft admissions among terminated retail chain employees. Unpublished technical report. Park Ridge, IL: London House.

Joy, D. S., & Jones, J. W. (1989). Relationship between the Personnel Selection Inventory and company shrinkage rates. Unpublished technical report. Park Ridge, IL: London House.

London House Management Consultants (1980). *The Personnel Selection Inventory* (PSI). Park Ridge, IL: London House Press.

McDaniel, M., & Jones, J. W. (1988). Predicting employee theft: A quantitative review of the validity of a standardized measure of dishonesty. *Journal of Business and Psychology*, 2(4), 327–345.

Moretti, D. M. (1980). Employee counterproductivity: Attitudinal predictors of industrial damage and waste. Paper presented at the Sixth Annual Meeting of the Society of Police and Criminal Psychology, Atlanta.

Moretti, D.M. (1982). The prediction of employee counterproductivity through attitude assessment. Paper presented at the 90th Annual Convention of the American Psychological Association, Washington, DC.

Moretti, D.M. (1983a). A brief report on the effectiveness of the Bank Personnel Selection Inventory. Unpublished technical report. Park Ridge, IL: London House.

Moretti, D. M. (1983b). The use of the Personnel Selection Inventory in screening airport employees: Comparisons with a preemployment polygraph examination. Unpublished technical report. Park Ridge, IL: London House.

Moretti, D. M. (1984a). Integrity testing in a southern department store: The demonstration of validity, cost-effectiveness, and legal compliance. Unpublished technical report. Park Ridge, IL: London House.

Moretti, D. M. (1984b). The validation of an integrity test for banks. Unpublished technical report. Park Ridge, IL: London House.

Moretti, D. M., Jones, J. W., & Terris, W. (1983). Integrity testing in the banking industry. Paper presented at the Bank Administration Institute's Conference on Bank Security, New Orleans.

O'Bannon, R. M., Goldinger, L. A., & Appleby, G. S. (1989). *Honesty and integrity testing: A practical guide*. Atlanta: Applied Information Resources.

Rafilson, F. M. (in press). Temporal stability of a pre-employment integrity test. *Psychological Reports*.

Sackett, P. R., & Harris, M. M. (1984). Honesty testing for personnel selection: A review and critique. *Personnel Psychology*, 37, 221–245.

Sackett, P. R., Burris, L. R., & Callahan, C. (1989). Integrity testing for personnel selection: An update. *Personnel Psychology*, 42, 491–529.

Sauser, W. I. (1985). London House Personnel Selection Inventory. In Mitchell, J. V. (ed.), *The Ninth Mental Measurements Yearbook*. Lincoln, NE: Buros Institute of Mental Measurements.

Slora, K. B. (1989). The Personnel Selection Inventory: Conformance to the APA Division 14's Principles for the Validation and Use of Personnel Selection Procedures. Unpublished technical report. Park Ridge, IL: London House.

Terris, W. (1979a). Attitudinal correlates of employee integrity: Theft related admissions made in preemployment polygraph examinations. *Journal of Security Administration*, 2, 30–39.

Terris, W. (1979b). Attitudinal correlates of theft, violence, and drug use. Paper presented at the 17th Interamerican Congress of Psychology, Lima, Peru.

Terris, W. (1985). Attitudinal correlates of employee integrity. *Journal of Police and Criminal Psychology*, 1(1), 60–68.

Terris, W., & Jones, J. W. (1980). Attitudinal and personality correlates of theft among supermarket employees. *Journal of Security Administration*, 3(2), 65–78.

Terris, W., & Jones, J. W. (1981). Using the PSI to screen for employee theft in a major department store chain: A preliminary report. Unpublished technical report. Park Ridge, IL: London House.

Terris, W., & Jones, J. W. (1982a). Psychological factors related to employees' theft in the convenience store industry. *Psychological Reports*, 51, 1219–1238.

Terris, W., & Jones, J. W. (1982b). Validation of the PSI with managerial and hourly employees in a fast food company. Technical Report 22. Park Ridge, IL: London House.

Terris, W., & Jones, J. W. (1983). Psychological correlates of employee theft in department stores. Technical Report 20. Park Ridge, IL: London House.

U.S. Department of Commerce (1972). *The economic impact of crimes against business*. Washington, DC: Government Printing Office.

Welchman, D. J., & Bae, R. P. (1983). The Personnel Selection Inventory: An empirical examination. Technical Report 14. Park Ridge, IL: London House.

Werner, S. H., & Ash, P. (1988). Reading grade level of the London House Personnel Selection Inventory (PSI). *Educational and Psychological Measurement*, 49(4), 921–927.

6

Attitude-Behavior Relations: A Theoretical and Empirical Analysis of Preemployment Integrity Tests

JOHN W. JONES

The Ajzen-Fishbein (1977) theory of attitude-behavior relationships, one of the most popular theories in the field of social psychology, explains why the correlations between attitude questionnaires and behavioral criteria range from low to high. These theoreticians found that attitudes are the best predictors of behavior when the attitudinal qualities being measured are congruent with the relevant behavior being predicted.

More specifically, Ajzen and Fishbein (1977) found that strong attitude-behavior relations are obtained only when there is high correspondence between the separate measures of attitude and behavior. According to this congruence theory, "An attitudinal predictor is said to correspond to the behavioral criterion to the extent that the attitudinal entity is identical in all, or nearly all four elements with the behavioral entity" (p. 89). The attitudes measured and the behaviors predicted may be congruent on four different elements:

1. *Target*: This is a person's attitude toward a target. A target is the focus or goal of a particular action; it can be an object, a person, or an institution. For example, company cash and merchandise are often the targets of theft by dishonest workers.

2. *Activity*: This predictor is one's attitude toward an action. That is, one is evaluating a specific action toward an object. Stealing, for instance, is an activity that can be directed toward company cash, merchandise, or property.

3. *Context*: This is a person's attitude toward the context in which an action takes place. Activities can occur at home, school, or the workplace. For example, employee theft occurs in the workplace.

4. *Time*: This is one's attitude toward an event at a particular time. This is an attitude toward a target and/or activity that has occurred, is occurring, or will occur. For instance, a job applicant might be asked to estimate how many employees will steal at work during the next six months.

Behavioral criteria (e.g., theft) that are to be predicted by attitudes always involve these four specific elements. A given action is always performed toward a specific target. This action toward a target always occurs in a given context and at a given time. An example of employee theft would have a cashier at a supermarket stealing cash from the register during the three-month probationary employment period. The action is stealing, the target is cash from the register, the context is the supermarket, and the time frame is during the three-month probationary period.

Empirical research on attitude-behavior relationships abounds. Ajzen and Fishbein (1977) found three types of relationships that were clearly supported by a review of scientific research. One type of relationship occurs when both the target and action elements of an attitude do not correspond to the target or action elements of the behavioral criterion. A lack of correspondence exists. Studies of this kind yield very low attitude-behavior correlations. For example, an attitude toward one's family (e.g., "My parents have often disapproved of my friends") taken from a personality test has no target or action elements that correspond to the target or action elements of a criterion variable such as "employee theft of cash or merchandise." Hence, the attitude-behavior correlation would be expected to equal zero or near zero.

A second type of relationship is partial correspondence: measures of attitude and behavior correspond with one of the two major elements (target or action) of the attitudinal and behavioral entities. Ajzen and Fishbein (1977) found that under conditions of partial correspondence, correlations between attitude and behavior will tend to be inconsistent, and even where they are significant, they will normally be quite low. For instance, the attitude about the degree of delinquency in one's behavior (e.g., "My troublesome behavior often causes problems") does not have a high degree of correspondence with the behavioral criterion "breaking company rules." In this case, there is a slight correspondence between the activity entities: troublesome behavior compared to company rules. Although some statistically significant correlations can be found, they will tend to be inconsistent and normally quite low.

In the third type of relationship, there is a high correspondence between attitudinal and behavioral entities. This results in strong correlations. The correspondence should be on two or more entities. For instance, an attitude toward theft of a particular object (e.g., "How often are employees tempted to take money from their company without permission?") has a high degree of correspondence with a behavioral criterion variable such as "engaging in on-the-job theft of company cash." There is high correspondence between both the target and activity entities: tempted to take company money without permission cor-

Table 6.1
Ajzen-Fishbein Theory of Attitude-Behavior Relations

Degree of Attitude–Behavior Congruence	Estimated Magnitude of Correlation
No Correspondence	Zero
Partial Correspondence	Low
High Correspondence	High

responds with engaging in on-the-job theft of company cash. High attitude-behavior correlations are found. A summary of the Ajzen-Fishbein attitude-behavior correspondence theory is presented in Table 6.1.

This theory has major implications in the area of test construction. For instance, more and more companies are using paper-and-pencil integrity tests for selecting honest and dependable employees. Employee theft is a serious and costly problem, which companies must grapple with (Hollinger & Clark, 1983).

TYPES OF INTEGRITY TESTS

Paul Sackett and associates (Sackett, Buris & Callahan, 1989) identified the emergence of two distinct types of integrity tests that are used to identify theft-prone and counterproductive job applicants: overt integrity tests and personality-based measures. Overt integrity tests inquire directly about job applicants' attitudes toward theft. They were primarily developed to control both the prevalence and magnitude of employee theft and similar forms of gross misconduct in the workplace (Terris, 1985). Personality-based tests were primarily designed to measure poor impulse control, lack of conscientiousness, and general delinquency in nonemployee populations (Gough, 1971, 1972).

Although published research indicates that overt integrity tests do predict employee theft (McDaniel & Jones, 1988), no published study shows a significant relationship between personality-based measures of delinquency and pure on-the-job theft criteria. Most personality-based tests are validated against a composite measure of on-the-job misconduct. While over 30 honesty tests have been identified (O'Bannon, Goldinger & Appleby, 1989), much of the validation research with overt integrity tests has been conducted with the Personal Selection Inventory (PSI) (cf. Sackett & Harris, 1984; Sackett, Buris & Callahan, 1989). The PSI Honesty scale has been found to predict the following criteria: (1) supervisors' ratings of employees' dishonesty, (2) applicants who are likely to get caught stealing once hired, (3) applicants who have a criminal history of theft and related offenses, and (4) applicants who are likely to make theft admissions in an anonymous testing situation (Joy, 1988). McDaniel and Jones (1988) summarized 23 studies in a meta-analysis and found that the average validity coefficient of the PSI Honesty scale equals 0.50. Overt integrity tests appear to have a high degree of attitude-behavior correspondence in predicting employee theft criteria.

Ash (1987, 1988) reviewed the literature available on a number of personality-based measures, including the Personnel Reaction Blank (PRB) (Gough, 1972) and the PDI Employment Inventory (EI) (Paajanen, 1986). Ash pointed out that the use of personality tests to assess criminality has yielded inconsistent results, especially in the employment context. Hence, it would be expected that personality-based measures would tend to lack correspondence with behavioral criteria such as on-the-job theft and therefore would yield lower validity coefficients than overt integrity tests.

A BETWEEN-TEST COMPARISON

Sackett and associates (1989) suggested that when a company is most interested in predicting theft criteria, overt integrity tests appear to be more appropriate. Unfortunately, these authors pointed out, a lack of head-to-head comparisons between the two types of integrity tests prevents us from drawing strong conclusions about the relative merits of these different types of tests. Frost and Rafilson (1989) were the first researchers to publish a study that directly compared a leading overt integrity test, the PSI, to a leading personality-based measure of delinquency, the PRB. These researchers examined the ability of these two tests to predict anonymous admissions of employee theft.

They hypothesized that the overt test would better predict theft criteria than the personality-based measure, for two reasons. First, overt integrity tests were designed primarily to predict theft, reduce employee pilferage, and hence control company shrinkage rates. Personality-based measures were originally developed to predict delinquency in the general adult population. Second, moderately high validity coefficients have been obtained between overt integrity tests and various theft criteria. No published studies exist that show that personality-based measures can predict pure theft criteria.

Sample

Their sample consisted of 105 employees who were employed in a wide variety of business occupations at the time of the study: manufacturing (11.4 percent), retail sales (21.9 percent), government (5.7 percent), restaurant (11.4 percent), construction (2.9 percent), health care (5.7 percent), and miscellaneous (41 percent). They averaged 30.7 hours (SD = 15) of employment per week. Their average age was 24.1 years (SD = 8). Approximately 52 percent of the sample were male, and 48 percent were female.

Tests

Overt Integrity Test. All employees completed the Honesty scale from the PSI (London House, 1980). The scale has a Spearman-Brown split-half reliability equal to .95 (Terris, 1979) and an average validity coefficient against various theft criteria equal to .50 (McDaniel & Jones, 1988). The scale was designed to measure job applicants' attitudes toward, perceptions of, and opinions about theft in the workplace. The Honesty scale measures the following attitudes toward theft: (1) tolerance of others who steal, (2) estimates about the extent of theft by others, (3) acceptance of common rationalizations for theft, and (4) ruminations about theft. Higher scores mean less tolerance for theft.

Personality-based Measure. The PRB (Gough, 1971, 1972) was one of the original personality-based measures of delinquency. Other personality-based measures seem to be patterned after it (e.g., the EI). It purports to measure dependability and conscientiousness. The PRB effectively discriminated between adult samples of delinquents and nondelinquents (Gough, 1971). Internal consistency coefficients have ranged from .65 to .95 depending on the type of sample studied (Gough, 1972). Higher scores mean more dependability.

Theft Criteria

Employees in the Frost-Rafilson study anonymously completed a nine-item theft criterion checklist. The alpha reliability coefficient for the theft checklist equaled .82. Types of behavior assessed with the theft subscale include (1) theft of money, property, and merchandise from the employer; (2) overcharging and shortchanging customers for personal gain; (3) changing company records to get paid for work not actually done; (4) actively helping other employees steal from the company; and (5) selling merchandise to friends and relatives at a reduced price. A five-point Likert-type scale was used for all items. Employees used the following scale to rate how often during the last six months they engaged in any of the relevant behaviors: 1 = Very Often (three or more times per week); 2 = Often (one or two times per week); 3 = Occasionally (one or two times in one month); 4 = Seldom (only once in six months); and 5 = Never. Hence, higher scores on the criterion checklist mean less theft.

Results and Comments

Frost and Rafilson found that although the overt honesty scale significantly predicted theft (r = .46, $p < .001$), the personality-based measure did not (r = .10, n.s.) (Figure 6.1). The difference between these two correlations was statistically significant ($p < .001$).

The results of the study support the notion that overt integrity tests should be the best predictors of on-the-job theft criteria (cf. Sackett, Burris & Callahan, 1988). These findings are consistent with the Ajzen-Fishbein theory of attitude-

Figure 6.1
Correlation of PRB and PSI with Theft Criteria

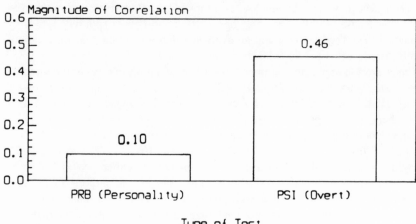

behavior relations: attitudes toward theft in the workplace should be better predictors of on-the-job theft criteria than attitudes toward delinquency in general.

DETERMINING CONGRUENCE

Another study was conducted to determine if the PSI has greater attitude-
behavior congruence with on-the-job theft criteria than the PRB.

Method

In this study, an unbiased psychometrician familiar with both overt integrity
tests and personality-based measures of delinquency examined all of the test
items on the 57-item PSI Honesty scale and the 42-item PRB. The psychometrician used a three-point Likert-type rating scale to document if a particular
attitudinal entity had any degree of correspondence with on-the-job theft criteria.
The rating scale ranged from 1 (very low or nonexistent congruence) to 3 (very
high congruence). Each of the following entities was rated:

1. *Theft Target*: Did the test item make reference to a particular object of theft, such as
   cash, merchandise, property, or information?

2. *Theft Activity*: Did the item make reference to theft-related or dishonest behavior?

3. *Employment Context*: Did the item make reference to or clearly imply on-the-job theft?

4. *Time Frame*: Did the item make reference to theft or dishonest behavior at a particular
   point in time?

Two other dependent variables were analyzed. The psychometrician used a three-point scale to rate if an item appeared to be job relevant. A rating of 1 meant that no part of the item, at face value, made reference to a job or work setting. A rating of 3 meant that the item definitely made reference to a job or work setting. An in-between rating of 2 meant that some people might construe the item as job relevant and some might not. Second, the five-item element scores (target, activity, context, time frame, and job relevancy) were summed to yield an overall item quality score. The overall quality score could theoretically range from 5 to 15. Higher scores meant greater attitude-behavior congruence and more job relevancy.

In order to gauge the reliability of the ratings, the psychometrician was asked to rate a random selection of 20 items four months after the first rating. The items were rated in terms of their congruence with a theft target and theft activity. Ten items were randomly selected from the PSI and 10 from the PRB. The overall correlation between the theft target ratings at time 1 and time 2 equaled 0.92 ($p < .01$). This magnitude of correlation was also found when correlating, separately, pairs of scores for the 10 PSI items ($r = .94$, $p < .01$) and the 10 PRB items ($r = .76$, $p < .05$).

The overall correlation between the theft activity ratings at time 1 and time 2 was also highly significant ($r = .95$, $p < .01$). Similar results were found when looking only at the PSI item pairings ($r = .93$, $p < .01$) and the PRB item pairings ($r = .92$, $p < .01$). The obtained reliability coefficients suggest that the psychometrician was giving consistent ratings across time.

Results and Discussion

The average item scores for each attitudinal entity as a function of type of test are summarized in Table 6.2. Inspection of the between-test differences shows that the overt integrity test has higher-quality items for predicting on-the-job theft than the personality-based measure. A graphic presentation of the between-test differences for the overall item quality score is presented in Figure 6.2

The entire population of test items was rated for each test. No statistical test of significance was necessary because there is no need to make an inference to a larger group of items. However, if one were to view the items as independent subjects, then a t-test could be used. All between-test differences are statistically significant ($p < .01$ in all cases) when using this latter approach. Arguments can be made to use or not use inferential statistics. The bottom line is that overt tests have more congruent items with theft criteria than do personality-based tests.

The obtained pattern of results needs to be replicated using different psychometricians. The rating procedure is very straightforward and appears to be reliable across time. Researchers and practitioners can easily use the three-point rating strategy to document the degree of congruence between attitudinal predictors and behavioral criteria of concern.

Table 6.2
Attitude-Behavior Congruence

Attitudinal Entity	Overt Integrity (N = 57 Items)	Personality-based Measure (N = 42 Items)
1. Theft Target:		
M =	2.3	1.1
SD =	0.9	0.3
2. Theft Activity:		
M =	2.6	1.1
SD =	0.7	0.3
3. Employment Context:		
M =	2.3	1.1
SD =	0.8	0.3
4. Timeframe:		
M =	1.8	1.1
SD =	1.0	0.3
5. Job Relevancy:		
M =	2.4	1.1
SD =	0.7	0.3
6. Overall Quality:		
M =	11.5	5.4
SD =	3.3	1.3

Higher scores mean greater attitude-behavior congruence. All between-test differences are statistically significant (p < .01 or less).

The results also suggested that the overt integrity test was a better predictor of theft in the Frost-Rafilson study (1989) because a higher degree of congruence existed between the test items and on-the-job theft criteria. This study should ideally be replicated using a predictive validity design. The Ajzen-Fishbein theory should prove useful when personnel psychologists design and validate personnel selection tests.

Figure 6.2
Attitude-Behavior Congruence Overall Score

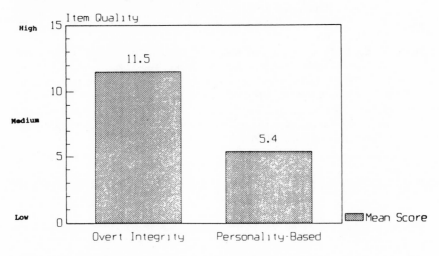

REFERENCES

Ajzen, I., & Fishbein, M. (1977). Attitude-behavior relations: A theoretical analysis and review of empirical research. *Psychological Bulletin* 84, 888–918.

Ash, P. (1987). A summary of personality-based measures of counterproductivity. Unpublished manuscript.

Ash, P. (1988). A history of honesty testing. Paper presented at the 1988 Convention of the American Psychological Association, Atlanta.

Frost, A. G., & Rafilson, F. M. (1989). Overt integrity tests versus personality-based measures of delinquency: An empirical comparison. *Journal of Business and Psychology*, 3 (3), 269–277.

Gough, H. G. (1971). The assessment of wayward impulse by means of the Personnel Reaction Blank. *Personnel Psychology*, 24, 669–677.

Gough, H. G. (1972). *Manual for the Personnel Reaction Blank*. Palo Alto, CA: Consulting Psychologists Press.

Hollinger, R. C., & Clark, J. P. (1983). *Theft by employees*. Lexington, MA: Lexington Books.

Joy, D. (1988). The use of the Personnel Selection Inventory to reduce employee theft. Technical Report 51. Park Ridge, IL: London House Press.

London House (1980). The Personnel Selection Inventory (PSI). Park Ridge, IL: London House Press.

McDaniel, M. A., & Jones, J. W. (1988). Predicting employee theft: A quantitative review of a standardized measure of dishonesty. *Journal of Business and Psychology*, 2, 327–345.

O'Bannon, R. M., Goldinger, L. A., & Appleby, G. S. (1989). *Honesty and integrity testing: A practical guide*. Atlanta: Applied Information Resources.

Paajanen, G. E. (1986). Development and validation of the PDI Employment Inventory. Paper presented at the 94th Annual Convention of the American Psychological Association, Washington, D.C.

Sackett, P. R., & Harris, M. E. (1984). Honesty testing for personnel selection: A review and critique. *Personnel Psychology*, 37, 221–246.

Sackett, P. R., Burris, L. R., & Callahan, C. (1989). Integrity testing for personnel selection: An update. *Personnel Psychology*, 42, 491–529.

Terris, W. (1979). Attitudinal correlates of employee integrity: Theft-related admissions made in preemployment polygraph examinations. *Journal of Security Administration*, 2, 30–39.

Terris, W. (1985). Attitudinal correlates of employee integrity. *Journal of Police and Criminal Psychology*, 1, 60–68.

7

Honesty Testing for Personnel Selection: A Quantitative Review

MICHAEL A. MCDANIEL AND JOHN W. JONES

There has been an increasing interest in the use of paper-and-pencil measures designed to identify dishonest job applicants (Sackett & Harris, 1984). The purpose of this chapter is to summarize the validity evidence for a published dishonesty measure, the Dishonesty subscale of the Personnel Selection Inventory (PSI) (London House, 1980). Terris (1985) has provided a narrative review of the validity of this scale. The research examined here employed meta-analysis methods (Hunter, Schmidt & Jackson, 1982) to summarize the validity evidence and to test the hypothesis that the validity covaries with a severity-of-consequences moderator. Specifically, we hypothesize that respondents who anticipate adverse consequences following accurate reporting of theft-related attitudes will be less likely than others to respond accurately and that the correlation between the predictor and the criterion will be lower.

METHOD

Validity studies involving the Dishonesty scale were obtained from its publisher. The senior research psychologist of the test publisher stated that the authors were given a complete set of all validity studies on the scale (personal communication, W. Terris, 1986). Thus, reporting bias (Schmidt, Hunter, Pearlman, & Hirsch, 1985) does not appear to be a problem in the research.

Hirsh and McDaniel (1986) have recommended that meta-analytic investigators explicitly state the reasons some research is excluded from the analysis to allow other researchers to reach their own conclusions regarding the adequacy of a meta-analytic study's decision rules. With the exceptions of the cases noted, all validity coefficients were included in this study when the zero-order correlation coefficients between the raw or percentile dishonesty scale scores and a theft criterion were reported. In operational use, the Dishonesty scale is one of three predictive scales in a screening battery (London House, 1980). Each scale has a recommended cutoff score; a respondent must exceed each cutoff score to receive a passing score on the battery. In 10 studies, the validity analyses were limited to the dichotomously scored (pass-fail) total battery score. Since no zero-order validity coefficient was available for the dishonesty measure, data from these 10 studies could not be included in the analysis. Also excluded were data from any study where only statistically significant coefficients were reported; had they been included, the results would have overestimated the mean population validity (Hirsh & McDaniel, 1986). None of the available studies reported any evidence of criterion contamination.

Six studies were not included because they did not include theft data. One study (Wiechman & Bae, 1983) was not included due to selective reporting of results. A study by Jones and Terris (1982) successfully contrasted the dishonesty scores of convicted felons with nonfelons. Data from this extreme groups approach, although interesting, were not judged appropriate for inclusion in our analysis. A study by Jones and Terris (1983) was not included for similar reasons.

Twenty-three independent samples from 17 studies met the decision rules established for this study. Nineteen of the samples consisted of employees or applicants. Four samples used high school or college students. Most of the samples were composed of retail employees in grocery, department, or home improvement stores. The remaining samples included two samples of nurses, one sample of warehouse workers, and one sample of Salvation Army workers. Several samples were not occupationally homogeneous.

Several theft criteria were available: self-report theft admissions, supervisory ratings of employees' theft, criminal history background investigations, polygraph examinations, and cash shortfalls. Eighteen of the 23 samples used self-report theft admission criteria. These 18 studies were concurrent studies requiring the subjects to complete both the Dishonesty scale and a self-report scale of theft behavior. In all but one of these studies, the data were collected anonymously. The studies included a diverse set of theft criteria. If many validity studies were available, we could have chosen criteria more selectively or prepared more detailed analyses by criterion type; however, given the number of coefficients available for analysis, we judged it best to include any data with a theft criterion.

Our analysis is a bare-bones meta-analysis (Schmidt et al., 1985) because it corrects the distribution of coefficients only for sampling error. This approach was taken for two reasons. First, we had no well-documented estimates for either the criterion reliabilities or the amount of range restriction. Second, a bare-bones analysis is very conservative. To the extent that the criterion measures were less than perfectly reliable and range restriction was operating, the results would underestimate the magnitude and the invariance of the estimated population validity. Whereas employment testing professionals are often skeptical of validity claims made for integrity measures (Sackett, 1985), a conservative analysis is the best approach for summarizing these validity data.

We hypothesized that respondents who anticipate adverse consequences following accurate reporting of theft-related attitudes will be less likely than others to respond accurately and that the correlation between the predictor and the criterion will be lower. Two study characteristics allow one to categorize the available studies roughly along this severity-of-consequences continuum. The first study characteristic is the anonymity of the Dishonesty scale responses. In general, one would expect that respondents whose responses are anonymous will be less likely to expect adverse consequences for responding accurately about their theft-related attitudes. The second study characteristic hypothesized to influence reporting accuracy and scale validity is whether the study participant is an applicant-employee or student. A participant who is a student and not a job applicant or employee should be less concerned about accurate responses because he or she need not worry about losing or obtaining a job. If the study participant is an applicant, one would expecct the person to be more concerned about adverse consequences from responding accurately.

RESULTS

Table 7.1 displays the results of the meta-analyses. The first column displays the study categories for the meta-analysis: all samples, samples with self-report criterion, samples with any criterion excluding self-report, samples where the subjects were employees or applicants, samples where the subjects were students, samples with a self-report criterion where the subjects were employees or applicants, samples with a self-report criterion where the subjects were students, samples where the respondents completed the Dishonesty scale anonymously, samples where the subjects' responses to the Dishonesty scale were not anonymous, samples where the subjects knew that their Dishonesty scale responses would be compared to another indicator of their honesty, and samples where the subjects did not know that their Dishonesty scale responses would be compared to another indicant of their dishonesty.

The second, third, and fourth columns display the number of samples in the analysis category, the total sample size, and the mean sample size. Columns 4 and 5 display the sample-size-weighted mean and standard deviation for the distribution of the observed coefficients. The expected sampling error for the distribution of observed coefficients is displayed in column 7, with column 8 displaying the percentage of observed variance that can be attributed to sampling error. Columns 9 and 10 display the standard deviation of the residual distribution and the lower ninetieth confidence value for the residual distribution.

The first analysis category includes data for all 23 samples. The mean coefficient is .50. The residual standard deviation is .09, which is about average

Table 7.1
Meta-Analyses of the Validity of the Dishonesty Scale

Analysis Categories	Number of r	Total Sample Size	Mean Sample Size	Observed Mean r	Observed SD	Sampling SD	% Var.	Residual SD	90% C.I.
All Samples - All Criteria									
1. All Samples All Criteria	23	1,806	79	.50	.12	.09	48	.09	.36
Analyses by Criterion Category									
2. Self-report Criteria	18	959	53	.53	.11	.10	82	.05	.47
3. All Other Criteria	5	847	169	.46	.13	.07	29	.11	.32
Analyses by Subject Category									
4. Employees/Applicants	19	1,463	77	.48	.13	.09	47	.09	.36
5. Students	4	343	86	.55	.08	.08	92	.02	.52
Analyses by Subject Category for Self-report Criteria									
6. Employees/Applicants	14	616	44	.52	.12	.11	81	.05	.45
7. Students	4	343	86	.55	.08	.08	92	.02	.52
Analyses by Predictor Anonymity Category									
8. Anonymous predictor	17	855	50	.54	.11	.10	82	.05	.48
9. Not Anonymous predictor	6	951	159	.45	.12	.07	33	.10	.33
Analyses by Knowledge of Criteria Category									
10. Samples where applicant knows of criterion	19	1,429	75	.54	.09	.08	84	.04	.50
11. Samples where applicant doesn't know of criterion	4	377	94	.33	.07	.09	100	.00	.33

Note: In this meta-analysis, the observed mean is not corrected. The residual standard deviation is the square root of the variance remaining after the correction of the observed variance for sampling error. Percentages of variance accounted for that exceeded 100% were truncated to 100%.

compared to the residual standard deviations found in validity generalization studies of cognitive ability measures (McDaniel, Hirsh, Schmidt, Raju & Hunter, 1986).

Analyses 2 and 3 compare the validities using self-report criteria versus all other criteria. Studies using self-report measures show higher mean validities than studies using other criteria. A comparison of the mean coefficients and the residual standard deviations for analyses 2 and 3, when judged against the comparable statistics for the analyses of all data (analysis 1), supports the moderator-like effect of this criterion distinction. Specifically, at least one mean coefficient (both here) in the moderator subgroups (e.g., the self-report samples are one subgroup, the other criteria samples are the second subgroup) is different from the mean of the total distribution (e.g., the distribution of all 23 coefficients), and the sample-size-weighted mean residual standard deviation of the subgroup distributions is lower than that of the total distribution. (For this and all moderator analyses presented, we remind readers of the tentative nature of the conclusions given the few coefficients available for analysis.)

Analyses 4 and 5 compare the validities of samples with student subjects versus employee or applicant samples. The validities for the student samples are higher than those for the employees or applicants. As with the criterion analysis, the pattern of means and residual standard deviations suggests the moderator-like effect of this categorization. Sufficient data existed for an examination of the categorization for samples with self-report criteria. Analyses 6 and 7 display these results. Like the previous categorization analyses, the student samples show higher validity than do the employee-applicant samples.

Analyses 8 and 9 show analyses broken out by the anonymity of subjects' responses to the Dishonesty scale. Those studies whose participants responded anonymously to the scale yielded higher validities than those studies where the responses were not anonymous. As in earlier analyses, the pattern of mean coefficients and residual standard deviations suggests that the respondents' anonymity may moderate the validity of the Dishonesty scale.

Analyses 10 and 11 address whether the subjects' knowledge that criterion data would be collected influences the validity of the dishonesty measure. A subject would know that the researchers had another indicant of the subject's dishonesty when the subject provided the criterion with a self-report theft questionnaire or when the subject knew that he or she would undergo a polygraph interrogation. If the study used a supervisory rating of theft or if an unobtrusive measure of employee theft was used as the criterion, subjects were considered to be unaware of the criterion. The analyses show that the validities are higher when respondents are aware that the investigator has another source of theft information that can be compared to their Dishonesty scale responses.

DISCUSSION

The results from these meta-analyses indicate that the validity of the Dishonesty scale is at useful levels regardless of the circumstances of its use. The measure achieves its highest validity when the subjects' responses are anonymous, when the criterion is self-reported, when the subjects are students, and when the respondent is aware that the investigator has another source of information on the subject's honesty. We argue that these moderators affect the validity of the Dishonesty scale by affecting the accuracy of the subject's responses. While the residual variance for the distribution of all studies is not large, the partitioning of the data into the hypothesized moderator subgroups reduces the size of the remaining variance.

The data refute the hypothesis that theft criteria are not reliable measures. If the criteria were very unreliable, the criteria correlations with the Dishonesty scale or any other variable would cluster around zero. This was not the case.

This meta-analysis demonstrates that the Dishonesty scale studies conducted to date report sufficient information such that, when cumulated, informative conclusions may be drawn. This does not imply, however, that there is no room for improvement in the studies' reporting practices. Future studies should report the manner in which the sample members were selected, the intercorrelations among the predictors, the mean and variance of the predictor, the intercorrelations among the criteria, the mean and variance of the criterion, the criterion reliability, and the zero-order validities for the theft scale. Estimates of the population mean and variance of the Dishonesty scale should also be calculated.

A more focused research effort would improve knowledge in this area. Future studies should examine whether validity covaries with criterion type, occupational group, and testing conditions (e.g., anonymity and awareness of alternative measures of an employee's honesty). Most of the studies in this review are based on anonymous, self-report criteria, which are substantially different from those obtained in operational settings and may overestimate the validity to be expected in operational settings. Thus, the generalization of these results to operational testing situations is in doubt. More research is needed using methods that mirror the conditions under which the test is operationally used.

REFERENCES

Hirsch, H. R., & McDaniel, M. A. (1986). Developing decision rules for meta-analysis. In M. A. McDaniel (chair), An overview and new directions in the Hunter, Schmidt, Jackson meta-analysis technique. Symposium presented at the First Annual Conference of the Society for I/O Psychology, Chicago.

Hunter, J. E., & Hunter, R. F. (1984). Validity and utility of alternative predictors of job performance. *Psychological Bulletin, 96,* 72–98.

Hunter, J. E., Schmidt, F. L., & Jackson, G. B. (1982). *Meta-analysis: Cumulating research findings across studies.* Beverly Hills, CA: Sage.

Jones, J. W., & Terris, W. (1982). Convicted felons' attitudes toward theft, violence, and illicit drug use. Paper presented at the Seventh Annual Convention of the Society of Police and Criminal Psychology, New Orleans.

Jones, J. W., & Terris, W. (1983). Human factors in organizations: 1. Screening nuclear security guard applicants for criminal potential. *American Nuclear Society Transactions*, 160–161.

London House (1980). *Personnel Selection Inventory Manual*. Park Ridge, IL: London House Press.

McDaniel, M. A., Hirsh, H. R., Schmidt, F. L., Raju, N. S., & Hunter, J. E. (1986). Interpreting the results of meta-analytic research: A comment on Schmitt, Gooding, Noe, and Kirsh (1984). *Personnel Psychology*, 39, 141–148.

Sackett, P. R. (1985). Honesty research and the person-situation debate. In W. Terris (ed.), *Employee theft: Research, theory, and applications*. Park Ridge, IL: London House Press.

Sackett, P. R., & Harris, M. M. (1984). Honesty testing for personnel selection: A review and critique. *Personnel Psychology*, 37, 221–246.

Schmidt, F. L., Hunter, J. E., Pearlman, K., & Hirsh, H. R. (1985). Forty questions and answers about validity generalization and meta-analysis. *Personnel Psychology*, 38, 697–798.

Terris, W. (1985). Personnel selection as a method to reduce employee theft. In W. Terris (ed.), *Employee theft: Research, theory, and applications*. Park Ridge, IL: London House Press.

Wiechman, D. J., & Bae, R. P. (1983). The Personnel Selection Inventory: An empirical examination. Technical Report No. 14. Park Ridge, IL: London House Press.

8

Honesty Testing: Estimating and Reducing the False Positive Rate

Scott L. Martin

Paper-and-pencil tests designed to predict employee theft and counterproductivity in the workplace are becoming increasingly popular among employers. The increased use of honesty tests is at least partly due to the fact that employee theft has increased over the past two decades (American Management Association, 1977; Bales, 1988; Jones, 1981; U.S. Department of Commerce, 1972). It has been estimated that the cost of internal theft to American businesses may exceed $40 billion per year (Palmiotto, 1983). In addition, as a result of the law prohibiting the use of polygraphs for preemployment screening by private employers, which took effect on December 27, 1988, the use of paper-and-pencil honesty tests is likely to become even more prevalent.

Controversy has surrounded the increased use of honesty testing in industry. An initial source of concern has been the research used to support the validity of honesty tests. Sackett and Harris (1984) and Sackett, Burris, and Callahan (1988) have examined the use of paper-and-pencil predictors of employee theft. At the time of the Sackett and Harris (1984) review, the data available to support the validity of honesty tests were refutable. However, the second review highlights more conclusive evidence supporting the validity of honesty tests. In contrast to the earlier review, this evidence was based on larger, predictive validation studies involving employees who were dismissed for theft and other forms of counterproductivity in the workplace. As a result, the authors find the evidence "more compelling" and conclude that honesty tests can help organizations predict employee theft in the workplace.

However, another major issue remains unresolved in the use of honesty tests. The scientific community has been reluctant to endorse honesty tests fully because of the rejection rate associated with these instruments. Specifically, there has been a concern with the failure rates, which have been found to range from 40 to 60 percent (Sackett et al., 1988). Given such figures, researchers and practitioners are interested in estimates of the false-positive rate (honest applicants who are identified as dishonest by the test).[1] In a tight labor market, many employers cannot afford to screen out 40 to 60 percent of their applicants and still have enough otherwise qualified candidates to fill available job openings.

This chapter is designed to highlight the proportion of false positives for two types of employee deviance and to provide suggestions for reducing the false-positive rate associated with honesty tests.

PROPORTION OF FALSE POSITIVES

The calculations required to determine the proportion of false positives are relatively straightforward using a direct application of Bayes's theorem. It is, of course, necessary to include estimates of various parameters based on data collected from the actual use of honesty tests in industry. The estimates to be used for the calculations are based on summary data provided by publishers of some of the more heavily researched honesty tests (e.g., Joy, 1986) and on data provided in the Sackett et al. (1988) review. Although the estimates used are reasonable and empirically based, they are not intended to represent the only estimates because the figures vary according to a variety of circumstances (e.g., type of honesty test, industry type, selection decision rules, geographical region). In addition, estimates are certain to be revised as more research is done in this area. As a result, a range of parameters will be used to provide alternative estimates of the false-positive rate.

An estimate of the probability of a positive test outcome (i.e., the test indicating that the applicant is dishonest) given that the applicant is dishonest is approximately .80. That is, using standard notation, $P (+|D) = .80$, where D represents dishonest. Second, if the applicant is honest, the probability of a negative outcome is estimated at roughly .80. Using notation, $P (-|H) = .80$, with H indicating honest.

It is also necessary to estimate the base rate or the proportion of "dishonest" applicants likely to apply for a job. Precise estimates of these figures are difficult to obtain and vary according to industry type and the specific criteria of interest (Hollinger & Clark, 1983). For this example, a general interpretation of employee theft will be used as the criterion. Used in this manner, employee theft reflects theft of company property, merchandise, and money. It also includes other types of theft such as misuse of discount privileges, damaging merchandise to purchase it with a discount, and getting paid for more hours than one has actually worked. Jones and Joy (1988) summarized 10 empirical studies comprised of a total of more than 130,000 subjects and found that the unweighted mean base rate for theft was 32 percent (SD = 16 percent). Thus, for the purpose of these calculations, a representative estimate of .32 will be used as the base rate for employee theft, $P(D) = .32$. (Tables 8.1 and 8.2 present the results of the following calculations using .16 and .48 as alternative estimates of the base rate. These figures represent one standard deviation below and above the mean, respectively.)

Incorporating these probabilities into a direct application of Bayes's theorem, we can estimate the probability that a job applicant with a positive (or theft prone) test result actually is dishonest. Where $P(+|\bar{D})$ is the probability of a positive test outcome given that the applicant is honest and $P(\bar{D})$ is the probability that the applicant is honest:

$$P(D|+) = \frac{P(+|D) \times P(D)}{P(+|D) \times P(D) + P(+|\bar{D}) \times P(\bar{D})}$$

$$= \frac{.80 \times .32}{.80 \times .32 + .20 \times .68}$$

$$= .65$$

Thus, if all applicants are tested and the estimated probabilities are representative, 35 percent of the applicants testing positive would be incorrectly identified as being dishonest.[2]

REDUCING THE FALSE-POSITIVE RATE

Employee Theft

The following example illustrates how the proportion of false positives can be reduced using employee theft as the criterion. Assume that 500 job applicants are to be screened using a paper-and-pencil honesty test. Using the same probabilities presented above, 32 percent of the 500 applicants, or 160, will be dishonest. The remaining 340 candidates will be honest. Of the 160 dishonest applicants, $160 \times .8$, or 128, will test positive (correctly identified as dishonest). Of the 340 honest applicants, $340 \times (1 - .8)$, or 68, will test positively (the test will incorrectly identify them as dishonest). Thus, 196 applicants (approximately 40 percent of the total applicant pool) will test positive, and, consistent with the results provided using Bayes's theorem, 35 percent (68/196) will be classified as false positives.

As an approach to reducing the proportion of false positives, why not screen all of the 196 applicants testing positive again using a second screening procedure? If the second screening procedure is independent from the first one, only $68 \times (1 - .8)$, or 14, honest applicants should test positive.[3] In addition, the second screening procedure should find $128 \times .8$, or 102, dishonest candidates testing positively. Therefore, 116 applicants will test positive, with only 12 percent (14/116) being incorrectly identified as dishonest. Thus, the false-positive rate has been reduced from 35 percent to 12 percent.

It is important to note that these percentages represent the number of false positives given a positive test outcome. That is, the denominator for these calculations represents only the positive test outcomes rather than the entire sample. Estimates of the false-positive rate for the total sample will be provided below. Although both types of estimates provide useful information, it is necessary to recognize which method has been used when estimates of the false-positive rate are presented. The false-positive rate based on only the positive test outcomes will be larger and does not indicate how many honest applicants have been incorrectly classified as dishonest. Alternative estimates of the reduction in the percentage of positive test outcomes that are false are provided in Table 8.1 using other reasonable estimates of the base rate and the two conditional probabilities.

Although the proportion of incorrect positive test outcomes has been reduced, it is necessary to consider the effect of multiple screening procedures from a broader perspective. In terms of the total applicant pool of 500, 14 percent (68/500) are originally classified as false positives, whereas only 3 percent (14/500) are incorrectly identified as dishonest when the second screening procedure is used. Thus, the percentage of false positives in the total sample has also been reduced significantly.

It is also necessary to consider the number of false-negative (dishonest applicants who are incorrectly classified as honest) decisions in the total sample. In the example, based on the initial test, $160 \times (1 - .8)$, or 32, applicants are incorrectly classified as honest. When the second screening procedure is used, $128 \times (1 - .8)$, or 26, additional dishonest applicants are classified as honest. In terms of the 500 applicants, 6 percent (32/500) are initially classified as false negatives, but the proportion of false negatives increases to 11 percent (58/500) when the second screening procedure is used. In order to reduce the proportion of false positives, the number of false-negative decisions has increased. This highlights the dilemma organizations are forced to confront. As companies reduce the number of low-risk or honest applicants who are rejected, they simultaneously expose themselves to more theft-prone or dishonest employees.

Although a degree of trade-off exists between the two types of errors, this clearly does not negate the overall utility of using multiple screening procedures. In the example, the total number of incorrect decisions (false positives and false negatives) has been reduced. The number of false positives was reduced from 68 applicants to 14 applicants, representing a difference of 54 applicants, or 11 percent ((68 − 14)/500). The false-negative rate increased from 32 applicants to 58 applicants, representing a difference of 26 applicants, or 5 percent ((58 − 32)/500). Thus, the total number of incorrect decisions was reduced by 6 percentage points ((54 − 26)/500). As a result, using the two screening procedures improved the overall accuracy of the decisions by 6 percent. In addition, this procedure provides organizations with more control over the type of error they wish to minimize. In this case, it was possible to reduce significantly the

Table 8.1
Alternative Estimates of the Reduction in the False-Positive Rate for Positive Test Outcomes for Theft

P(+|D)[a]	P(-|H)[b]	P(D)[c]	% Positive Outcomes which are False: with first screening	with second screening
.80	.80	.32	35%	12%
.80	.80	.16	57%	25%
.80	.80	.48	21%	6%
.70	.70	.32	48%	28%
.70	.70	.16	69%	49%
.70	.70	.48	32%	17%
.90	.90	.32	19%	3%
.90	.90	.16	37%	6%
.90	.90	.48	11%	1%

These figures represent the percentage of false positive outcomes given a positive test outcome.

[a] $P(+|D)$ = Probability of a positive test outcome given that the applicant is dishonest (i.e., a dishonest applicant correctly identified as dishonest).

[b] $P(-|H)$ = Probability of a negative test outcome given that the applicant is honest (i.e., an honest applicant correctly identified as honest).

[c] $P(D)$ = Probability that an applicant is dishonest (i.e., the base rate).

Table 8.2
Alternative Estimates of the Reduction in the False-Positive Rate and the Number of Incorrect Decisions for the Total Sample for Theft

			Total % False Positive and Incorrect Decisions:	
$P(+|D)$[a]	$P(-|H)$[b]	$P(D)$[c]	with first screening	with second screening
.80	.80	.32	14% (20%)	3% (14%)
.80	.80	.16	17% (20%)	3% (9%)
.80	.80	.48	10% (20%)	2% (19%)
.70	.70	.32	20% (30%)	6% (22%)
.70	.70	.16	25% (30%)	8% (16%)
.70	.70	.48	16% (30%)	5% (29%)
.90	.90	.32	7% (10%)	1% (7%)
.90	.90	.16	8% (10%)	1% (4%)
.90	.90	.48	5% (10%)	1% (10%)

These figures represent the percentage of false positive and incorrect decisions for the total applicant pool. Incorrect decisions include false positive and false negative decisions and appear in parentheses.

[a] $P(+|D)$ = Probability of a positive test outcome given that the applicant is dishonest (i.e., a dishonest applicant correctly identified as dishonest).

[b] $P(-|H)$ = Probability of a negative test outcome given that the applicant is honest (i.e., an honest applicant correctly identified as honest).

[c] $P(D)$ = Probability that an applicant is dishonest (i.e., the base rate).

proportion of false positives. Table 8.2 illustrates the percentage of false positives and incorrect decisions (false positives and false negatives) for the total sample using alternative estimates of the base rate and the two conditional probabilities.

Production Deviance

Another example will be used to illustrate the benefits and caveats of using multiple screening procedures and to highlight the importance of understanding the criteria of interest with regard to the field of integrity testing. For this example, the criterion will involve what is referred to as production deviance. Production deviance reflects a variety of inappropriate behaviors, such as coming to work late or leaving early, using sick leave when one is not actually sick, working under the influence of illicit drugs, and intentionally doing slow or sloppy work. Paper-and-pencil honesty tests were designed to predict employee theft, as well as production deviance in general.

Assume the two conditional probabilities are the same as above. That is, the probability of a positive test outcome given that the applicant is "dishonest" or deviant is .80, and if the applicant is "honest," the probability of a negative outcome is .80. Research suggests that an alternative estimate of the base rate be used for production deviance. Based on four studies with over 9,000 subjects, Jones and Joy (1988) found the unweighted mean base rate to be 75% (SD = 8 percent) for the various types of production deviance. As would be expected, this estimate is substantially higher than that for employee theft.

Incorporating these estimates into a direct application of Bayes's theorem, only 8 percent of applicants testing positive would be incorrectly identified as dishonest or deviant. Using the same set of calculations already presented and a total applicant pool of 500, only 5 percent (25/500) of the applicants would be classified as false positives. Because of the high base rate of .75 for production deviance, the proportion of false positives is extremely low and would be quite acceptable under most circumstances.

For illustrative purposes, however, assume that we follow the same procedures as presented above in order to reduce further the false positive rate. That is, all applicants who tested positive on the first screening procedure are subjected to a second screening procedure, which is equally effective. If this is done, only 1 percent, or 5, of the 500 applicants would be incorrectly identified as dishonest or deviant. Thus, the false-positive rate has been reduced by 4 percentage points (from 5 percent to 1 percent). The total false-negative rate, however, has increased from 15 percent (75/500) to 27 percent (135/500)—a difference of 12 percent. Although the false-positive rate has been reduced, this reduction is quite costly to the employer in terms of overall decision-making accuracy. The increase in false negatives is greater than the decrease in false positives. The total number of incorrect decisions (false positives and false negatives) has increased from 20 percent to 28 percent using the second screening procedure. Thus, attempting to reduce the false-positive rate further should not be recommended in this context unless false-positive errors are viewed as extremely serious. Table 8.3 presents the percentage of false positives and incorrect decisions for the total sample using alternative estimates of the best rate (i.e., plus and minus one standard deviation) and the two conditional probabilities.

Given the base rate in this scenario, more attractive benefits could be provided if there was an interest in reducing the proportion of false negatives. Based on the sample of 500 applicants and the calculations presented, the overall false-negative rate after administering the first screening procedure is 15 percent (75/500). In order to reduce the false-negative rate, applicants who scored negatively on the first screening procedure would be screened a second time. If all of the applicants who tested negative on the first screening procedure are screened again, the false-negative rate would be only 3 percent (15/500). Along with this decrease in false negatives, it is expected that the false-positive rate will increase. In this case, the false-positive rate would increase from 5 percent (25/500) to only 9 percent (45/500). As a result, the false-negative rate has been reduced significantly, and the total number of incorrect decisions has been reduced from 20 percent to 12 percent. Table 8.4 presents the reduction in false-negative and incorrect decision errors for the total applicant pool using alternative estimates of the base rate and the two conditional probabilities.

Thus, multiple screening procedures can be used to reduce the proportion of false-positive or false-negative decision errors. However, as this example was designed to illustrate, it is imperative to consider all parameters in the model and the magnitude of all decision outcomes in order to make an informed decision regarding the benefits of this procedure.

DEVELOPING COMPLEMENTARY TESTING PROCEDURES

The calculations were designed to highlight the benefit of repeating screening procedures, which, when considered alone, may be only moderately effective. In certain circumstances (e.g., testing for AIDS) such benefits can be obtained by simply repeating the same testing procedure. Unfortunately, this is unlikely to be the case with repeated administrations of an honesty test. There are presumably systematic response patterns that, for the most part, would reoccur during follow-up administrations of the same test. As a result, the honest applicants who were classified as dishonest would provide similar responses and would again be classified as dishonest. Therefore, follow-up assessments of integrity must capitalize on the different methods available for identifying dishonest applicants.

Sackett et al. (1988) examined various methods of identifying potentially dishonest employees. They identified a number of overt integrity tests, which consist of specific items related to one's attitude toward theft (e.g., "Do you agree that low wages will force honest employees to take money from their employers without authorization?" "How often have you been tempted to take

Table 8.3
Alternative Estimates of the Reduction in the False-Positive Rate and the Number of Incorrect Decisions for the Total Sample for Production Deviance

$P(+|D)$[a]	$P(-|H)$[b]	$P(D)$[c]	Total % False Positive and Incorrect Decisions: with first screening	with second screening
.80	.80	.75	5% (20%)	1% (28%)
.80	.80	.67	7% (20%)	1% (25%)
.80	.80	.83	3% (20%)	1% (31%)
.70	.70	.75	8% (30%)	2% (40%)
.70	.70	.67	10% (30%)	3% (37%)
.70	.70	.83	5% (30%)	2% (44%)
.90	.90	.75	3% (10%)	0% (14%)
.90	.90	.67	3% (10%)	0% (13%)
.90	.90	.83	2% (10%)	0% (16%)

These figures represent the percentage of false positive and incorrect decisions for the total applicant pool. Incorrect decisions include false positive and false negative decisions and appear in parentheses.

[a] $P(+|D)$ = Probability of a positive test outcome given that the applicant is deviant (i.e., a deviant applicant correctly identified as deviant).

[b] $P(-|H)$ = Probability of a negative test outcome given that the applicant is honest (i.e., an honest applicant correctly identified as honest).

[c] $P(D)$ = Probability that an applicant is deviant (i.e., the base rate).

Table 8.4
Alternative Estimates of the Reduction in the False-Negative Rate and the Number of Incorrect Decisions for the Total Sample for Production Deviance

P(+|D)[a]	P(-|H)[b]	P(D)[c]	Total % False Negative and Incorrect Decisions: with first screening	with second screening
.80	.80	.75	15% (20%)	3% (12%)
.80	.80	.67	13% (20%)	3% (15%)
.80	.80	.83	17% (20%)	3% (9%)
.70	.70	.75	22% (30%)	7% (20%)
.70	.70	.67	20% (30%)	6% (23%)
.70	.70	.83	25% (30%)	7% (16%)
.90	.90	.75	7% (10%)	1% (6%)
.90	.90	.67	7% (10%)	1% (7%)
.90	.90	.83	8% (10%)	1% (4%)

These figures represent the percentage of false negative and incorrect decisions for the total applicant pool. Incorrect decisions include false positive and false negative decisions and appear in parentheses.

[a] P(+|D) = Probability of a positive test outcome given that the applicant is deviant (i.e., a deviant applicant correctly identified as deviant).

[b] P(-|H) = Probability of a negative test outcome given that the applicant is honest (i.e., an honest applicant correctly identified as honest).

[c] P(D) = Probability that an applicant is deviant (i.e., the base rate).

some item without paying for it?''). Some overt integrity tests are also designed to elicit admissions of past theft.

It appears, however, that alternative methods of assessing the integrity of job applicants may be available. For instance, Sackett et al. (1988) identified personality-based measures, which are more general and do not include explicit references to theft. These instruments are designed to assess broader personality traits (e.g., self-restraint, nonconformance, social insensitivity), which have been found to be predictive of employee theft as well as other counterproductive work behaviors. Wilson (1988) has developed structured integrity interviewing procedures designed to identify job applicants who are at risk for dishonest and counterproductive behavior in the workplace. Sackett (1985) has indicated that a variety of projective instruments are available for predicting employee honesty. Although no research was found to support the validity of integrity interviews or projective instruments as predictors of theft, such alternative approaches have the potential to be useful in advancing the assessment of employee integrity.

Future research in the area of honesty testing should take advantage of these alternative measures of assessing dishonesty in attempting to reduce the false-positive rate. Although some of the existing tests may be highly correlated with each other, others may not demonstrate strong relationships. At this time, however, such comments are purely speculative. The point to be made is that with the exception of Rafilson and Frost (1988), the empirical research required to address these issues is not available. Additional research should examine the relationships between the different types of tests and continue to explore the utility of additional methods of assessing honesty.

Multiple measures need not be absolutely independent in order to improve the utility of honesty testing. To be sure, the benefits derived from combining predictor variables with low (not necessarily zero) intercorrelations have been well documented for the general multiple correlation model (see, for instance, Ghiselli, Campbell & Zedeck, 1981).

Finally, for the purposes of demonstration, the example provided in this chapter used a noncompensatory or multiple hurdle selection model. It should be noted, however, that the intended message would remain valid for compensatory models as well. For instance, consider again the first example using employee theft as the criterion. Based on the estimated parameters, the first screening procedure produces a phi coefficient of .57.[4] After the second screening is administered, the phi coefficient improves to .66. As an alternative selection model, a compensatory model might have been appropriate. Multiple regression is compensatory and will be used here for illustrative purposes (strictly speaking, multiple regression would not be appropriate because of the dichotomous criterion). In this case, the two different screening procedures would serve as two predictor variables in the multiple regression equation. As above, given the estimated parameters, each screening procedure considered alone would correlate .57 with the criterion. When the two procedures are used simultaneously in a regression equation, the multiple R increases to .70. This value is similar to the final phi coefficient of .66 found when using the multiple hurdle selection model.

The correlation coefficients for the two selection models were compared to illustrate that the benefits associated with multiple screening procedures generalize to compensatory selection models. However, it should be clear that the type of selection model used does not depend on these statistics. Compensatory selection models assume that low scores on one predictor can be offset by high scores on another. If this assumption is untenable, other selection models, such as a multiple hurdle approach, must be used.

SUMMARY

Bayes's theorem was used as an alternative approach to estimating the false-positive rate for tests of employee theft and counterproductivity. Examples were provided to illustrate how follow-up screening procedures can reduce either false-positive or false-negative decision errors, as well as the total number of incorrect decisions. A review of the relevant literature appears to indicate that continued research in the area of integrity testing can provide organizations with alternative methods of identifying dishonest applicants.

NOTES

The author would like to thank Bruce Fisher, Jack Jones, Maureen McConnell, and Bob Vance for their helpful comments during the preparation of this manuscript.

1. In this context, positive or negative refers to the outcome of the test rather than to an accept-reject selection decision. A positive outcome indicates that a test has classified an applicant as dishonest (i.e., at risk for dishonest behaviors at work given the need and opportunity). Honest applicants who are incorrectly identified as dishonest constitute false-positive decision errors.

2. In practice, it is important to make a distinction between the false-positive rate and labeling applicants as dishonest. Test administrators are trained to understand that all psychological tests produce errors in prediction (i.e., false positives and false negatives) and that no applicant should be labeled as dishonest.

3. In this context, an independent screening procedure refers to an alternative measure that is equally effective in identifying honest and dishonest applicants. This does not imply that the results produced by the two screenings are independent or uncorrelated. Many honest and dishonest applicants would be correctly classified by both measures. For this example, the two screening procedures are correlated .33.

4. Although this validity coefficient may appear relatively high, it was computed using an estimate of the base rate obtained directly from base rate studies, which is expected to be higher and more accurate than would be realized in actual criterion-related validity studies. In addition, the meta-analysis conducted by McDaniel and Jones (1988) revealed a mean validity coefficient of .50.

REFERENCES

American Management Association (1977). *Crimes against business project: Background, findings, and recommendations*. New York: American Management Association.

Bales, J. (1988). Integrity tests: Honest results? *APA Monitor*, August, pp. 1, 4.

Brown, T. S., Jones, J. W., Terris, W., & Steffy, B. D. (1987). The impact of pre-employment integrity testing on employee turnover and inventory shrinkage losses. *Journal of Business and Psychology*, 2(2), 136–149.

Ghiselli, E. E., Campbell, J. P., & Zedeck, S. (1981). *Measurement theory for the behavioral sciences*. San Francisco: W. H. Freeman and Co.

Hollinger, R. C., & Clark, J. P. (1983). *Theft by employees*. Lexington, MA: Lexington Books.

Jones, J. W. (1981). Attitudinal correlates of employee theft of drugs and hospital supplies among nursing personnel. *Journal of Nursing Research*, 30, 349–351.

Jones, J. W., & Joy, D. S. (1988). Employee deviance base rates: A summary of empirical research. Manuscript submitted for publication.

Joy, D. S. (1986). The use of the Personnel Selection Inventory to reduce employee theft. Manuscript submitted for publication.

McDaniel, M. A., & Jones, J. W. (1988). Predicting employee theft: A quantitative review of the validity of a standardized measure of dishonesty. *Journal of Business and Psychology*, 2(4), 327–345.

Palmiotto, M. J. (1983). Labor, government and court reaction to detection of deception services in the private sector. *Journal of Security Administration*, 6, 31–42.

Frost, A. G., & Rafilson, F. M. (1989). Overt integrity tests versus personality-based measures of delinquency: Am empirical comparison. *Journal of Business and Psychology*, 3(3), 269–277.

Sackett, P. R. (1985). Honesty testing for personnel selection. *Personnel Administrator*, 30, 67–76, 121.

Sackett, P. R., Burris, L. R., & Callahan, C. (1988). Integrity testing for personnel selection: An update. Manuscript submitted for publication.

Sackett, P. R., & Harris, M. H. (1984). Honesty testing for personnal selection: A review and critique. *Personnel Psychology*, 37, 221–245.

U.S. Department of Commerce (1972). *The economic impact of crimes against business*. Washington, D.C.: Government Printing Office.

Wilson, C. (1988). New developments in selection interviewing. Paper presented at the Training Conference for Human Resource Professionals, New York, December.

9

Empirical Investigation of Job Applicants' Reactions to Taking a Preemployment Honesty Test

JOHN W. JONES AND DENNIS S. JOY

Employee theft is widespread and difficult to detect, and its existence is widely accepted by security researchers and professionals. Hollinger and Clark (1983) found that the average percentage of employees who admitted to theft in the workplace was 41.8 percent for retail sector employees, 32.2 for hospital employees, and 26.2 for those employed in manufacturing. Slora (1988) conducted an anonymous survey among fast food employees and found that 62 percent admitted to some type of property or cash theft, and 78 percent admitted to time theft (e.g., faking illness and calling in sick, leaving work early without permission). These studies are a first step toward accurately quantifying the total frequency and cost of employee theft.

Many companies have attempted to control the employee theft problem through preemployment screening. The use of paper-and-pencil honesty tests in this process has become increasingly common (Ash, 1988; Sackett & Harris, 1984). Standardized honesty tests that have been constructed to meet legal and professional guidelines tend to exhibit high reliability and useful levels of validity. McDaniel and Jones (1988) summarized 23 studies in a meta-analysis and found that the average validity coefficient of a leading honesty test equals .50. Yet despite acceptable levels of test validity and statistically documented reductions in shrinkage and theft losses (e.g., Terris & Jones, 1982; Brown, Jones, Terris & Steffy, 1987), some companies are hesitant to implement preemployment honesty tests, for a number of reasons. One is that they think job applicants will view such tests as offensive—the subject of this chapter.

Ryan and Sackett (1987) were the first researchers to assess scientifically test takers' reactions to preemployment honesty tests. In their study, 148 college students completed a paper-and-pencil honesty test and a subsequent 10-item questionnaire that assessed their reactions to it. (The majority of the students had had work experience.) The questionnaire used a five-point scale (agree-disagree) to such questions as, "This type of test is an invasion of privacy," and "I'd refuse to take such a test, even if it meant losing a chance at the job." Ryan and Sackett concluded that "reaction to the honesty test was less negative than many organizations considering the use of these tests might think. While some subjects found the test objectionable, the majority saw the test as an appropriate management tool" (p. 255). About 6 percent of subjects "Strongly Agreed" that they would resent being asked to take an honesty test, about 5 percent of subjects "Strongly Agreed" that this type of test was an invasion of privacy, and about 2 percent of subjects "Strongly Agreed" that they would refuse to take such a test, even if it meant losing a chance at the job.

Two pilot studies have empirically investigated job applicants' reactions to taking a preemployment honesty test, both conducted with actual job applicants in order to maximize the relevancy of the findings. Both were designed to determine if applicants who scored below standards on an honesty test objected to the use of the test more so than applicants who scored above standards.

STUDY 1

The main purpose of this study was to assess how many job applicants were offended by preemployment honesty tests. Another purpose was to understand better the differences between the applicants who found honesty tests to be offensive and the applicants who more readily accepted their use. This second issue was not addressed by Ryan and Sackett (1987). It is possible that job applicants are more likely to be offended by preemployment honesty tests if they feel the test might accurately identify them as being at risk to steal. The following hypotheses were put forth:

1. The majority of job applicants would not complain about or object to having to take a preemployment honesty test (cf. Ryan & Sackett, 1987).

2. Applicants who score below standards on the honesty test will complain more than applicants who score above standards, even though the applicants do not know their scores.

METHOD

Job Applicants

Two hundred and twenty-four job applicants from various retail stores completed a standard preemployment honesty test as part of their hiring process.

The majority of applicants were applying for jobs in the Midwest. Although applicants were not required to record their age, sex, or race on the test, the test administrators reported that approximately 48 percent of the applicants were males and 52 percent were females.

Preemployment Honesty Test

All applicants completed the Honesty Scale from the London House Personnel Selection Inventory (PSI) (London House, 1980), a leading paper-and-pencil honesty test listed in the *Buros Mental Measurements Yearbook*. The PSI Honesty scale has a Spearman-Brown split-half reliability of .95 (Terris, 1979). Sackett and Harris (1984) have reviewed a number of PSI validation studies. McDaniel and Jones (1988) summarized 23 studies in a meta-analysis and estimated an average validity coefficient against various theft criteria of .50. Over 65 test validation studies have been conducted with the PSI showing that honesty scores are significantly related to a number of theft-related criteria (Joy, 1988).

Procedure

All applicants completed the PSI as part of the hiring process. Applicants did not have access to their honesty test scores during the study. Therefore, they did not know if they scored below or above national standards. Applicants should not have felt offended at having "passed" or "failed" the test since they did not know their test outcome. Therefore, they should have based their reactions predominantly on the process of taking such a test.

At the end of the test, before turning in the test booklet, applicants were instructed to record any comments or objections they had about taking the PSI. Typically, their comments related to test length, discomfort at having to take an employment test in general, and a belief that the test was too "prying." The completed comments sections were reviewed by the researchers for objections. Thus, the study maintained a nonobtrusive design. However, some applicants might not have taken the time to write comments or have been fully motivated to complete this section truthfully due to an obvious demand characteristic that accompanies this study (e.g., "If I give candid comments, I might not be hired"). Again, this was merely a first attempt to understand better applicants' reactions to an honesty test.

Design and Statistical Analysis

A 2 × 2 (Passed/Failed × No Objection/Objection) chi-square analysis was computed. Applicants passed or failed the PSI based on nationally accepted cutoffs that typically result in a 60 percent passing rate (cf. Terris, 1979). Personnel experts rated the applicants' comments as being "objectionable" if the comments reflected any negative attitudes toward the PSI or the test process

Table 9.1
Job Applicants' General Reactions to an Honesty Test

	"Passed" Test	"Failed" Test	Totals
No Objections to Test	114	70	184
Objections to Test	7	33	40
Totals	121	103	224

χ^2 [1] = 26.1, p < .01

r phi = .32

(e.g., "I do not know why I have to take this kind of test for such a petty job"). The applicants' comments were rated "not objectionable" if they reflected neutral (e.g., "I have no comments about this test") or positive (e.g., "I hope you find these answers helpful") sentiments about taking the test. All subjects completed the comments section, although responses ranged from brief statements to full paragraphs. Again, applicants did not have access to either their PSI scores or the ratings of their comments.

RESULTS AND DISCUSSION

The main results, summarized in Table 9.1, reveal that 82 percent of all applicants reported no objections to taking the preemployment honesty test. These results are consistent with the findings of Ryan and Sackett (1987) and extend their work from college students to actual job applicants.

A statistically significant 2 × 2 chi-square analysis was obtained (X^2 [1] = 26.1, p < .01, r phi = .32). That is, applicants were more likely to complain about taking an honesty test if it turned out that they scored below standards on the test than if they passed. More specifically, about 18 percent of the total applicant sample objected to some part of the honesty testing procedure. A full 83 percent of this group of objectors scored below standards on the honesty test.

STUDY 2

One major limitation of study 1 was that applicants were asked to write a narrative statement describing their reactions toward taking the honesty test.

Some applicants might not have taken the time to describe their reactions fully toward the test or given fully candid answers. Study 2 was conducted to replicate the findings of study 1 and to use a standard rating form (cf. Ryan & Sackett, 1987) instead of an open comments section as a method to quantify applicants' reactions to taking a preemployment honesty test.

Study 2 was a field study conducted with one of the largest fast food restaurant chains in the country. When the company began contemplating using a preemployment honesty test to select manager trainees, it became interested in whether these applicants would find the test offensive. The company was also curious as to whether applicants would view the request to take the test as an invasion of privacy and if the use of an honesty test would reflect negatively on the company. Study 2 empirically investigated these types of issues and examined if applicants who held more negative views of honesty tests were more likely to be those who scored below standards on the test. The same hypotheses put forth in study 1 were made here.

METHOD

Job Applicants

In this study, 226 manager trainee applicants from throughout the United States completed an honesty test as part of their hiring process. The applicants were being considered for training by a fast food restaurant chain. Demographic information such as age, sex, and race was not asked on the test and therefore could not be analyzed. However, test administrators reported that approximately 85 percent of the applicants were males and 15 percent were females.

Procedure

The applicants completed the PSI Honesty scale and scored above or below standards using the same cutoff scores as in study 1. The applicants did not have access to their test scores at any time during the study.

Applicants also completed a slightly modified version of the test-taker reaction questionnaire developed and used by Ryan and Sackett (1987). The questionnaire was slightly reworded so that it would be applicable to job applicants rather than college students. Each item was rated on a 5-point Likert-type scale ranging from "Agree Strongly" (1) to "Disagree Strongly" (5). Items 1, 3, 9, and 10 were worded so that higher scores meant more negative attitudes toward the test. Items 2, 4, 5, 6, 7, and 8 were worded so that higher scores meant more positive attitudes. The 10 items are presented in Table 9.2.

For all between-group analyses reported in Table 9.3, items 1, 3, 9, and 10 were reverse scored so that higher scores reflect greater acceptance of the honesty test. Moreover, the 10 items were summed to yield an overall test-taker reaction

Table 9.2
Precentage Choosing Each Response on the Reaction Questionnaire

(N = 226 Manager Trainee Applicants)

Item	Agree Strongly	Agree Somewhat	Neither Agree nor Disagree	Disagree Somewhat	Disagree Strongly
1. It is perfectly appropriate for an employer to administer such questionnaire.	60	30	7	2	1
2. I would refuse to take such a questionnaire, even if it meant losing a chance at a job.	3	1	8	18	70
3. I would enjoy being asked to take such a questionnaire.	38	25	29	6	2
4. This type of questionnaire is an invasion of privacy.	1	10	20	24	45
5. If I had two comparable job offers, I would reject the company that used such a questionnaire.	1	1	18	19	61
6. I resent being asked to take such a questionnaire	3	0	19	14	64
7. A questionnaire such as this is an inappropriate selection procedure.	1	4	13	34	48
8. Administering a questionnaire such as this reflects negatively on the organization.	3	2	13	24	58
9. Being asked to take such a questionnaire would not affect my view of the organization.	60	20	9	5	6
10. Questionnaires such as this are routinely used in industry today.	45	35	18	2	0

Table 9.3
Job Applicants' Specific Reactions to an Honesty Test

Item *	Overall (N = 226)		"Pass Group" (N = 169)		"Fall Group" (N = 57)			
	X̄	S.D.	X̄	S.D.	X̄	S.D.	t	p**
1)	4.47	.78	4.50	.80	4.37	.72	1.13	.130
2)	4.50	.93	4.57	.89	4.28	1.03	2.07	.019
3)	3.91	1.05	4.01	1.07	3.61	.94	2.46	.007
4)	4.01	1.09	4.08	1.08	3.79	1.10	1.77	.039
5)	4.38	.90	4.49	.85	4.05	.97	3.21	.001
6)	4.34	1.01	4.41	1.00	4.14	1.04	1.73	.042
7)	4.24	.90	4.32	.89	4.00	.91	2.34	.010
8)	4.32	.97	4.35	.99	4.26	.90	.62	.268
9)	4.23	1.17	4.24	1.22	4.21	1.01	.18	.429
10)	4.20	.86	4.27	.85	4.02	.88	1.90	.029
Total score	42.61	5.80	43.24	5.61	40.74	5.97	2.87	.002

* All items were coded so that higher scores mean greater acceptance.

** One-tailed tests of significance were used since directional hypotheses were forwarded.

score. The final score could theoretically range from 10 to 50. A score of 10 would represent a very strong negative reaction toward the honesty test, and a score of 50 would represent a very strong positive reaction. The alpha reliability coefficient of the Ryan-Sackett test-taker questionnaire equaled .80.

RESULTS AND DISCUSSION

The percentage of applicants choosing each response on the test-taker reaction questionnaire is summarized in Table 9.2, which shows that applicants' responses to each item were more positive than negative. This pattern of results is consistent with study 1 and also generalizes the findings of Ryan and Sackett (1987) from college students to employment applicants.

Descriptive statistics for each of the questionnaire items and the total questionnaire score are presented in Table 9.3. All items were coded so that higher scores reflect greater acceptance of the honesty test. For 9 of the 10 items, the item means were above 4.0. Also, the average total score was 42.61 (SD = 5.8). These findings support the notion that honesty tests were perceived much more positively than negatively.

A finer review of some of the major findings in Table 9.2 shows that about 80 percent of the applicants agreed to some extent that it was appropriate for an employer to use honesty tests. About 69 percent disagreed with the position that honesty tests are an invasion of privacy, and another 20 percent were neutral in their opinions toward the privacy issue. Finally, about 82 percent disagreed with the notion that the use of honesty tests reflects negatively on the organization. In fact, about 90 percent thought that this type of questionnaire is routinely used by industry today.

Demand characteristics might have influenced some applicants' responses to the test-taker questionnaire. Future research should attempt to account for any demand characteristics that may influence applicants' ratings of their reactions toward taking an honesty test. A conservative interpretation of the results is that the majority of applicants did not report adverse reactions toward the test or negative perceptions of the organization that administered the test. These results need to be replicated with other types of applicant samples.

Study 1 showed that applicants are more likely to view honesty tests as being offensive if they score below standards on the test. Using a previously established cutoff score for the honesty scale, the applicant sample was divided into those "passing" the PSI ($N = 169$) and those "failing" the inventory ($N = 57$). Independent t-tests were computed for each of the 10 questionnaire items, as well as the total scale score. These between-group differences are also summarized in Table 9.3. Significant differences between the "passing" and "failing" groups were found for 7 of the 10 items and for the total reaction score. These results are in the predicted direction and replicate the findings in study 1. That is, the applicants with poorer scores on the honesty test were apparently more motivated to express dissatisfaction with taking the test.

Although the below-standard group held more negative or defensive views compared to the above-standard group, their reactions were still in the range where they agreed the test was fairly acceptable and nonoffensive. Even for the items where there were no significant between-group differences, average scores for both groups were at the high or positive end of the scale. Hence, while there are differences in reactions between the two groups of job applicants, the test was perceived more positively than negatively by both groups. Since there was substantial overlap in the two groups' distribution of scores, these findings may have more theoretical significance than practical application.

POST HOC ANALYSIS

One might speculate that the reason the applicants in the below-standard group were slightly more offended was that they were angry at having failed the test and being misclassified. This argument is weak, however. Since the applicants were blind to their pass-fail status on the honesty test, they did not know if they scored above or below standards.

Table 9.4 also reveals that some subjects in study 2 made admissions of past

Table 9.4
Post Hoc Analysis

Test Outcome

Theft Status	Below Standards	Above Standards
Theft Admissions	M = 40.95 (N = 40)	M = 43.59 (N = 22)
No Admissions	M = 40.24 (N = 17)	M = 43.19 (N = 147)

Analysis of Variance

Source of Variance:	d.f.	F	Significance
Main Effects:	2	4.205	.016
Theft Status	1	.257	.613
Test Outcome	1	7.048	.009
Status x Outcome Interaction:	1	.022	.882
Explained	3	2.811	.040
Residual	222		
Total	225		

employee theft in an unscored section of the PSI booklet. One might hypothesize that below-standard subjects who did not make an admission of past theft would be more offended than below-standard subjects who did make an admission. This hypothesis is based on the notion that someone who admitted to a history of theft and scored below standards might feel properly classified with the test. However, if this person scored below standards and did not make a theft admission, there is the chance that he or she would feel misclassified as a false positive (someone who scores below standards on the honesty test yet would never steal in the workplace). The dependent variable in Table 9.4 is the overall offensiveness score that was analyzed in Table 9.3.

A review of Table 9.4 shows a nonsignificant F-ratio was obtained for the theft-status-by-test outcome interaction. This finding does not support the contention that below-standard applicants who did not make an admission of theft would feel most offended. Again, the analysis in Table 9.4 was probably unnecessary since applicants were unaware of their test scores.

GENERAL DISCUSSION

Studies 1 and 2 have a few practical implications, although more research is needed in this area using improved research designs. First, organizations can feel more assured that the majority of employment applicants will probably not report major objections to taking honesty tests. If applicants do raise objections, then they are slightly more likely not to pass company standards on the test because of their more tolerant attitudes toward theft. The applicants who score below standards might object to the test because they perceive that the hiring company will not tolerate on-the-job theft, as evidenced by the fact that the company uses preemployment honesty tests. (Hollinger and Clark [1983] claim that employees are able to detect readily if an employer is truly committed to controlling employee theft, and such a perception creates a deterrent effect against employee counterproductivity.)

Additional research is warranted in this relatively new area of inquiry. Very little research exists on how job applicants react to taking any type of employment test. For example, how would job applicants rate honesty tests in relation to other types of employment tests (e.g., cognitive ability tests)?

Jones (1989) recently found that a leading overt honesty test was significantly less offensive than two personality-based measures of delinquency and speculated this was due to the obvious job relatedness of the overt honesty test. In fact, Jones obtained a statistically significant correlation between ratings of job relatedness and offensiveness for a number of different test items ($r = .58$).

Test administrators can also be surveyed to assess their perceptions of how job applicants react to preemployment honesty tests. Calhoun (1988) recently surveyed eight restaurant managers who administered an honesty test to 181 job applicants applying for work. In his survey, all eight managers agreed that applicants were "very willing" to take the honesty test. Moreover, all eight indicated that it was very easy to combine honesty test scores with the interview results. Surveying test administrators can serve as another research method to gauge test takers' reactions to honesty tests if the demand characteristics on the test administrators can be accounted for.

Honesty tests are reliable and valid, and quasi-experiments suggest they are capable of reducing theft-related losses in organizations (McDaniel & Jones, 1988). Honesty tests have been used by industry for over 20 years (Ash, 1988). Moreover, this research and that conducted by Ryan and Sackett (1987) suggest that the majority of applicants will probably not be offended when asked to take a preemployment honesty test. The information in this study serves as a useful adjunct to the reliability, validity, test fairness, and loss reduction studies that have been the focus of recent honesty test research. Empirical research is starting to disprove the perception that honesty tests are offensive to applicants. Misconceptions about any personnel selection procedures should always be scientifically tested before they are inappropriately accepted as truth.

REFERENCES

Ash, P. (1988). The history of honesty testing. Paper presented at the Annual Conference of the American Psychological Association, Atlanta, August.

Brown, T. S., Jones, J. W., Terris, W., & Steffy, B. D. (1987). The impact of pre-employment integrity testing on employee turnover and inventory shrinkage losses. *Journal of Business and Psychology*, 2, 136–149.

Calhoun, C. (1988). *Pre-employment honesty testing: A pilot program*. Mobile, AL: Morrison's Specialty Restaurants.

Hollinger, R., & Clark, J. (1983). *Theft by employees*. Lexington, MA: Lexington Books.

Jones, J. W. (1989). Overt integrity tests versus personality measures of delinquency: Job-relatedness, offensiveness and invasiveness. Unpublished manuscript.

Joy, D. (1988). The use of the Personnel Selection Inventory to reduce employee theft. Technical Report 51. Park Ridge, IL: London House Press.

London House (1980). *The Personnel Selection Inventory (PSI)*. Park Ridge, IL: London House Press.

McDaniel, M. A., & Jones, J. W. (1988). Predicting employee theft: A quantitative review of the validity of a standardized measure of honesty. *Journal of Business and Psychology*, 2 (4), 327–345.

Ryan, A. M., & Sackett, P. R. (1987). Pre-employment honesty testing: Fakability, reactions of test takers, and company image. *Journal of Business and Psychology*, 1 (3), 248–256.

Sackett, P. R., & Harris, M. E. (1984). Honesty testing for personnel selection: A review and critique. *Personnel Psychology*, 37, 221–246.

Slora, K. (1988). Employee theft in the fast food industry: Preliminary findings. Technical Report 2. Risk Management Department. Park Ridge, IL: London House Press.

Terris, W. (1979). Attitudinal correlates of employee integrity: Theft-related admissions made in pre-employment polygraph examinations. *Journal of Security Administration*, 2, 30–39.

Terris, W., & Jones, J. W. (1982). Psychological factors related to employees' theft in the convenience store industry. *Psychological Reports*, 51, 1219–1238.

10

The Organizational Climate of Honesty

JOHN W. JONES AND WILLIAM TERRIS

The London House Personnel Selection Inventory (PSI) (London House, 1980a, 1980b) reliably identifies job applicants who, if hired, will engage in on-the-job theft, violence, and drug abuse. The PSI contains test items that measure job applicants' attitudes, values, perceptions, and opinions toward theft (Honesty scale), violence, (Non-violence scale), and drugs (Drug Avoidance scale). The validity of the PSI has been established (cf. McDaniel & Jones, 1988).

The three PSI subscales measure psychological traits that characterize counterproductive and deviant employees. The hiring of more honest employees should logically lead to better organizational climates of honesty. Organizational climate refers to the "personality" or "psychological character" of a work environment (Dubrin, 1974). The organizational climate helps to shape employees' attitudes about the company, and it influences their behavior (Forehand & Gilmer, 1964).

Researchers have studied organizational climates of honesty (i.e., theft proneness) in various retail settings (cf. Cherrington & Cherrington, 1981; Jones & Terris, 1982b; Terris & Jones, 1982) using valid and reliable integrity tests that measure attitudes and cognitions toward theft. They found that employees with tolerant attitudes toward theft typically worked in stores with higher levels of shortages, internal theft, and turnover, and employees with intolerant attitudes toward theft usually worked for stores with lower levels of inventory shortages and internal theft.

The purpose of this study was threefold. First, an effort was made to document incident rates of employee theft in the restaurant industry. Next, it was hypothesized that significantly more employees in the 15 problematic restaurants would make theft admissions compared to the employees in 15 nonproblematic restaurants. Finally, it was hypothesized that the 15 problematic restaurants would have significantly poorer organizational climates of honesty compared to the 15 nonproblematic restaurants.

METHODS

Subjects

A sample of 521 male and female employees from a leading West Coast restaurant chain anonymously completed a psychological test that measured attitudes toward theft, violence, and drug abuse. These employees represented 30 different restaurant locations. All job positions were represented in this study.

Psychometric Measure of Honesty

Subjects completed the PSI. The PSI contains an Honesty scale that measures attitudes, values, and perceptions toward theft and dishonesty in the workplace. A person who scores poorly on it (poorer scores mean greater theft proneness) generally exhibits more rumination over theft activities (e.g., "How often in recent years have you simply thought about taking money without actually doing it?"); more projection of theft in others (e.g., "How many executives steal from their companies?"); greater rationalization of theft acts (e.g., "Will everyone steal if the conditions are right?"); less punitive attitudes toward thieves (e.g., "A young person was caught stealing $50.00 in cash from an employer. If you were his employer what would you do?"); and more interthief loyalty (e.g., "If you were caught stealing would you tell on the people who helped you?"). Other relevant attitudes are also assessed. Items that assess these same types of attitudes are also contained in both the Non-violence and the Drug Avoidance scales of the PSI, which has been scientifically validated in a series of studies (cf. McDaniel & Jones, 1988).

Three types of scores were derived and analyzed from the PSI:

1. Confidence Scores: These scores give a ranking of a subject's theft potential by measuring attitudes toward theft. These scores can range from 1 to 100. The higher the confidence score is, the greater is the probability that a subject is at low risk to steal. Confidence scores were also computed for both the PSI violence and drug abuse scales.

2. Organizational Climate of Honesty: This measure is the average confidence score for a particular restaurant. If a restaurant has a high honesty climate score, then most of the staff at this location have intolerant, unfavorable, and punitive attitudes toward theft and therefore are at low risk to steal from their employer.

3. Organizational Climate of Counterproductivity. A subject's Honesty, Non-violence, and Drug Avoidance scale scores were summed and averaged for a particular restaurant to yield an organizational climate of counterproductivity measure. Higher climate scores mean less potential for employee counterproductivity.

Design and Statistical Analyses

Restaurant chain executives selected 15 problematic restaurants and 15 non-problematic restaurants for between-group comparisons. Between-group analyses were computed using an F-test statistic. Standardized computer programs were used for all statistical analyses. The following variables were considered when grouping the stores:

1. Internal theft (subjective).
2. Cash overages/Shortages.
3. Employee turnover.
4. Profit center income.
5. Cost controls.

Procedure

The following outline was used as a step-by-step guide for conducting the study:

1. Restaurant executives did not give the researchers the store numbers of the 15 problematic restaurants or the 15 nonproblematic restaurants until all data were coded and descriptive statistics were computed to ensure objectivity and totally reduce bias.
2. Managers of the 30 restaurants participating in this study were given PSI booklets and a supplemental questionnaire used to collect demographic information.
3. The managers of the participating restaurants had a 1-hour meeting at their restaurant where all of their employees were present. The managers did not know the exact purpose of the study. A personnel department employee administered the PSI to all of the restaurant employees at this meeting. This person simply told the employees that the study was being conducted because the restaurant chain was interested in their attitudes toward work.
4. Employees were told that the information they provided would not be put in their files, and in fact, employees were asked not to put their names anywhere on the test booklet. When they finished the survey, they put their completed test booklets in a box on the examiner's table. Before the employees turned in the booklet, they made sure that they completed all PSI items and an adverse impact card used to assess compliance with the Equal Employment Opportunity Commission's selection standards.
5. Once the employee put the completed booklet in the box, the test administrator took out all completed booklets, put them in a large envelope, and wrote the restaurant's unit number and location on the outside of the envelope.
6. Once the 30 packets of data were collected, they were forwarded to the senior author,

who had no way of knowing if a restaurant was classified as being problematic or nonproblematic.

7. The PSI data were coded for computer analyses. A summary of scores for each restaurant was then forwarded to the restaurant chain's personnel department.

8. The researchers were provided with the restaurant numbers of the 15 "good" and 15 "bad" units. Final inferential statistics were then computed.

RESULTS

Amount of Theft

Table 10.1 presents a breakdown of the estimated dollar amount of all theft by the type of restaurant (problematic or nonproblematic). Employee theft admissions ranged from $25 to over $500 for both groups. These admissions are more than likely underestimates, however, since most employee thieves want to conceal their theft behavior.

Table 10.2 presents the percentage of employees making anonymous theft admissions as a function of type of restaurant. Results show that 32.5 percent of all subjects admitted to stealing company merchandise and property, 11.3 percent admitted to stealing company cash, and 25 percent admitted to buying stolen merchandise and property.

As anticipated, employees in the problematic restaurants admitted to considerably more theft than employees in the 15 nonproblematic restaurants. Between-group analyses on all three criterion variables were statistically significant ($p <$ .05 in all three analyses) (Table 10.2).

Organizational Climate of Honesty

The major finding showed that the organizational climate of honesty scores were lower (lower scores mean greater theft proneness) for the 15 problematic restaurants compared to the 15 nonproblematic restaurants. This between-group difference was statistically significant using both the parametric t-test ($t(28) =$ 2.6, $p <$ .025) and the nonparametric Wilcoxn Rank-Sum test ($W(15/15) =$ 177, $p <$ .01).

Between-group analyses on both the Non-violence and the Drug-avoidance climate scores were not statistically significant; however, the mean differences were in the predicted direction. This latter set of findings is to be expected since the restaurants were primarily selected and grouped on theft-related criteria. The following analysis was based on the overall organizational climate of counterproductivity scores.

Overall Climate of Counterproductivity

All three PSI subscale scores were summed up and averaged for each subject to yield an individual's overall counterproductivity score, reflecting an individ-

Table 10.1
Estimated Amount of Theft

Dollar Value of Merchandise/Property Theft by Type of Restaurant

$ - Value	15 Problematic Restaurants		15 Non-Problematic Restaurants	
	N	%	N	%
No Admissions	115	62.0%	234	70.5%
$25 - $50	52	28.0%	68	21.0%
$51 - $250	7	4.0%	7	2.0%
$251 - $500	0	0.0%	1	0.3%
$501 - $5,000+	1	0.5%	4	1.2%
Admitted Theft; Unsure of $-Amt.	11	6.0%	17	5.0%
Totals	186	100.0%	331	100.0%

Dollar Value of Cash Theft by Type of Restaurant

$ - Value	15 Problematic Restaurants		15 Non-Problematic Restaurants	
	N	%	N	%
No Admissions	154	82.4%	307	92.2%
$25 - $50	19	10.2%	15	4.5%
$51 - $250	5	2.7%	5	1.5%
$251 - $500	0	0.0%	0	0.0%
$501 - $5,000+	1	0.5%	1	0.3%
Admitted Theft; Unsure of $-Amt.	8	4.3%	5	1.5%
Totals	187	100.0%	333	100.0%

(Sample sizes differ slightly due to missing data.)

Table 10.2
Employees Making Theft Admissions

Type of Theft	Overall	15 Problematic Restaurants	15 Non-Problematic Restaurants	χ^2
Merchandise and Property	32.5% (168/517)	38.2% (71/186)	29.5% (97/331)	4.3*
Company Cash	11.3% (59/520)	17.6% (33/187)	7.8% (26/333)	11.6**
Bought Stolen Merchandise and Property	26.0% (136/520)	32.1% (60/187)	22.8% (76/333)	5.3*

Sample sizes differ slightly across analyses due to missing data. Also, the theft admissions are most likely <u>underestimates</u> since research subjects have a tendency to minimize the true amount of their employee theft. Still, the statistically significant trends reveal that more theft is taking place in the 15 problematic units than in the 15 non-problematic units.

*p < .05, d.f. = 1

**p < .01, d.f. = 1

ual's attitudes toward theft, violence, and drug abuse. Next, all counterproductivity scores within a single restaurant were summed up and averaged to yield an overall climate score for that unit. Again higher scores mean less potential for employee counterproductivity within the restaurant.

The overall counterproductivity climate scores for the 15 problematic restaurants (M = 60.8, S.D. = 3.4) were significantly lower (i.e., poorer) than the overall counterproductivity climate scores for the 15 nonproblematic units (M = 64.0, SD = 6.4). This between-group difference was statistically significant using both the parametric (t(28) = 1.72, p < .05, 1-tailed) and the nonparametric (W(15/15) = 182, p < .05) statistical tests.

Table 10.3 presents a chi-square analysis that examined the degree of relationship between the overall counterproductivity climate scores and type of restaurant. A mean split was computed on these climate scores (M = 62.4, SD = 5.3). This yielded 17 restaurants with below-average climates of counterproductivity and 13 restaurants with above-average climates. Analyses showed that 85 percent (11/13) of the above-average restaurants were rated as being nonproblematic compared to only 24 percent of the below-average restaurants. This

Table 10.3
Chi-Square Analysis: Comparison of Overall Integrity Climate Scores with Type of Restaurant

Overall Integrity Climate Scores

Type of Restaurant	< 62.4	> 62.4	
Problematic	4	11	15
Non-Problematic	13	2	15
	17	13	30

Percent Agreement: 24/30 = 80%

Statistical Analysis: X^2 (1) = 11, $\underline{p}$ < .001; Phi-Coefficient = +.61.

A mean-split was computed on the overall integrity climate scores. This yielded an above-average group of units (N = 13) and a below-average group of units (N = 17) for between-group comparison.

difference was statistically significant ($X^2(1) = 11$, $p < .001$), yielding a phi coefficient of $+0.61$.

Adverse Impact Analyses

The PSI had no adverse impact against any protected group. Consistent with other research, females had significantly less tolerant attitudes toward theft, violence, and drug abuse than males. In addition, there were no statistically significant differences between PSI pass-fail rates as a function of race or ethnic group. A variety of PSI cutoff standards were used in these analyses. This set of findings was consistent with other PSI adverse impact studies.

Supplemental Analyses

The employees from the 15 nonproblematic restaurants ($N = 334$) had significantly less tolerant attitudes toward theft, as measured by the PSI Honesty scale, compared to the employees from the 15 problematic restaurants ($N = 187$)(M = 53.9, SD = 24.0 versus M = 47.6, SD = 22.4; F(1/519) = 8.6, $p < .004$). The employees from the nonproblematic restaurants also had less tolerant attitudes toward violence and drug abuse, although these between-group differences were not statistically significant.

Some subjects did not indicate whether they were supervisors or nonsupervisors; however, 342 subjects did respond. Results showed that the supervisors ($N = 76$; $M = 65.1$, S.D. $= 13.0$) had significantly less tolerant attitudes toward drug abuse compared to the nonsupervisors ($N = 266$; $M = 60.9$, S.D. $= 13.5$) ($F(1/340) = 6.0$, p, $<. 02$.) These two groups did not significantly differ in their attitudes toward theft and violence.

DISCUSSION

Obtained results showed that an appreciable number of employees from both the problematic and the nonproblematic restaurants made anonymous employee theft admissions. However, a significantly higher percentage of employees from the problematic restaurants anonymously admitted to employee theft compared to the employees from the nonproblematic restaurants. This finding confirms the company's suspicion that more employee theft is taking place in the problematic restaurants.

The major finding showed that the problematic restaurants were staffed by employees having more dishonest attitudes toward theft compared to the nonproblematic restaurants. This difference was statistically significant. That is, the "typical" employee in the problematic restaurants (1) was more tempted to steal, (2) endorsed more of the common rationalizations for theft, (3) was less punitive toward thieves, (4) thought more about theft-related activities, (5) attributed more theft to others, (6) exhibited more interthief loyalty, and (7) felt more vulnerable to peer pressure to steal compared to the average employee in the nonproblematic restaurants. This finding, coupled with the finding that more employees in the problematic restaurants admitted to employee theft, indicates the need for hiring honest employees. The results support the notion that organizational climates of dishonesty facilitate employee theft, while organized climates of honesty tend to deter employee theft.

The findings are especially meaningful since the restaurant chain executives who grouped the restaurants were not aware of the employees' PSI test scores. Similarly, the London House researchers who coded and scored the PSI were not aware of a restaurant's grouping until after the organizational climate of honesty scores was computed for each restaurant. This was truly a blind research design.

The results have implications in two areas. First, preemployment integrity tests can be used to screen out job applicants who are at high risk to engage in employee theft due to their tolerant attitudes toward theft. Such screening efforts could conceivably improve a restaurant's overall climate of honesty and therefore reduce the losses that can be attributed to employee theft. Results from two large-scale research projects show that the use of professionally developed integrity tests can significantly reduce theft-related losses (Jones & Terris, 1982a, 1982b; Terris & Jones, 1983).

Second, the results of this study have implications for the use of integrity surveys to monitor current employees. Current employees who steal from their employer tend to be (1) more tolerant of theft, (2) aware of more coworker theft, (3) more prone to drug abuse, (4) more burned-out or stressed, and (5) more dissatisfied with their jobs compared to honest employees (Jones & Terris, 1982c). The London House Employee Attitude Inventory (EAI) (London House, 1982a, 1982b) was specifically developed to assess anonymously current employees who might be engaged in on-the-job theft and counterproductivity. The EAI is used to identify high-risk employee groups, departments, or locations that could benefit from a preemployment integrity testing program.

This study showed that the 15 problematic restaurants employed a greater percentage of workers who (1) made admissions of employee theft and (2) had tolerant attitudes toward theft compared to the 15 nonproblematic restaurants. It was concluded that preemployment tests could be used to screen out job applicants who are at high risk to steal due to their tolerant attitudes toward theft.

REFERENCES

Cherrington, D. J., & Cherrington, J. O. (1981). The climate of honesty in retail stores. Paper presented at the 89th Annual Meeting of the American Psychological Association, Los Angeles, California, August.

Durbin, A. J. (1974). *Fundamentals of organizational behavior*. New York: Pergamon Press.

Forehand, G. A., & Gilmer, B. V. (1964). Environmental variation in studies of organizational behavior. *Psychological Bulletin*, 71, 316–382.

Jones, J. W. (1982). Psychological predictors of employee theft. Paper presented at the 90th Annual Meeting of the American Psychological Association, Washington, DC, August 23–27.

Jones, J. W., & Terris, W. (1982a). The use of the PSI to reduce employee theft in department stores: A program evaluation study. Paper presented at the Ninth Annual Scientific Conference of the Society of Police and Criminal Psychology, Nashville, October 28–30.

Jones, J. W., & Terris, W. (1982b). Predicting employee theft in home improvement centers. Paper presented at the Annual Meeting of the Academy of Criminal Justice Sciences, Louisville, March 23–27.

Jones, J. W., & Terris W. (1982c) The Employee Attitude Inventory: A validity study on theft by current employees. Paper presented at the Ninth Annual Meeting of the Society of Police and Criminal Psychology, Nashville, October 28–30.

London House (1980a). *The Personnel Selection Inventory (PSI)*. Park Ridge, IL: London House.

London House (1980b). *The PSI Test Administration Manual*. Park Ridge, IL: London House.

London House (1982a). *The Employee Attitude Inventory-6*. Park Ridge, IL: London House.

London House (1982b). *Test Manual: The Employee Attitude Inventory*. Park Ridge, IL: London House.

McDaniel, M. A., & Jones, J. W. (1988). Predicting employee theft: A quantitative review of a standardized measure of honesty. *Journal of Business and Psychology*, 2, 327–345.

Terris, W., & Jones, J. W. (1982). *Preemployment screening to reduce employee theft in department stores: Three separate studies*. Park Ridge, IL: London House Press.

Terris, W., & Jones, J. W. (1983). Psychological predictors of employee theft in the convenience store industry. *Psychological Reports*, 51, 1219–1238.

III

FUTURE DIRECTIONS

11

Development of a Standardized Measure to Predict Employee Productivity

FRED M. RAFILSON

The problem of counterproductive employees has reached epidemic proportions and is costing companies considerable financial loss. For example, nonviolent crimes against American business cost $50 billion a year, the equivalent of Exxon Corporation's annual sales (Palimotto, 1983). Even more alarming is the estimate that approximately one-third of all business failures are due to employee theft and dishonesty (Morgenstern, 1977). According to Hollinger and Clark (1983), approximately 40 percent of employees may exhibit some form of dishonesty at work. Significant financial losses may also result from such behaviors as poor job performance, inadequate customer relations skills, absenteeism, tardiness, high turnover, on-the-job accidents, violations of company policy, and on-the-job drug use.

Identifying potentially counterproductive employees before hiring them is a major challenge facing employers. To date, various methods have been pursued to detect tendencies toward counterproductivity, including polygraph screening; biographical data analysis; special keys for standard personality tests; clear-purpose honesty tests, which typically include specific questions about attitudes toward and admissions of theft behavior; and specially developed personality tests (Ash, 1988). This chapter will focus on the development and validation of the London House Employment Productivity Index (EPI–3) (London House, 1986; Terris, 1986), a broad-based personality-oriented measure designed to predict the successful employee.

DEVELOPMENT OF THE EPI–3

Preemployment polygraph testing, which seems doomed to imminent demise, was one of the early attempts to identify job applicants at high risk for engaging in counterproductive behavior (e.g., theft, drug abuse, excessive absenteeism) once hired. Paper-and-pencil tests, designed to identify potentially counterproductive applicants, are becoming more dominant in this ever-expanding market. Recent state legal developments (Massachusetts Polygraph Act, Chapter 149, Section 19-B, of the State of Massachusetts, approved as amended, effective 9/30/86) prohibit the use of "preemployment lie detector tests, *including written examinations*, to render a diagnostic opinion regarding the honesty of an individual." Indeed, overt honesty tests have a more limited scope, focusing more on industrial security issues than general employee productivity.

In recent years, employers have expressed interest in a psychological test that would screen in employees who are likely to be highly productive, successful workers—those unlikely to be fired because of poor performance, excessive absenteeism, or other reasons (e.g., rule breaking). They are conscientious, hard working, and possess a strong work ethic. They would not engage in inappropriate behaviors in the workplace such as using drugs during work hours or engaging in employee sabotage. As the costs of employee selection and training continue to increase, many employers would like a screening test designed to identify individuals who are likely to remain on the job for long periods of time. Moreover, some human resource professionals have expressed an interest in tests that are less offensive than the more overt honesty tests. The EPI–3 was developed in response to these needs and is appropriate for situations where overt honesty tests cannot be used, such as the Massachusetts situation.

The EPI–3 was developed by selecting validated items from the London House Personnel Selection Inventory (PSI) (London House, 1986), which consistently predicts reliable, productive work behavior. Only PSI items that make no reference to honesty or theft were selected for the EPI–3. The validity of the PSI series has been well established in over 65 studies to date. In the area of employee counterproductivity, research (Alvord, 1985; Brown, Jones, Terris & Steffy, 1987; Brown & Joy, 1985; Jones, 1980; Moretti, 1980, 1986) has indicated that PSI scores were significantly related to various forms of on-the-job counterproductivity (e.g., employee theft, damage or destruction of company property, waste of supplies, company shrinkage, absenteeism and tardiness, employee reprimands and suspensions, drug and alcohol use on the job). Additional items were developed to measure other various important attributes (e.g., dependability, productivity, interpersonal cooperation).

RELIABILITY OF EPI–3 SCALES

A large sample of employees ($N = 3,251$) from various industries and occupations, including retail, hotel/motel, restaurant, and grocery, was used to calculate the reliabilities and conduct the original item analyses of the EPI–3 subscales.

The Dependability scale measures applicants' willingness to obey company rules while completing the work assigned, as well as the likelihood that applicants will show up for work on schedule once employed. Sample items are: "How many employees don't call in when they stay home from work?" and "How often do you really try hard to do well at work or school?" This scale was designed to identify more responsible, productive employees. The reliability of this scale (coefficient alpha) has been calculated at .84.

The Drug Avoidance scale measures the likelihood that applicants will not use illegal drugs on the job once employed. On-the-job drug use leads to poor work performance and industrial accidents. This scale consists of both attitudinal and behavioral items that have demonstrated high degrees of success in predicting on-the-job drug use. Sample items include "How many people use marijuana socially?" and "How often do you drink alcoholic beverages?" The reliability of this scale (coefficient alpha) has been calculated at .72. The validity of this scale has been well documented using job-related criteria (Alvord, 1985; Brown, Jones, Terris & Steffy, 1987; Jones, 1979a, 1979b, 1979c, 1980, 1982; Jones & Terris, 1983; Joy, Frost & Cook, 1987; Terris, 1979a, 1979b, 1985).

The Interpersonal Cooperation scale measures the likelihood that applicants will be courteous and cooperate with others once employed. This includes cooperation with supervisors, coworkers, vendors, and customers. Sample items include "How often have you thought of hitting someone who really deserved it?" and "How often do you lose your temper?" The reliability of this scale (coefficient alpha) has been calculated at .83.

Information from these three subscales contributes to an overall composite scale, the Productivity Index. Personnel selection decisions are based on the use of this composite index, whose reliability (coefficient alpha) has been calculated at .91. The subscale scores are used mainly for supplementary information, and the overall index is used for personnel selection.

Another version of the Employment Productivity Index, the EPI–3S, contains all of the above scales and an additional safety scale (described in depth in Jones & Wuebker, 1988).

In addition, the EPI–3 contains a Validity scale that assesses accuracy of response. This scale has been constructed to detect patterns of responses that are unlikely to occur when applicants both understand the inventory and answer the questions in a careful manner. The scale identifies rare response patterns on individual items. An item response is considered rare if less than 2 percent of the population responds in that manner. If applicants make too many rare responses, we can conclude that their test booklet was not accurately completed. Research has shown that this scale can detect 95 percent of all test booklets completed in a random, careless, or distorted manner (Rafilson, 1988).

Table 11.1

Percentage of Applicants Accepted or Rejected by the EPI–3

Composite Productivity Index Standard Used	ACCEPTED		REJECTED		
	(N = 651) Successful Employees	(N=585) Fired Employees	(N = 651) Successful Employees	(N=585) Fired Employees	2 X
40	78.2	61.9	21.8	38.1	39.3*
45	72.7	55.3	27.3	44.7	39.3*
50	59.9	38.7	40.1	61.3	54.0*

* p ≤ .000

(Note: counterproductive employees were classified into three groups;
Fired for poor work performance (N=329);
Fired for absenteeism or tardiness (N=172);
Fired for violations of rules/policies (N=84))

VALIDITY

Predictive Validity

In the largest predictive validation study to date of the EPI–3 (Terris, 1986), 1,236 applicants in a retail setting completed the EPI–3 and were hired regardless of their scores. After six months, employees' job status was assessed. Six hundred and fifty-one "successful employees" were identified who worked a minimum amount of time and were not fired for any reason. These employees had successful work performance records and consistently showed up for work on time. Three other groups were also identified: (1) 329 employees who were fired for poor performance, (2) 172 employees who were fired for excessive absenteeism or tardiness, and (3) 84 employees who were fired for other reasons (e.g., violation of company rules). Using several cutoff score standards, the EPI–3 acceptance rate of the successful group was compared to the EPI–3 acceptance rates for all of the termination groups combined. For each set of cutoff scores, the acceptance rates of the termination group were significantly lower than the acceptance rates of the successful group. The acceptance rates for the group of successful employees ranged between 60 and 78 percent, depending on cutoff score. The acceptance rates for the group of counterproductive employees ranged between 39 and 70 percent. This represents a significant difference in acceptance rates for successful versus counterproductive employees (chi-square values range from 39.3 to 54.0, $p < .0001$ in all cases) (Table 11.1).

In a second predictive validation study by Joy and Frost (1987), a sample of 167 applicants for jobs to a large discount retail chain completed the EPI–3 as part of the preemployment hiring process. Test scores were not used in making

Table 11.2
Correlations between EPI Scales and Work Performance Dimensions

Performance Dimensions	EPI Scales			Overall Productivity Index
	Dependability	Interpersonal Cooperation	Drug Avoidance	
Customer Service	.253** (126)	.171* (126)	N.S.	.178* (126)
Employee Relations	.170** (163)	.170** (163)	N.S.	N.S.
Safety/Sanitation	.191** (162)	.201** (162)	.172** (162)	.229** (162)
Absenteeism/Tardiness	N.S.	N.S.	.205** (143)	.217** (143)
Employee Conduct	.170** (159)	.190** (159)	.131* (159)	.200** (159)
Productivity	.254** (159)	.153* (159)	.160* (159)	.174** (159)

* $p < .05$
** $p < .01$

hiring decisions. Approximately three months later, supervisors evaluated the job performance of these employees using a standardized performance appraisal form. Completed performance appraisal forms were returned for the 167 applicants, and these data were used for correlation analyses. The testing procedure was completely independent of the rating procedure. Because only corporate executives had access to test scores, neither test administrators nor supervisors were aware of applicants' EPI–3 scores.

The performance appraisal forms were organized into six dimensions: Customer Service (6 items: e.g., "Does this employee consistently give pleasant service?"), Employee Relations (4 items: e.g., "Does this employee make an effort to get along with his/her co-workers?"), Absenteeism and Tardiness (5 items: e.g., "Does this employee come late to work?"), Employee Conduct (11 items: e.g., "Does the employee comply with rules and regulations?"), Productivity (7 items: e.g., "How often does this employee try to do a good job?"), and Safety/Sanitation (5 items: e.g., "Does this employee have many accidents on the job?"). The range of options on each performance item was from 1 (never) to 5 (very often). Scores were determined for each of these dimensions by averaging the supervisors' ratings for all of the contributing items. All of these performance ratings were coded so that a higher value represented better performance. Since higher scores are also better on the EPI–3, positive correlations were expected.

The first analysis examined correlations between the EPI–3 scales and each of the performance dimensions (Table 11.2). Nineteen of 24 correlations were significant (using a one-tailed test) at the .05 level. All significant correlations

Table 11.3
Multiple Correlations between EPI Scales and Work Performance Dimensions

EPI SCALES

Performance Dimensions	Dependability, Interpersonal Cooperation, Drug Avoidance
Customer Service	R = .259* $F(3,122) = 2.92$
Employee Relations	R = .187 $F(3,159) = 1.93$
Safety/Sanitation	R = .227* $F(3,158) = 2.86$
Absenteeism/Tardiness	R = .207 $F(3,139) = 2.06$
Employee Conduct	R = .197 $F(3,155) = 3.99$
Productivity	R = .268** $F(3,155) = 3.99$

* $p < .05$
** $p < .01$

(Note: performance dimension scores were computed for each
subject only if none of the items that comprise that dimension
were missing)

were in the expected direction; as EPI–3 test scores increased, so did the supervisors' ratings of these individuals' performance.

Table 11.3 shows the multiple correlations between the three EPI–3 subscales and total scores on each of the performance dimensions. The EPI–3 scales showed a significant relationship with Customer Service ($R = .259$, $p < .05$), Safety/Sanitation ($R = .227$, $p < .05$), and Productivity ($R = .268$, $p < .01$).

A narrative summary of these results indicates that the Dependability scale should help to select employees who will consistently give pleasant service, be more courteous and enthusiastic when initiating contact with customers, and be less likely to argue with coworkers or spread rumors or gossip that may cause trouble at work. This scale was also found to identify employees who try harder to do a good job, contribute to a team effort, and are likely to be praised for doing an outstanding job.

Use of the interpersonal Cooperation scale was found to predict employees who try harder to get along with fellow workers and are more likely to do the work assigned without getting angry or annoyed when told what to do. This scale also identified people who are less likely to argue with their supervisors.

Use of the Drug Avoidance scale was found to identify employees who are less likely to leave work early without permission or not to show up for work when scheduled. These employees took fewer sick days and were less likely to abuse alcohol or other drugs while at work.

The composite Productivity index was best able to predict employees who did not ignore work orders or were not involved in the use or sale of alcohol or drugs on the job. These employees suffered fewer injuries on the job and practiced better personal hygiene and grooming. Hence, a number of important areas of performances can be improved through the use of the EPI–3. The results of this predictive validity study provide further evidence that the EPI–3 is a valid and useful predictor of future on-the-job behavior.

Concurrent Validity

A final study by Rafilson (1987) used 247 male and female college students, employed part time and full time in various companies, as subjects. All subjects completed the EPI–3, as well as an anonymous questionnaire that assessed 45 different forms of counterproductive behaviors employees might possibly have engaged in while on the job. Hence, this is a concurrent (both the test and the criterion data were collected at the same time) criterion-related validation study.

The purpose of the analysis was to examine the frequency and extent of the subjects' counterproductive behaviors in the workplace and correlations between the EPI–3 scales and the counterproductivity data from the anonymous questionnaire. All subjects scored in the acceptable range on the accuracy scale and were included in the analysis.

The anonymous questionnaire assessed admissions of counterproductivity in five areas: Time Deviance (missed work because of physical illness, came to work late, left work early without permission, etc.), Co-worker Relations (spread rumors or gossip that may have caused trouble at work; argued with customers, coworkers, or supervisors; etc.), Drug Abuse (came to work hung over from alcohol or drugs, etc), Merchandise/Property Damage (damaged company merchandise, property, or equipment accidentally but did not report it; etc.), and Work Quality (i.e., did work badly or incorrectly on purpose, did slow or sloppy work on purpose, etc.).

Subjects' scores were computed as the average of the item responses for each of the five areas of counterproductivity. In addition, a Total Counterproductivity Score was computed for each subject by averaging the responses from all 45 items on the admissions questionnaire. Scores for all counterproductivity dimensions were coded so that a higher value represented more productive behavior and a lower value represented more counterproductive behavior. Positive correlations were expected because on all EPI–3 scales, higher scores are more favorable.

Subjects' admissions of counterproductive behavior were frequent. Fifty-six percent ($N = 144$) of the subjects admitted to using company supplies or equipment for personal use on a regular basis. Thirty-two percent ($N = 81$) admitted to having argued with customers, coworkers, or supervisors at least occasionally. Twenty-four percent ($N = 59$) admitted to engaging in drug use or alcohol consumption while on the job, and 14 percent ($N = 35$) admitted to having falsified a company document for personal gain. The subjects' Total Counter-productivity Scores indicated that 15 percent ($N = 41$) of the employees re-peatedly engaged in some form of counterproductive behavior at work.

All correlations with the counterproductivity data were significant in the pre-dicted direction at the .01 level or beyond (Table 11.4). As the EPI–3 test scores increased, the frequency of productive behaviors in the workplace also increased.

Multiple correlations of the EPI–3 Dependability, Drug Avoidance, and In-terpersonal Cooperation scales with each of the counterproductivity dimensions were all highly significant at the .001 level (Table 11.5). Significant correlations range from $R = .317$ (Merchandise/Property Damage) to $R = .517$ (Drug Abuse).

The results of the three studies demonstrated significant relationships between EPI–3 scores and work behavior. Subjects who made fewer admissions of coun-terproductivity were more likely to have acceptable EPI–3 scores. Productive workers tend to score higher on dependability, drug avoidance, and interpersonal cooperation.

ADVERSE IMPACT

A large study was recently conducted to examine the EPI–3 pass-fail rates for protected sex and racial groups. For this analysis 4,065 applicants completed the EPI–3. The highest passing rate for a racial group (whites) was compared to the passing rates of blacks and Hispanics. In addition, male and female passing rates were compared. All passing rates were well within the four-fifths rule established by the Equal Employment Opportunity Commission for employee selection (DeGroot, Flenberg & Kadane, 1986) (Table 11.6). Thus, the EPI–3 does not exhibit adverse impact against any protected group.

UTILITY ANALYSIS

Although equations for determining the economic or dollar impact of a se-lection procedure have been available for many years, only recently have re-searchers developed practical methods for management to use. These methods are thoroughly described in Schmidt, Hunter, McKenzie, and Muldrow (1979), Hunter and Schmidt (1982, 1983), and Schmidt and Rauschenberger (1986). Utility analyses estimate the return on investment a company can expect from implementing a valid personnel selection program.

An illustrative utility analysis was computed using retail clerks as the targeted job. For this utility analysis, the following variables are needed: TV (validity of the selection procedure or test), NS (number of employees selected), SR (selection ratio of the procedure used), SDy (standard deviation of selected employees'

Table 11.4
Correlations of EPI-3 Scales with Counterproductivity Data

EPI-3 Scales	Counter-productivity	Time Deviance	Co-worker Relations	Drug Abuse	Merchandise/Property-Damage and Waste	Work Quality
Dependability	r = .450** N = 225	r = .419** N = 232	r = .307** N = 236	r = .409** N = 236	r = .311** N = 233	r = .378** N = 234
Interpersonal Cooperation	r = .380** N = 225	r = .338** N = 232	r = .344** N = 236	r = .354*** N = 236	r = .242** N = 233	r = .306** N = 234
Drug Avoidance	r = .357** N = 225	r = .409** N = 232	r = .230** N = 236	r = .498** N = 236	r = .214** N = 233	r = .157* N = 234
Productivity Index	r = .414** N = 225	r = .426** N = 232	r = .308** N = 236	r = .486** N = 236	r = .271** N = 233	r = .248** N = 234

* $p < .01$
** $p < .001$

(Note: higher criteria scores mean less counterproductivity)

Table 11.5
Multiple Correlations of the EPI-3 Scales with Counterproductivity Data

EPI-3 Scales	Counter-productivity Score	Time Deviance	Co-worker Relations	Drug Abuse	Merchandise/Property-Damage and Waste	Workmanship
Dependability						
Interpersonal Cooperation	$R = .484^*$ $F(3,238)$ $=23.5$	$R = .478^*$ $F(3,238)$ $= 23.5$	$R = .350^*$ $F(3,243)$ $= 11.3$	$R = .517^*$ $F(3,242)$ $= 29.4$	$R = .317^*$ $F(3,240)$ $= 8.9$	$R = .407^*$ $F(3,241)$ $= 16.0$
Drug Avoidance						

* $p < .001$

Table 11.6
EPI–3 Adverse Impact Analysis

RACIAL ANALYSIS

EPI-3	Recommended Standard		Percent Passing	
		White	Black	Hispanic
Composite Score	40	79%	76%	77%

SEX ANALYSIS

EPI-3	Recommended Standard	Percent Passing	
		Male	Female
Composite Score	40	77%	80%

annual salaries); Zx (average standard score on the test of those selected), and C (cost of selection for each employee). For the purpose of this analysis, the validity of the EPI–3 is computed as the average multiple correlation, weighted by sample size, of the EPI–3 predictor scales with work "productivity" data from studies 2 and 3 ($R = .268, N = 155; R = .484, N = 238$). This coefficient is calculated at .40.

For this example, assume that 100 retail clerks will be selected with a .70 selection ratio. This ratio is quite common when using the EPI–3 for selection. The average salary of our retail clerk employees is $15,000, and we will use a conservative estimate of $6,000 (40 percent of annual salary) as the standard deviation of the employees' annual salary for the equation (Hunter & Schmidt, 1983). The average standard score on the test of those selected can be estimated based on the selection ratio and the height of the normal curve at that proportion. The final variable, the cost of administering the EPI–3, is estimated at $12 per test booklet per applicant. The following equations are used for this analysis (based on Schmidt & Rauschenberger, 1986):

$$UT = (TV*SDy*Zx) - C/SR = \$1,182.86$$
$$TUT = (NS*TV*SDy*Zx) - NS(C/SR) = \$118,285.72,$$

where UT is the gain in productivity in dollars from the use of the selection procedure per year per clerk and TUT is the total gain in productivity in dollars per year for all those selected.

The results of this analysis are quite compelling. In this example, retail clerks make an average of $15,000 per year in a company that hired 100 new clerks using the EPI–3 at an average cost of $12 per applicant. The gain in productivity due to the use of the EPI–3 as a selection procedure would be $1,182.86 per clerk per year and $118,285.72 per year for the total group of 100. These are impressive bottom line figures and document the expected utility of the EPI–3. (Of course, the expected financial gain would be much higher for larger retail corporations that screen tens of thousands of applicants annually.)

CONCLUSION

The EPI–3 is a scientifically sound personnel selection instrument with useful levels of validity and utility. Moreover, it exhibits no adverse impact against protected groups.

The EPI–3 has several useful applications. This instrument is appropriate where theft is not a major concern for employers, yet improved productivity is. The EPI–3 can provide employers with invaluable information about their applicants that has been shown to be predictive of employee retention, work performance, and productivity in general.

Use of an instrument such as the EPI–3 raises several ethical issues. The role of personnel psychologists in our society is not to pass judgement on the character of an individual. That role belongs to the courts, the judges, and juries. The duty of personnel specialists is to assess job applicants' attitudes accurately and to determine, through research and scientific investigation, the degree to which those attitudes are predictive of successful performance in the workplace. This goal can be achieved only through rigorous efforts to determine the validity of the EPI–3 or any psychological inventory for its specific purpose. Fair administration of the instrument to applicants of all racial and sex groups, as well as the consistent application of uniform standards (cutoffs) to all individuals, is also of key importance. These goals can be consistently achieved through training of those who use the EPI–3. Users need to be trained in test interpretation, handling of individual test results, and confidentiality issues. Only through intensive efforts in these areas can we maintain our ethical code and our high standards for the practice of psychology in organizations.

REFERENCES

Ash, P. (1988). A history of honesty testing. Paper presented at the 1988 convention of the American Psychological Association, Atlanta, August 13.

Alvord, G. (1985). Validation of the Personnel Selection Inventory as a screening test for bus operators. *Journal of Security Administration*, 8(1), 37–47.

Berte, D. L., Moretti, D. M., Jusko, R., & Leonard, J. (1981). An Investigation of a combined withdrawal and counterproductive behavior decision process model. Paper presented at the Annual Conference of the American Academy of Management, San Diego.

Brown, T. S., Jones, J. W., Terris, W., & Steffy, B. (1987). The Impact of preemployment integrity testing on employee turnover and inventory shrinkage losses. *Journal of Business and Psychology*, 2(2).

Brown, T. S., & Joy, D. S. (1985). The predictive validity of the Personnel Selection

Inventory in the grocery industry. Unpublished technical report. Park Ridge, IL: London House.

Commerce Clearing House. Paragraph 24175. Chapter 149. Section 19-B of the general laws of the State of Massachusetts.

DeGroot, M. M., Fienberg, S. E., & Kadane, J. B. (1986). *Statistics and the law.* New York: Wiley.

Hollinger, R. C., & Clark, J. P. (1983). *Theft by employees.* Lexington, MA: Heath.

Hunter, J. E., & Schmidt, F. L. (1982). Fitting people to jobs: The impact of personnel selection on national productivity. In M. D. Dunnette and E. O. Fleishman (eds.), *Human capacity assessment.* Hillsdale, NJ: Erlbaum.

Hunter, J. E., & Schmidt, F. L. (1983). Qualifying the effects of psychological interventions on employee job performance and work force productivity. *American Psychologists,* 78, 473–478.

Jones, J. W. (1979a). Employee alcohol abuse in the workplace. Paper presented at the Fifth Annual Convention of the Society of Police and Criminal Psychology, Chicago.

Jones, J. W. (1979b). Employee deviance: Attitudinal correlates of theft and on-the-job alcohol abuse. Paper presented at the Fifth Annual Convention of the Society of Police and Criminal Psychology, Chicago.

Jones, J. W. (1979c). Predictors of prealcoholism. Paper presented at the 17th Interamerican Congress of Psychology, Lima, Peru.

Jones, J. W. (1980). Attitudinal correlates of employees' deviance: Theft, alcohol use, and nonprescribed drug abuse. *Psychological Reports,* 47, 71–77.

Jones, J. W. (1982). Correlates of police misconduct: Violence and alcohol use on the job. Paper presented at the Annual Meeting of Society of Police and Criminal Psychology, Atlanta. Technical Report 7. Park Ridge, IL: London House.

Jones, J. W., & Terris, W. (1983). Personality correlates of theft and drug abuse among job applicants. *Proceedings of the Third International Conference on the 16PF Test,* 85–94.

Jones, J. W., & Wuebker, L. J. (1988). Accident prevention through personnel selection. Paper submitted to the *Journal of Business and Psychology,* 3(2), 187–198.

Joy, D. S., & Frost, A. G. (1987). The prediction of employee performance using the Employment Productivity Index. Unpublished technical report. Park Ridge, IL: London House.

Joy, D. S., Frost, A. G., & Cook, M. S. (1987). Predicting counterproductive behaviors at a major metropolitan transit authority using the Personnel Selection Inventory. Technical Report 63. Park Ridge, IL: London House.

London House (1986a). *The Personnel Selection Inventory (PSI).* Park Ridge, IL: London House Press.

London House (1986b). *The Employment Productivity Index (EPI).* Park Ridge, IL: London House Press.

Moretti, D. M. (1980). Employee counterproductivity: Attitudinal predictors of industrial damage and waste. Paper presented at the Sixth Annual Meeting of the Society of Police and Criminal Psychology, Atlanta.

Moretti, D. M. (1986). The prediction of employee counterproductivity through attitude assessment. *Journal of Business and Psychology,* 1(2), 134–147.

Morgenstern, D. (1977). *Blue collar theft in business and industry.* Springfield, VA: National Technical Information Service.

Palimotto, M. J. (1983). Labor, government and court reaction to detection of deception services in the private sector. *Journal of Security Administration*, 6(1), 31–42.

Rafilson, F. M. (1987). The Employment Productivity Index: A concurrent validation study. Unpublished technical report. Park Ridge, IL: London House.

Rafilson, F. M. (1988). Random response analysis of a validity (accuracy) scale. Unpublished technical report. Park Ridge, IL: London House.

Schmidt, F. L., Hunter, J. E., McKenzie, R., and Muldrow, T. (1979). The impact of valid selection procedures on workforce productivity. *Journal of Applied Psychology, 64*, 609–626.

Schmidt, F. L., & Rauschenberger, J. (1986). Utility analysis for practitioners: A workshop. Presented at the First Annual Conference of the Society for Industrial and Organizational Psychology, Chicago.

Terris, W. (1979a). Attitudinal correlates of employee integrity: Theft related admissions made in preemployment polygraph examinations. *Journal of Security Administration, 2*, 30–39.

Terris, W. (1979b). Attitudinal correlates of theft, violence, and drug use. Paper presented at the 17th Interamerican Congress of Psychology, Lima, Peru.

Terris, W. (1985). Attitudinal correlates of employee integrity. *Journal of Police and Criminal Psychology, 1*,(1), 60–68.

Terris, W. (1986). The development and validation of the EPI–3. Unpublished research abstract. Park Ridge, IL: London House.

12

Psychological Correlates of Illicit Drug Use among Job Applicants

JOHN W. JONES, DENNIS S. JOY, AND WILLIAM TERRIS

Recent survey research (e.g., NIDA, 1989) indicates that 32 percent of the 18- to 25-year-old adult population used illicit drugs in the past year and 18 percent used a drug in the past month. Many of these young adults are preparing to enter the work force if they are not already employed. Among a group of 20- to 40-year-old employees, 22 percent have used an illicit drug in the past year, and 12 percent have used an illicit drug in the past month. Drug-abusing employees seem to prefer marijuana and cocaine (Newcomb, 1988). Although the exact prevalence rate of on-the-job drug use is unknown (Crown & Rosse, 1988), the existence of employee drug use during paid work hours is undisputed (Backer, 1987).

The cost of employee illicit drug use to American industries exceeds $8 billion a year (Levy, 1972). Harris (1976) estimated losses in excess of $40 billion a year because of drug-abusing and problem-drinking employees. Both alcohol and drug abuse at work are related to industrial accidents, absenteeism, theft, and other forms of employee counterproductivity (Harwood, Napolitano, Kristiansen & Collins, 1984). Hence, a need exists to screen out job applicants who are at highest risk to abuse illicit drugs in the workplace while selecting in applicants at lowest risk to use illicit drugs (cf. Normand, Salyards & Mahoney, 1990). The purpose of the study reported in this chapter was to determine if psychological tests used for personnel selection can successfully predict a wide range of drug abuse criteria.

SELECTION TESTS

Both the Personnel Selection Inventory (PSI) (London House Press, 1980a, 1980b, 1983) and the Sixteen Personality Factor Questionnaire (16PF) (Cattel, Eber & Tatsuoka, 1970) can be used to identify job applicants with criminal potential. The PSI includes a job-related scale that measures work applicants' attitudes, values, and perceptions toward on-the-job drug use. The validity of this scale has been established using a number of different validation strategies. For example, Jones and Rafilson (1988) showed that chronic illicit drug users scored significantly poorer on the PSI Drug Avoidance scale compared to typical drugstore and retail store job applicants (F = 42.4, p < .001). The chronic drug users had more tolerant attitudes toward drug use in the workplace compared to non-drug-abusing job applicants. A summary of other validity studies conducted with the Drug-avoidance scale is shown in Table 12.1. Drug scale scores have significantly predicted a number of job-related criteria (Table 12.2).

Research on the PSI drug scale shows that the "typical" illicit drug abuser (1) is more tempted to use drugs, (2) engages in many of the common rationalizations for drug use, (3) would punish drug users and dealers less, (4) often thinks about drug use, (5) attributes more drug use to others, (6) shows more loyalty to drug users, and (7) is more vulnerable to peer pressure to use drugs (cf. Terris, 1979). The PSI Violence and Honesty scales, two additional job-related scales, measure similar attitudes and cognitions (Jones, 1980; Terris, 1979).

The 16PF test, which measures 16 primary personality factors, was designed to predict a variety of antisocial behaviors, including criminal behavior and drug addiction (Krug, 1981). In one study, Kochkin (1981) administered both an integrity test that measured theft proneness and the 16PF to 176 job applicants. He found that the dishonest applicants (1) had lower ego strength (C−); (2) were more dominant, as evidenced by aggressiveness, competitiveness, and stubbornness (E+); (3) had weaker superego strength (G−); (4) were more apprehensive and insecure (0+); and (5) were more tense, frustrated, and overwrought (Q+) compared to honest applicants. Therefore, integrity tests such as the PSI and personality tests such as the 16PF can be used to identify work applicants who are at risk to engage in drug abuse and other forms of counterproductivity (e.g., theft, violence, unsafe behavior).

Certain people have a greater need than others to seek stimulation, excitement, or risky adventures. Zuckerman (1979) developed a personality test measure of sensation seeking to discriminate high- from low-sensation seekers. Research with his Sensation Seeking Scale (SSS) shows that high-sensation seekers include not only parchutists but also certain criminal types and illicit drug abusers. The high-sensation-seeking personality type appears to be at risk to abuse drugs in the workplace.

The purpose of this study was to identify reliable personality correlates of employee drug abuse. Job applicants' scores from the PSI, the 16PF, and the

Table 12.1
Drug-Avoidance Scale Validation Summary

STUDY	SAMPLE	CRITERIA	VALIDITY LEVEL
Terris (1979)	College Students (N = 146)	1) $ Value Theft 2) # Criminal Admissions 3) # Violence Admissions 4) Drugs ever used	r = .36*** r = .43*** r = .42*** r = .20*
Jones (1979)	College Students (N = 146)	1) Weekly alcohol consumption rate 2) # Times intoxicated 3) # Alcohol related problems	r = .29*** r = .28*** r = .31***
Jones (1979)	Employees from two retail food stores (N = 22/14)	# Drinks on food breaks	r = .46*
Jones (1979)	Retail food store employees (N = 36)	1) $ Theft of merchandise 2) # Drinks on-the-job 3) # Days alcohol consumed on-the-job	r = .33* r = .39* r = .41*
Moretti (1980)	Warehouse and supermarket employees (N = 25/20)	1) $ Amount of stolen merchandise 2) # Criminal behaviors	r = .58* r = .68**
Jones (1982)	Police officers (N = 53)	1) # Times came to work hungover 2) # Drinks consumed on-the-job 3) # Days alcohol consumed on-the-job 4) # Drinks consumed on lunch/supper break	r = .29* r = .39** r = .34* r = .35*
Jones (1980)	Employees from a medical book co., manufacturing co., & a food service company (N = 19/11/9)	1) $ Theft 2) # Times came hungover from alcohol 3) # Times came intoxicated from drug use	r = .32* r = .29* r = .46**
Terris & Jones (1980)	Employees from two retail food stores (N = 27/15)	Total employee theft (cash & merchandise)	r = .66**
Jones (1981ᵃ)	Nurses from a hospital trauma emergency room (N = 34)	1) $ Theft general supplies 2) $ Theft medical supplies 3) $ Total theft	r = .38* r = .36* r = .46**
Jones (1981ᵇ)	College students (N = 74)	Drug admissions	r = .29*
Moretti (1986)	Grocery store employees and hospital employees (N = 132/64)	Employee counter-productivity index	r = .42**

Table 12.1 (continued)

STUDY	SAMPLE	CRITERIA	VALIDITY LEVEL
Jones & Terris (1983)	Convenience store job applicants (N = 104)	1) # Theft crimes 2) # Drug crimes 3) # Illicit drugs used	$r = .27^{**}$ $r = .45^{**}$ $r = .30^{**}$
Terris (1985)	Job applicants for various positions of trust (N = 470)	1) Polygraph admissions of theft 2) Polygraph admissions of violent behavior 3) Polygraph admissions of marijuana use 4) Polygraph admissions of other drug use	$r = .26^{*}$ $r = .15^{*}$ $r = .46^{*}$ $r = .40^{*}$
Jones & Scruggs (1981)	High school students (N = 45)	1) Chemical abuse 2) Theft crimes 3) Violent crimes	$r = .42^{**}$ $r = .37^{*}$ $r = .32^{*}$
Frost & Joy (1987)	Employees from a nursing home for handicapped children (N = 49)	Standardized Measures of Emotional Instability 1) Rationalization 2) Inferiority 3) Hostility 4) Depression 5) Fear & anxiety 6) Organic reaction 7) Projection 8) Sexual adjustment 9) Withdrawal 10) Internal adjustment 11) External adjustment 12) Somatic adjustment 13) Job performance	 $r = .35^{**}$ $r = .50^{***}$ $r = .45^{***}$ $r = .53^{***}$ $r = .42^{**}$ $r = .39^{**}$ $r = .36^{**}$ $r = .43^{***}$ $r = .33^{**}$ $r = .43^{***}$ $r = .47^{***}$ $r = .44^{***}$ $r = .36^{**}$
Joy & Rafilson (1988)	Grocery store employees (cashiers) (N = 357)	Supervisors' rating of job performance 1) Customer service dimension 2) Employee conduct dimension 3) Productivity dimension 4) Employee rank	 $r = .23^{***}$ $r = .17^{***}$ $r = .20^{**}$ $r = .18^{**}$
Joy & Werner (1988)	Drug store employees (N = 304)	Supervisors' rating of employee quality top 33% <u>vs</u> bottom 33%	Top groups scored significantly higher than the bottom group on Drug Avoidance Scale $t = 2.85^{**}$
Jones & Rafilson (1988)	Chronic drug users retail store applicants drug store applicants (N = 96)	Comparison of PSI Drug Scale scores: Chronic drug users <u>vs</u> applicants	Chronic drug abusers scored significantly lower than job applicants on Drug Avoidance Scale $F = 42.10^{***}$
Brown, Jones Terris & Steffy (1987)	Chain of 21 Home Improvement Centers (N = approx. 4,000)	Comparison of average number of drug related terminations before and after PSI implementation	Pre-test average 19 terms/year Post-test average 4.5 terms/year $t = 4.44^{*}$

Table 12.1 (continued)

STUDY	SAMPLE	CRITERIA	VALIDITY LEVEL
Joy, Werner & Jones (1989)	Job applicants from a major hotel corporation (N = 4,746)	Admissions of drug use 1) Current Users 2) Experimental users 3) Non-users	Significant differences on Drug Avoidance Scale among all groups. Current users scored lowest. Group making No Drug Admissions Use scored highest. F = 373***
Joy & Werner (1990)	Manufacturing applicants (N = 357)	Medical drug screening (Urinanalysis)	Group positive on medical drug screen scored significantly lower on PSI Drug Avoidance Scale than did group negative on medical drug screen t = 1.9*

Table 12.2
Criteria Predicted with Drug-Avoidance Scale

Drug Abuse Criteria:

* Chronic drug use

* High Intoxication rate

* Drug-related criminal admissions

* Violent behavior

* Positive urinalysis results

* Emotional Instability

Job-related Criteria:

* Coming to work hungover

* Coming to work Intoxicated

* Drug-related terminations

* Poor Job performance

* Extended work breaks

* Poor customer service

* Theft of cash and merchandise

SSS were correlated with their admissions of past drug use. Psychological tests need to be validated against such criteria so that a valid test battery can be selected to screen out high-risk applicants. Job applicants with a history of drug abuse are at greatest risk to engage in future acts of on-the-job drug abuse (cf.

Monahan, 1981). A secondary goal of this study was to examine the personality correlates of employee theft.

CASE STUDY _____

METHOD

One hundred and four convenience store job applicants (45 males and 59 females) completed the PSI (Form 4), the 16PF (Form A), and the SSS (Form 5) during a preemployment interview. This battery took approximately 1 1/2 to 2 hours to complete. The average age of the applicants was 26.3 years (SD = 9.2).

In this study, raw data were recoded so that higher scores on the PSI Drug-avoidance, Non-violence, and Honesty scales meant poorer or more tolerant attitudes toward drug abuse, violence, and theft, respectively. Higher scores on the PSI Distortion scale meant more attempts to "fake good." The 16PF has 16 personality scales. The scoring strategy for the 16PF raw scores is summarized in Table 12.3. Finally, higher scores on the SSS mean greater sensation seeking and risk-taking tendencies. Scores from the PSI, the 16PF, and the SSS served as predictor variables.

All applicants also completed a behavioral checklist that measured past criminal history. Three forms of criminal behavior were measured: the total number of drug crimes ever committed (e.g., drunken driving, underage drinking, buying and selling marijuana, buying and selling other illegal drugs), the total number of theft crimes ever committed (e.g., breaking and entering, stealing cars, shoplifting, cashing stolen checks, using stolen credit cards, writing bad checks, selling stolen property), and all the illicit drugs (e.g., marijuana, heroin, cocaine, opium, mescaline) ever used for social or experimental reasons. Applicants were told to answer this section truthfully since any attempts to lie or deceive are grounds for disqualification or dismissal. Higher scores on the criterion checklist mean more criminal admissions.

RESULTS AND DISCUSSION

Means, standard deviations, and ranges for both the predictor and the criterion variables are presented in Table 12.4. Fifty-seven percent of the applicants admitted to one or more drug crimes, and 21 percent admitted to two or more drug crimes. In addition, 55 percent admitted using one or more illegal drugs. Fourteen percent used two or more illegal substances. Forty percent of the applicants admitted to one or more theft crimes. Fourteen percent admitted to two or more theft crimes.

A profile of a work applicant with a history of drug-related crimes can be constructed from Table 12.5. Significant correlations at the .01 level show that

Table 12.3
Description of 16PF Scales

16-PF Scale	Lower Score Description	Higher Score Description
A	Reserved	Outgoing
B	Less Intelligent	More Intelligent
C	Lower Ego Strength	Higher Ego Strength
E	Submissive	Dominant
F	Serious	Happy-go-lucky
G	Weaker Superego Strength	Stronger Superego Strength
H	Timid	Venturesome
I	Tough-minded	Sensitive
L	Trusting	Suspicious
M	Practical	Imaginative
N	Forthright	Shrewd
O	Self-assured	Apprehensive
Q_1	Conservative	Experimenting
Q_2	Group-dependent	Self-sufficient
Q_3	Uncontrolled	Controlled
Q_4	Relaxed	Tense

the applicant at risk to abuse illicit drugs has (1) strong sensation-seeking tendencies and a desire to take risks (SSS), (2) an extremely dominant personality, as characterized by aggressiveness and stubbornness (16PF scale E+), (3) tolerant attitudes toward illicit on-the-job drug use (PSI Drug-avoidance scale), (4) a less serious and a more happy-go-lucky approach to life (16PF scale F+), (5) tolerant attitudes toward workplace theft (PSI Honesty scale), and (6) an average or above-average level of intellectual functioning (16PF scale B+). The applicant who admitted using a variety of illicit drugs had stronger sensation-seeking tendencies (SSS), tolerant attitudes about drug use (PSI Drug scale), and a more happy-go-lucky approach to life (16PF scale F+).

A psychological profile of a job applicant with a history of theft can also be constructed from Table 12.5. Statistically significant correlations at the .01 level show that the applicant with a history of theft has (1) dishonest and tolerant

Table 12.4
Means and Standard Deviations on Predictor and Criterion Variables (N = 104)

Predictors Scales:	$\bar{X}$	SD	Range
PSI Scales[a]:			
PSI Drug-Avoidance	21.1	5.5	10 to 35
PSI Non-violence	15.3	3.8	1 to 22
PSI Honesty	40.2	11.0	5 to 60
PSI Distortion	20.5	5.6	5 to 30
Sensation Seeking Scale:	12.5	5.6	0 to 23
16-PF Scales:			
A Warmth	10.4	3.2	1 to 20
B Intelligence	7.1	1.9	0 to 11
C Emotional Stability	16.8	4.0	2 to 24
E Dominance	10.6	3.5	1 to 20
F Impulsivity	12.6	3.6	2 to 22
G Conformity	13.8	3.3	0 to 20
H Boldness	14.2	5.1	0 to 25
I Sensitivity	11.4	3.2	2 to 18
L Suspiciousness	6.6	3.3	0 to 15
M Imagination	10.5	3.0	0 to 18
N Shrewdness	11.0	3.2	0 to 18
O Insecurity	10.3	4.1	0 to 23
Q_1 Radicalism	8.6	3.4	0 to 17
Q_2 Self sufficiency	10.1	3.2	0 to 18
Q_3 Self-discipline	14.8	3.3	0 to 20
Q_4 Tension	9.9	4.3	0 to 20
Criteria			
No. Drug Crimes	1.0	1.1	0 to 5
No. Drug Used	1.1	1.9	0 to 11
Frequency of Drug Use	1.8	0.9	1 to 4
No Theft Crimes	0.8	1.2	0 to 5

* For this study, the PSI scales were coded so that _higher_ scores mean _greater_ counterproductivity.   Raw scores were analyzed.

attitudes toward on-the-job theft (PSI Honesty scale), (2) tolerant attitudes toward illicit drug use (PSI Drug-avoidance scale), (3) sensation-seeking and risk-taking tendencies (SSS), (4) a dominant approach to life, as characterized by aggressiveness, competitiveness, and stubbornness (16PF scale E+), and (5) weaker superego strength, as evidenced by a tendency to be a quitter, an undependable person, and a rule breaker (16PF scale G−).

The three criterion measures were moderately intercorrelated. The theft crimes scores reliably correlated with both the drug crimes (r[102] = .43, $p <$ .01) and

Table 12.5
Relationship of PSI, Sensation Seeking Questionnaire, and 16 PF Scores to Drug Abuse and Theft

	• Drugs Crimes	• Drugs Used	• Theft Crimes
PSI Scales:			
Drug-Avoidance	.45**	.30**	.27**
Honesty	.26**	.11	.45**
Non-violence	.22*	.17	.20*
Distortion	-.19	-.09	-.26**
Sensation Seeking	.57**	.38**	.27**
16-PF Scales:			
A	-.10	-.10	-.14
B	.26**	.21*	-.02
C	.15	.01	-.11
E	.46**	.22*	.29**
F	.35**	.26**	.22*
G	.06	.04	-.26**
H	.15	.08	-.02
I	-.16	.08	-.23*
L	.16	.16	.16
M	.01	-.15	-.01
N	-.22*	-.22*	-.19
O	-.11	.09	.06
Q_1	.21*	-.02	.06
Q_2	.03	-.12	-.03
Q_3	-.10	-.11	-.22*
Q_4	.03	.04	.21*
Multiple-R	.70**	.60**	.57*

*p< .05
**p< .01

the illicit drug use scores (r[102] = .20 p < .05), and the drug crimes scores significantly correlated with the illicit drug use scores (r[102] = .49, p < .01). Hence, applicants who use illicit drugs are probably more likely to steal in the workplace when confronted with both the need and the opportunity to steal.

Presentation of the full intercorrelation matrix is beyond the scope of this chapter. Still, one of the main correlations is worthy of mention. The PSI Drug-avoidance scales scores reliably correlated with the Sensation Seeking Scores (r = .51, p < .01). Hence, the applicant most likely to abuse illicit drugs in the workplace, as measured by the PSI Drug-avoidance scale, is one at highest risk to engage in thrill-seeking and potentially dangerous behavior, probably as a way to escape boredom and increase excitement in life.

The correlations in Table 12.5 indicate that scale scores from the PSI, the 16PF, and the SSS significantly correlated with the three criterion measures. Tentative personality profiles and cognitive styles of job applicants with histories of drug abuse and/or theft were constructed. This study needs to be replicated and extended using larger sample sizes and a heterogeneous selection of businesses. These results support the notion that preemployment psychological tests can be used to screen out job applicants who are at risk to use drugs and/or steal in the workplace.

REFERENCES

Backer, T. E. (1987). *Strategic planning for workplace drug abuse problems*. Rockville, MD: National Institute on Drug Abuse.

Brown, T. S., Jones, J. W., Terris, W., & Steffy, B. D. (1987). The impact of preemployment integrity testing on employee turnover and inventory shrinkage losses. *Journal of Business and Psychology*, 2(2).

Cattel, R. B., Eber, H. W., & Tatsuoka, M. M. (1970). *Handbook for the Sixteen Personality Factor Questionnaire (16-PF)*. Champaign, IL: Institute for Personality and Ability Testing.

Crown, D. F., & Rosse, J. G. (1988). A critical review of the assumptions underlying drug testing. *Journal of Business and Psychology*, 3, 22–41.

Frost, A. G., & Joy, D. S. (1987). The Use of Personnel Selection Inventory and the EMO questionnaire in the selection of child care workers. Unpublished technical report. Park Ridge, IL: London House.

Harris, O. J. (1976). *Managing people at work: Concepts and Interpersonal behavior*. New York: Wiley.

Harwood, H. J., Napolitano, D. M., Kristiansen, P. L., & Collins, J. J. (1984). *Economic costs to society of alcohol and drug abuse and mental illness: 1980*. Research Triangle Park, NC: Research Triangle Institute.

Jones, J. W. (1979a). Predictors of prealcoholism. Paper presented at the 17th Interamerican Congress of Psychology, Lima, Peru.

Jones, J. W. (1979b). Employee alcohol abuse in the workplace. Paper presented at the Fifth Annual Convention of the Society of Police and Criminal Psychology, Chicago.

Jones, J. W. (1979c). Employee deviance: Attitudinal correlates of theft and on-the-job alcohol abuse. Paper presented at the Fifth Annual Convention of the Society of Police and Criminal Psychology, Chicago.

Jones, J. W. (1980). Attitudinal correlates of employee deviance: Theft, alcohol use, and nonprescribed drug use. *Psychological Reports*, 47, 71–77.

Jones, J. W. (1981a). Attitudinal correlates of employee theft of drugs and hospital supplies among nursing personnel. *Journal of Nursing Research*, 30(6), 349–351.

Jones, J. W. (1981b). Personality profiles of endorsers of nuclear crime. Paper presented at the 89th Annual Convention of the American Psychological Association, Division of Military Psychology, Los Angeles.

Jones, J. W. (1982). Correlates of police misconduct: Violence and alcohol use on the job. Paper presented at the Annual Meeting of Society of Police and Criminal Psychology, Atlanta.

Jones, J. W., & Rafilson, F. M. (1988). *Chronic drug users' attitudes toward delinquency in the workplace*. Technical Report 77. Park Ridge, IL: London House Press.

Jones, J. W., & Scruggs, D. P. (1981). Psychologically profiling endorsers of nuclear crime and sabotage. Paper presented at the 53d Annual Convention of the Midwestern Psychological Association.

Jones, J. W., & Terris, W. (1983). Personality correlates of theft and drug abuse among job applicants. *Proceedings of the Third International Conference on the 16PF Test*, 85–94.

Joy, D. S., & Rafilson, F. M. (1988). Validation of the Personnel Selection Inventory (PSI–7S) for the grocery industry. Unpublished technical report. Park Ridge, IL: London House.

Joy, D. S., & Werner, S. H. (1988). The concurrent validity of the Personnel Selection Inventory (PSI–7) in a major drug store chain. Unpublished technical report. Park Ridge, IL: London House.

Joy, D. S., & Werner, S. H. (1990). Effectiveness of the Personnel Selection Inventory in the Identification of current drug use: A comparison with a medical drug screening procedure. Unpublished technical report. Park Ridge, IL: London House.

Joy, D. S., Werner, S. H., & Jones, J. W. (1989). Impact, legal compliance, and return on investment of the Personnel Selection Inventory for a major hotel corporation. Unpublished technical report. Park Ridge, IL: London House.

Kochkin, S. (1981). *Some by-products associated with screening applicants with an integrity test*. Chicago: United Airlines Human Resources Department, June.

Krug, S. (1981). *Interpreting 16 PF profile patterns*. Champaign, IL: Institute for Personality and Ability Testing.

Levy, S. J. (1972). Drug abuse in business: Telling it like it is. *Personnel, 49*, 8.

London House (1980a). *The Personnel Selection Inventory*. Park Ridge, IL: London House Press.

London House (1980b). *Test administration and analysis instruction manual: The London Personnel Selection Inventory*. Park Ridge, IL.

London House (1983). *The Personnel Selection Inventory: Research studies*. Park Ridge, IL: London House Press.

Monahan, J. (1981). *Predicting violent behavior*. Beverly Hills: Sage Publications.

Moretti, D. M. (1980). Employee counterproductivity: Attitudinal predictors of industrial damage and waste. Paper presented at the Sixth Annual Meeting of the Society of Police and Criminal Psychology, Atlanta.

Moretti, D. M. (1986). The prediction of employee counterproductivity through attitude assessment. *Journal of Business and Psychology*, 1(2), 134–147.

Newcomb, M. D. (1988). *Drug use in the workplace: Risk factors for disruptive substance use among young adults*. Dover, MA: Auburn House.

NIDA (1989). Highlights of the 1988 National Household survey on drug abuse. *National Institute on Drug Abuse Capsules*, August. C–86–13, Rockville, MD: NIDA.

Normand, J., Salyards, S. & Mahoney, J. J. (1990). An evaluation of preemployment drug testing. Unpublished manuscript. Washington, DC: U.S. Postal Service.

Terris, W. (1979a). Attitudinal correlates of employee integrity: Theft related admissions made in preemployment polygraph examinations. *Journal of Security Administration*, 2, 30–39.

Terris, W. (1979b). Attitudinal correlates of theft, violence, and drug use. Paper presented at the 17th Interamerican Congress of Psychology, Lima, Peru.

Terris, W. (1985). Attitudinal correlates of employee integrity. *Journal of Police and Criminal Psychology*, 1(1), 60–68.

Terris, W., & Jones, J. W. (1980). Attitudinal and personality correlates of theft among supermarket employees. *Journal of Security Administration*, 3(2), 65–78.

Zuckerman, M. (1979). *Sensation seeking: Beyond the optimal level of arousal*. New York: Lawrence Erlbaum Associates.

13

The Prediction of On-the-Job Violence

KAREN B. SLORA, DENNIS S. JOY, JOHN W. JONES, AND
WILLIAM TERRIS

As negligent hiring suits, often based on the misconduct of employees, increase, employers seek means of being able to identify those persons most likely to engage in disruptive or assaultive behaviors. Not only is the potential of a lawsuit costly, but the perceived goodwill and public image of a company is tarnished when it is found that one of its employees has assaulted or violently argued with a customer. Even fairly mundane acts, such as arguing with a customer, can result in losses in that both repeat business and the reputation of the company are threatened.

On-the-job violence is not limited to extremely aggressive criminal acts, such as rape or assault. Of concern to most employers is the more commonplace violence and aggressiveness toward customers such as volatile arguments and fights. Such acts can drive business away and directly hurt the bottom line. Such violent work behaviors are not infrequent. A recent anonymous survey of employees from six supermarket chains (Slora, 1989; Slora & Boye, 1989) showed that 37 percent admitted to arguing with customers, 4 percent to fighting with customers, and 7 percent to fighting with coworkers or supervisors within the past six months.

Table 13.1 provides a representation of how on-the-job violent behavior can range from least injurious and costly violence to more extreme and harmful on-the-job violence. Companies are interested in controlling all types of on-the-job violence in order to improve the bottom line, lower insurance costs, and avoid legal suits.

Table 13.1
Examples of On-the-Job Violence

Least Injurious	Moderately Injurious	Highly Injurious
Behavior		
* Plays mean pranks	* Refuses to comply with work rules	* Attacks customers
* Occasionally argues with customers, coworkers, or supervisors	* Intentionally damages or wastes company property or merchandise	* Assaults other employees or supervisors
* Swears at others	* Engages in sabotage	* Has anger-related accidents
* Shows excessive belligerence	* Vandalizes facilities	* Assaults or rapes
* Spreads harmful rumors or gossip	* Argues frequently with customers	* Engages in arson
* Refuses to cooperate with supervisor	* Argues frequently with co-workers and/or supervisor	* Murders
* Breaks minor rules	* Steals for revenge	* Uses unauthorized weapons

What are employers to do? Firing employees after commission of such aggressive acts is too late; the damage to persons and company image has already been done. What is needed is a way to predict which job applicants are most likely to engage in violent work behaviors. Some of these ways are reviewed below.

Criminal background checks of job applicants identify only those persons who have been apprehended and prosecuted for violence; such checks do not account for actions not subject to legal attention or to hostile work behaviors that are either not detected or ignored. There is also an increasing tendency not to rely on reference checks since previous employers may be unwilling to provide negative information about an applicant. An option may be the assessment of applicants' attitudinal predispositions to engage in violent work behaviors using psychological inventories. The usefulness of this approach hinges largely on whether violent work behaviors can be accurately predicted.

The purpose of this chapter is twofold. The first is to argue that the conclusion drawn by some researchers (e.g., Inwald, 1989) that violence cannot be predicted is erroneous. Such a conclusion is based on methodologically unsound research that uses an inappropriate prediction model, a limited definition of violence and restricted samples, and weak predictors. The second purpose is to present evidence that work-related violence can be reliably predicted when appropriate predictor models, sound methodology, and standardized instruments are used.

THE PROBLEM OF THE PREDICTION MODEL

Most research in the area of the prediction of violence has focused on the prediction of whether a specific individual, usually a prisoner or mental patient, is likely to engage in violent acts in the future. This approach uses the clinical model of prediction and is used by therapists, clinicians, and others who make decisions on a case-by-case basis.

Some researchers in the area of criminal violence have lamented that anywhere from half to three-fourths of persons judged to be "dangerous" using a clinical model do not commit violent acts in the specified time frames (i.e., false positives). That is, more people are identified as dangerous than borne out by their behaviors. Other researchers, such as Walters (1980), point out that this may be due to the strong clinical bias toward minimizing false negatives. That is, clinicians take a conservative approach rather than letting one slip through the cracks. Also, studies do not account for violent actions that may occur after the conclusion of the data collection. That is, the time frame for prediction may not be long enough for violent behaviors to show themselves. Thus, there is a tendency to overclassify violence by identifying too many persons as violent. Citing the evidence for a disproportionate number of false positives as evidence that violence cannot be predicted is therefore a circular argument since violence is usually overclassified.

The clinical model of prediction is not appropriate for selecting individuals for employment. The statistical, or actuarial, model is more appropriate for such research and applied purposes. Personnel selection uses a statistical model of prediction. (The clinical and statistical models of prediction were described by Paul Meehl in 1954.) The statistical model is based on actuarial data and is intended to determine the likelihood a person will engage in certain behaviors or display certain characteristics. For example, insurance companies use the statistical model in determining mortality or accident rates (Behrens, 1989). The goal of such a model is to determine the occurrence of events across a population given certain characteristics (e.g., auto accidents, smoking, overeating). The statistical model is the appropriate one to use when selecting employees from a pool of applicants. In the employment setting, such a model is used to determine the statistical likelihood employees will be productive members of the organization.

THE PROBLEM OF DEFINITION AND SAMPLES

Following the clinical model, the definition of violence used by some researchers is often narrow and not applicable to the job setting. Typically violence is considered some type of dangerousness to others, usually defined as severe bodily injury. Thus, much of the research has focused on being able to predict which mental patients or prisoners represent a threat to the community when released. As such, clinicians and others who make judgments about violence are perceived as serving as social control agents.

There has been a reliance on using samples of persons apprehended for criminal acts of aggression such as battery and assault offenses. This represents only a small portion of on-the-job violent activities (Table 13.1). Moreover, these samples account only for those who are caught and whose actions are serious enough to warrant criminal arrest. In fact, researchers such as those of the National Victimization Panel (Department of Justice, 1978, reported in Monahan, 1982) speculate that over half of all violent crimes are never reported to police. Even when more conservative estimates are used, much violent crime is never reported. Monahan (1982) sums up, "One could conclude, therefore, that two out of three violent crimes in the United States are reported to the police; of these one results in an arrest" (p. 158). Clearly reliance on arrest records for estimating base rates of violent acts may seriously underestimate the true extent of criminal violent actions.

There is, moreover, a distinction between hostile and instrumental aggression that researchers do not consistently cite. Hostile aggression refers to actions intended to injure the intended target. Instrumental aggression refers to injurious actions performed as a means of attaining another goal (e.g., to obtain some goods, social approval). Hostile aggression is generally considered due to poor impulse control and a lack of temper control.

Many research studies have focused on hostile aggression. For example, Berkowitz (1978) interviewed 65 violent criminal offenders and concluded that their violent actions "were often the result of angry outbursts intended primarily to hurt." However, it appears likely that many acts of on-the-job violence may be due to instrumental aggression intended to gain attention, social approval, goods, time off from work, or the like. However, employees with poor impulse and temper control who are provoked may also engage in violent acts typical of hostile aggression.

The lack of a consensus of what constitutes violence has resulted in a lack of standardized report instruments in criterion measurement. In addition, criteria have tended to emphasize criminal arrests and do not include other more frequent examples of violence. Thus, mundane but important acts, such as fighting and arguing with customers or coworkers, are often not measured.

Perhaps a more meaningful approach to understanding on-the-job violence is to consider aggression as a continuum of injurious behaviors. The behaviors could be verbal or physical aggressiveness. At the most extreme, obviously injurious actions such as assault or rape would be considered examples of violence. At the lower end, one could consider less serious but still potentially injurious activities, such as pushing and shoving, arguing, and the like. It is the upper end that is brought to the attention of the police. However, actions at all points of this continuum concern employers because such employees drive customers, and business, away and therefore directly affect a company's bottom line.

THE PROBLEM OF THE WEAK PREDICTOR

Validation studies with predictor variables often used in studies of violence have several shortcomings (see Monahan, 1982, for a review). There is often a restricted range in that only a selected sample of the general population is tested (e.g., violent criminals). With little variability in the predictor, one would not expect substantial correlations with any criterion of violence. In addition, researchers often do not indicate the precise diagnostic criteria or do not use standardized predictor instruments. Subjective clinical judgment may result in unreliable diagnostic criteria. Thus, this makes it difficult to replicate studies and makes conclusions drawn from a specific study less credible given that different methods of measurement are used across studies.

Despite the limitations, studies that have used standard psychological instruments have tended to show that violence can be predicted to some extent. For example, Megargee (1979) devised a typology of prison populations based on the Minnesota Multiphasic Personality Inventory (MMPI) (Dahlstrom, Welsh & Dahlstrom, 1972; Graham, 1977). Megargee and colleagues were able to identify 10 MMPI profile types within a prisoner population. A cross-validation by Edinger (1979) further supported the ability of this standardized instrument to predict instances of violent behaviors as expressed by type of criminal records of the prisoners. In addition, the types of rule infractions and aggressiveness (e.g., verbal aggression, pilfering, group defiance) displayed by the prisoners also varied across the typology produced by the MMPI classifications. Bohn (1978) describes how this MMPI typology was used to classify prisoners into dormitories based on their aggressiveness. He found a significant decrease in the instances of violence due to these placements, thus highlighting the practical implications of predicting violent behavior.

Other studies using standardized instruments have found a similar pattern of results. For example, the California Psychological Inventory (CPI) (Gough, 1957, 1969, 1975) has been successfully used with criminals and juvenile delinquents. As described by Groth-Marnat (1984), several studies have found significant differences in the CPI profiles of violent and nonviolent offenders. In addition, Gough and his colleagues (Gough, Wenk & Rozynko, 1965) were able to develop a mathematical equation based on CPI scores that predicts parole success for delinquents.

Another widely used personality test, the Sixteen Personality Factor Questionnaire (16PF) (Cattel, Eber & Tatsuoka, 1970), has been found to predict violent actions. For example, White, McAdoo, and Megargee (1973) used 16PF scores as a means of determining the validity of a version of Megargee's MMPI typology. In this construct validation study, they found that the 16PF scores differed from one another in the expected directions. In yet another study with the 16PF, Wardell (1982) found that an inhibition factor based on 16PF scores was strongly related to violent and aggressive tendencies in a prison sample. Cattell (1989) also describes a pattern of 16PF scores that seems linked to acts of violence.

Yet another standardized instrument, the Sensation Seeking Scale (SSS) (Zuckerman, 1979), consistently shows a strong relationship to physically risky activities. Comparisons between delinquents or criminals and normals have found differences in their sensation-seeking scores. Also, aggression as measured by another instrument, the Personality Research Form (PRF) (Jackson, 1967), was found to be related significantly to sensation seeking in a 1975 study by Zuckerman (described in Zuckerman, 1979). Thus, a standardized measure of sensation seeking has been shown to be related to violence. It appears that when standardized predictors are used, there is a substantial relationship to violence criteria that can prove useful in applied settings. (It should be noted that the studies described relied on prison and hospital samples and did not use samples drawn from the general population or from work settings.)

The studies show that a sound assessment to predict the likelihood of on-the-job violence should incorporate several key elements: (1) the instrument should be validated using groups of employees and applicants, (2) the instrument should be standardized, (3) violence criteria should be job related, and (4) a program of research should be able to replicate the relationship between the instrument and on-the-job violence.

SCREENING FOR ON-THE-JOB VIOLENCE

Scales that measure a person's predisposition to engage in violent on-the-job activities are included on versions of the London House Personnel Selection

Inventory (PSI) (London House, 1980), a paper-and-pencil preemployment test designed to determine those persons likely to engage in counterproductive work activities. The items measure perceptions of the prevalence and acceptance of deviant actions and the likelihood the individual will engage in such behaviors in the future. The PSI is a reliable and well-validated instrument supported by a program of research (O'Bannon, Goldinger & Appleby, 1989; Sackett, Burris & Callahan, 1989).

Various versions of this instrument contain three measures of on-the-job violence: (1) the Nonviolence scale, (2) the Interpersonal Cooperation scale, and (3) the Customer Relations scale. The first scale was designed to predict the widest range of on-the-job violence (e.g., physical assault, intentional damage and waste, hostile customer relations) and is the prototype for the other two derivative scales. The other two scales, modifications of the Nonviolence scale, tend to measure primarily the risk of hostile and aggressive interpersonal relations with customers, coworkers, and supervisors. The three scales are highly intercorrelated.

Many studies show that the PSI Nonviolence scale is related to a variety of violent job behaviors. The scale has been found to be related to admissions of violence and criminal history (Jones, 1981; Terris, 1979; Terris & Jones, 1984), alcohol abuse (Jones, 1979a, 1979b), damaged and wasted merchandise and property (Moretti, 1980), arguing with supervisors, coworkers, or customers (Jones, 1983), polygraph admissions of past violence (Terris, 1985), and clinical diagnostic scales (Frost & Joy, 1987), to name a few. Also, Nonviolence scores have been found to be related to a measure of job safety consciousness (Wuebker, 1987). Research samples have included employees and applicants from food stores (Jones, 1979b; Moretti, 1980), warehouses and supermarkets (Moretti, 1980), a large police force (Jones, 1980), drugstores (Jones & Terris, 1981), department stores (Terris & Jones, 1984), hospitals (Moretti, 1986), and public transportation companies (Alvord, 1985; Joy, Frost & Cook, 1987).

Other modified Nonviolence scales on the PSI have found meaningful relationships to work behaviors. These modified violence scales also measure tendencies to act in hostile and overtly aggressive ways as they relate to dealing with customers and with employees. For example, the Employee/Customer Relations scale of the PSI-7 (a special version of the PSI designed for retail applications) is intended to measure a person's tendency to cooperate with customers and the likelihood of arguing or threatening customers. This modified measure of violence has been found to distinguish between exemplary and counterproductive groups based on supervisory ratings of overall employee quality in a drugstore chain (Joy & Werner, 1988). Another study (Joy & Rafilson, 1988a) found this scale to distinguish between top and bottom performers based on supervisory ratings of employee performance, including customer service, employee conduct, production, and overall employee ranking. Similar findings were obtained in another study in the auto rental industry (Joy, Frost & Boomhower, 1987). The findings showed significant relationships between the modified violence scale and supervisory ratings of productivity, customer relations, supervision, overall performance, and willingness to rehire the employee. Further, this scale successfully distinguished between top and bottom performers for customer relations, supervision, and overall quality ratings.

Another modified violence scale, Interpersonal Cooperation, is included on the Employment Productivity Index (EPI) (London House, 1986), a measure designed to screen in successful employees. In one study, 167 job applicants completed the EPI, and supervisory ratings were then obtained for these employees three months after they were hired (Joy & Frost, 1987). Significant correlations were obtained between the scores on this modified violence scale and supervisory ratings of customer service, employee relations, compliance with safety rules, employee conduct, and productivity. In addition, this scale was related to being angered or annoyed, trying to get along with coworkers, and arguing with supervisors. Rafilson (1988) describes another study in which 247 employed college students completed the EPI and an anonymous questionnaire concerning their work behaviors. Significant correlations were obtained between the modified violence scale and counterproductivity, time deviance, coworker relations, drug abuse, waste and damage of merchandise, and a composite measure of work quality. Thirty-two percent of this sample admitted to having argued at least occasionally with customers, coworkers, or supervisors.

Several different studies have been used to establish the relationship between standardized preemployment violence scales and on-the job violence (Table 13.2). Multiple approaches, using different study designs, are desired in any program of research to ensure that the conclusions from the studies are not due to the same type of method. For example, in one type of design, a contrasted-groups approach was used to show the PSI Nonviolence scale successfully distinguished between a group of convicted felons and drugstore and department store applicants (Jones & Terris, 1981). In another study (Moretti, 1980), warehouse and supermarket employees were asked to complete anonymously an inventory describing their damage and waste of company property and merchandise. Substantial validity coefficients were found between their PSI Nonviolence scores and the admitted dollar amount of damaged, wasted, and stolen company merchandise or property. In yet another study (Jones, 1983), the number of times employees argued with supervisors, coworkers, and customers was highly correlated with PSI Nonviolence scores. Using a construct validity approach (Frost & Joy, 1987), the PSI Nonviolence scores of nursing home employees were found to be related significantly to a number of clinical diagnostic scales, including hostility, projection, and adjustment to others. These studies show that on-the-job violence can be predicted when an appropriate standardized instrument is used.

SUMMARY

A review of the literature has shown that on-the-job violence can be predicted. Previous reviews and studies have yielded contrary conclusions, in large part

Table 13.2
Summary of Validation Research for Three Versions of the Nonviolence Scale

	Approximate Reliability (Alpha = .80)		
STUDY	SAMPLE	CRITERIA	VALIDITY LEVEL
TR 02 Terris (1979)	College Students (N = 146)	Admissions of violent behavior	r = .59***
TR 06 Moretti (1980)	Warehouse & Supermarket Employees (N = 31)	1) $ amount of damaged merchandise/property 2) $ amount of wasted materials/supplies	r = .49* r = .49*
TR 07 Jones (1980)	Police Officers (N = 53)	# of times expressed desire to physically assualt a suspect	r = .33*
TR 10 Jones (1983)	Employees from Medical Book Publishing Co., Food Service Co., Manufacturing Co. (N = 39)	1) # of times argued with supervisors, fellow employees, or customers 2) # of times physically fought with supervisors, fellow employees or customers	r = .57** r = .43**
TR 18 Jones (1982)	College Students (N = 74)	Violent crime admissions	r = .51**
TR 26 Moretti (1986)	Grocery Store and Hospital Employees (N = 196)	Employee counterproductivity ratings	r = .61***
TR 41 Terris (1985)	Applicants for positions of trust (N = 470)	Admissions of violent behavior	r = .25*
TR 54 Jones & Fay (1987)	Adult-Child Care Workers (N = 54)	1) Suspensions 2) Counterproductivity Index 3) Reprimands for poor job performance	r = .22** r = .20** r = .12*
TR 63 Joy, Frost & Cook (1987)	Public Transportation Authority Employees (N = 229)	1) Suspensions 2) Counterproductivity Index	r = .16* r = .14*
TR 68 Joy & Rafilson (1988a)	Grocery Store Cashiers (N = 362)	Supervisors' ratings 1) Customer Service 2) Productvity Best vs worst employees based on supervisors' ratings	r = .25*** r = .21** Best employees scored significantly higher than worst employees on Customer Relations Scale

Table 13.2 (continued)

STUDY	SAMPLE	CRITERIA	VALIDITY LEVEL
		1) Customer Service	t = 2.75**
		2) Employee Conduct	t = 2.49**
		3) Productivity	t = 2.15**
TR 55 Joy, Frost & Boomhower (1987)	Automobile Rental Agents (N = 204)	Supervisors' ratings: 1) Productivity 2) Customer Relations 3) Responsiveness to Supervision 4) Overall Performance 5) If employee left would you like to re-hire	r = .28* r = .35** r = .38** r = .38** r = .26* Best employees scored significantly higher than worst employees on Customer Relations Scale.
		6) Best <u>vs</u> poorest customer relations skills	t = 14.30**
		7) Best <u>vs</u> poorest cooperation with supervisors	t = 7.77**
TR 52 Frost & Joy (1987)	Nursing Home Employees (N = 49)	Standardized measures of emotional stability 1) Rationalization 2) Inferiority Feelings 3) Hostility 4) Depression 5) Fear & Anxiety 6) Organic Reaction 7) Projection 8) Internal Adjustment 9) External Adjustment 10) Somatic Adjustment	 r = .26* r = .33* r = .24* r = .34** r = .31* r = .37** r = .34** r = .27* r = .30* r = .31*
TR 72 Joy & Werner (1988)	Drug Store Employees (N = 304)	Supervisors' ratings Overall Quality Top 33% <u>vs</u> Bottom 33%	Top group scored higher than bottom group on Customer Relations Scale t = 3.28***
TR 71 Joy & Rafilson (1988)	Employees from a Chain of Consumer Electronics Store (N = 461)	Supervisors' ratings Exemplary <u>vs</u> Counterproductive Employees	Exemplary employees scored significantly higher than counterproductive employees on Customer Relations Scale t = 1.90*
TR 66 Jones & Joy (1987)	Adults convicted of sexual offenses against minors & adult childcare workers (N = 99)	1) Sexual offenders of minors (N = 33) 2) Adult childcare workers (N = 66)	t = 5.51**

* p < .05
** p < .01
*** p < .001

due to placing too much emphasis on studies plagued by shortcomings that compromise the studies' findings. These include the use of inappropriate and constricted samples, problems in study design, and limitations of the clinical model of prediction. When these problems are addressed, standardized instruments and an actuarial model have been found to be related significantly to violence in both clinical and work settings.

For employers, job-relevant behaviors such as aggressive dealings with customers should be considered in any measure of violence. The research has shown that persons will reveal violent tendencies on psychological assessment instruments and that many job-relevant violent acts may go undetected using conventional methods. Thus, the ability to predict on-the-job violence offers hope to employers in controlling the many costs of counterproductivity.

REFERENCES

Alvord, G. (1985). Validation of the Personnel Selection Inventory as a screening test for bus operators. *Journal of Security Administration* 8(1), 37–47.

Behrens, G. M. (1989). Predicting violence: A reply to Inwald. Unpublished research note. Park Ridge, IL: London House.

Berkowitz, L. (1978). Is criminal violence normative behavior? Hostile and instrumental aggression in violent incidents. *Journal of Research in Crime and Delinquency*, 15 (2), 148–161.

Bohn, M. J., Jr. (1978). Classification of offenders in an institution for young adults. Paper presented at the 19th International Congress of Applied Psychology, Munich, July 31.

Cattel, R. B., Eber, H. W., & Tatsuoka, M. M. (1970). *Handbook for the Sixteen Personality Factor Questionnaire*. Champaign, IL: Institute for Personality and Abilities Testing.

Cattell, H. B. (1989). *The 16PF: Personality in depth*. Champaign, IL: IPAT.

Dahlstrom, W. G., Welsh, G. S., & Dahlstrom, L. E. (1972). *An MMPI handbook: Volume I: Clinical interpretation*. Minneapolis: University of Minnesota Press.

Edinger, J. D. (1979). Cross-validation of the Megargee MMPI typology for prisoners. *Journal of Clinical and Consulting Psychology*, 47, 234–242.

Frost, A. G., & Joy, D. S. (1987). *The use of the Personnel Selection Inventory and the Emo Questionnaire in the selection of child care workers*. Technical Report 52. Park Ridge, IL: London House.

Gough, H. G. (1957). *California Psychological Inventory Manual*. Palo Alto, CA: Consulting Psychologists Press.

Gough, H. G. (1969). *Manual for the California Psychological Inventory*. Rev. ed. Palo Alto, CA: Consulting Psychologists Press.

Gough, H. G. (1975). *Manual for the California Psychological Inventory*. Rev. ed. Palo Alto, CA: Consulting Psychologists Press.

Gough, H. G., Wenk, E. A., & Rozynko, V. V. (1965). Parole outcome as predicted from the CPI, the MMPI, and a base expectancy table. *Journal of Abnormal Psychology*, 70, 432–441.

Graham, J. R. (1977). *The MMPI: A practical guide.* New York: Oxford University Press.

Groth-Marnat, G. (1984). *Handbook of psychological assessment.* New York: Van Nostrand Reinhold.

Inwald, R. (1989). How to detect those "little white lies" or "seven deadly sins" of honesty test vendors. *Corporate Security Digest,* 3 (36), 1–7.

Jackson, D. N. (1967). *Personality Research Form manual.* Goshen, NY: Research Psychologists Press.

Jones, J. W. (1979a). Predictors of prealcoholism. Paper presented at the 17th Interamerican Congress of Psychology, Lima, Peru.

Jones, J. W. (1979b). Employee alcohol abuse in the workplace. Paper presented at the Fifth Annual Convention of the Society of Police and Criminal Psychology, Chicago.

Jones, J. W. (1980). Correlates of police misconduct: Violence and alcohol use on the job. Technical Report 7. Park Ridge, IL: London House.

Jones, J. W. (1981). Personality profiles of endorsers of nuclear crime. Paper presented at the 89th Annual Convention of the American Psychological Association, Division of Military Psychology, Los Angeles.

Jones, J. W. (1983). Attitudinal correlates of employee violence. Technical Report 10. Park Ridge, IL: London House.

Jones, J. W., & Fay, L. (1987). *Predicting child abuse potential with the Personnel Selection Inventory for childcare workers.* St. Paul, MN: St. Paul Companies.

Jones, J. W., & Joy, D. S. (1987). Use of the Personnel Selection Inventory for childcare workers: A summary. Technical Report 66. Park Ridge, IL: London House.

Jones, J. W., & Terris, W. (1981). Convicted felons' attitudes toward theft, violence and illicit drug use. Paper presented at the Seventh Annual Convention of the Society of Police and Criminal Psychology, New Orleans.

Joy, D. S., & Frost, A. G. (1987). The prediction of employee performance using the Employment Productivity Index. EPI Technical Report 2. Park Ridge, IL: London House.

Joy, D. S., Frost, A. G., & Boomhower, D. (1987). Using the Personnel Selection Inventory (PSI–7S) to predict successful performance of employees in the automobile rental industry. Technical Report 55. Park Ridge, IL: London House.

Joy, D. S., Frost, A. G., & Cook, M. S. (1987). Predicting counterproductive behaviors at a major metropolitan transit authority using the Personnel Selection Inventory. Technical Report 63. Park Ridge, IL: London House.

Joy, D. S., & Rafilson, F. M. (1988a). Validation of the Personnel Selection Inventory (PSI–7S) for the grocery industry. Technical Report 68. Park Ridge, IL: London House.

Joy, D. S., & Rafilson, F. M. (1988b). Validation of the Personnel Selection Inventory for consumer electronics stores. Technical Report 71. Park Ridge, IL: London House.

Joy, D. S., & Werner, S. H. (1988). The concurrent validity of the Personnel Selection Inventory (PSI–7) in a major drug store chain. Technical Report 72. Park Ridge, IL: London House.

London House (1986). *The Employment Productivity Index.* Park Ridge, IL: London House.

London House (1980). *Personnel Selection Inventory.* Park Ridge, IL: London House.

Meehl, P. E. (1954). *Clinical versus statistical prediction*. Minneapolis: University of Minnesota Press.

Megargee, E. I. (1979). Development and validation of an MMPI-based system for classifying criminal offenders. In James N. Butcher (ed.), *New developments in the use of the MMPI* (303–324). Minneapolis: University of Minnesota Press.

Monahan, J. (1982). The prediction of violent behavior: Developments in psychology and law. *Psychology and Law*, 2, 147–176.

Moretti, D. M. (1980). Employee counterproductivity: Attitudinal predictors of industrial damage and waste. Paper presented at the Sixth Annual Meeting of the Society of Police and Criminal Psychology, Atlanta.

Moretti, D. M. (1986). The prediction of employee counterproductivity through attitude assessment. *Journal of Business and Psychology*, 1(2), 134–147.

O'Bannon, R. M., Goldinger, L. A., & Appleby, G. S. (1989). *Honesty and integrity testing: A practical guide*. Atlanta: Applied Information Resources.

Rafilson, F. M. (1988). Development of a standardized measure to predict employee productivity. *Journal of Business and Psychology*, 3, 199–213.

Sackett, P. R., Burris, L. R., & Callahan, C. (1989). Integrity testing for personnel selection: An update. *Personnel Psychology*, 42, 491–529.

Slora, K. B. (1989). An empirical approach to determining employee deviance base rates. *Journal of Business and Psychology*, 4, (2), 199–219.

Slora, K. B., & Boye, M. W. (1989). Employee theft in the supermarket industry: Final report of findings. Technical Report 2. Park Ridge, IL: London House.

Terris, W. (1979). *Attitudinal correlates of theft, violence, and drug use*. Paper presented at the 17th Interamerican Congress of Psychology, Lima, Peru.

Terris, W. (1985). Attitudinal correlates of employee integrity. *Journal of Police and Criminal Psychology*, 1(1), 60–68.

Terris, W., & Jones, J. W. (1984). Psychological correlates of employee theft in department stores. Technical Report 20. Park Ridge, IL: London House.

Walters, H. A. (1980). Dangerousness. In R. H. Woody (Ed.), *Encyclopedia of clinical assessment*, 1104–1111. San Francisco: Jossey-Bass Publishers.

Wardell, D. M. (1982). The concept of inhibition in personality theory and clinical assessment. Paper presented at the Second International Conference on the 16PF. Champaign, IL: IPAT.

White, W. C., McAdoo, W. G., & Megargee, E. I. (1973). Personality factors associated with over- and undercontrolled offenders. *Journal of Personality Assessment*, 37(5), 473–478.

Wuebker, L. J. (1987). The Safety Locus of Control scale: A construct validation study. Unpublished manuscript.

Zuckerman, M. (1975). Manual and research report for the Sensation Seeking Scale. Unpublished manuscript, 1975.

Zuckerman, M. (1979). *Sensation seeking: Beyond the optimal level of arousal*. Hillsdale, NJ: Lawrence Erlbaum Associates.

14

A Personnel Selection Approach to Industrial Safety

JOHN W. JONES

Work-related accidents, ranging from slips and falls to motor vehicle mishaps, cost employers billions of dollars every year (National Safety Council, 1983). They threaten the company's profitability due to lost production, disability payments, and higher insurance premiums (Huber, 1987). This chapter focuses on the personnel selection approach to safety, an approach that allows employers to screen job applicants for safety-sensitive positions. It reviews two personnel selection inventories developed for companies needing to staff a wide variety of safety-sensitive positions.

PERSONNEL SELECTION INVENTORY: SAFETY VERSION

The personnel selection approach allows employers to screen job applicants for positions where on-the-job injuries are easily incurred if proper safety rules and precautions are not followed. High-accident-risk applicants can be identified and screened out. Applicants identified as high risks for accidents due to individual differences in attitudes and personality can also be placed in less hazardous jobs or placed in special safety training programs designed to reduce their susceptibility to accidents. This chapter focuses on the assessment of attitudes and personality traits that research has shown are associated with differential accident susceptibility.

London House (1988) developed the Personnel Selection Inventory—Form 3S

(PSI-3S) to screen in employment applicants who exhibit high levels of safety consciousness. The PSI-3S has four subscales that can conceivably reduce industrial accident rates: the Honesty, Non-violence, Drug-avoidance, and Safety Locus of Control subscales. (The PSI-3S also has a Distortion subscale that measures job applicants' tendencies to give candid answers.) The PSI-3S subscales and their reliability coefficients are described in Table 14.1.

The Honesty subscale is traditionally used to assess applicants' potential for stealing in the workplace. However, research shows that honesty correlates with safety attitudes too (Wuebker, 1987). That is, persons with more tolerant attitudes toward theft and counterproductivity also have lower levels of safety consciousness and are more inclined to break company rules. The Non-violence subscale assesses applicants' tendencies to engage in violent, emotionally unstable behavior. This scale has predicted industrial damage and waste in past research (Moretti, 1983). Research has also linked on-the-job alcohol and drug use to industrial accidents (Jones, 1980). Hence, it can be posited that applicants who score poorer on the Drug-avoidance scale are at greater risk to have drug-related industrial accidents. Extensive validation research has been conducted on these three subscales, and they have consistently predicted a wide range of counterproductive work behaviors (cf. Terris, 1985).

The PSI-3S also includes a Safety Locus of Control scale designed to predict industrial accidents (Jones & Wuebker, 1985, 1988). The safety scale, a relatively new addition to the PSI-3S, consistently predicts a wide range of accident criteria. The scale includes test items that are based on the personality construct "locus of control" (Rotter, 1966). Applicants with "internal" safety locus of control beliefs expect a contingent relationship between personal actions and any accidents they may or may not have. Job candidates with "external" safety control orientations believe that accidents and injuries are caused by forces outside their control, such as bad luck or negligent company practices.

Ten criterion-related validation studies consistently document that internal scorers have significantly fewer on-the-job accidents than external scorers (cf. Jones & Wuebker, 1985, 1988). Moreover, two time-series studies document that companies that use the PSI-3S should expect a reduction in workplace accidents.

A 41-month time-series analysis (pre-PSI phase = 23 months; PSI phase = 18 months) was conducted with a large national trucking firm. Paid insurance losses were reduced from a monthly average of \$25,600 in the pre-PSI phase to a monthly average of \$5,400 in the PSI phase ($p < .05$). The average number of lost workdays was reduced by 50 percent: from 161 days per month in the pre-PSI phase to 79 days per month in the PSI phase ($p < .05$).

The trucking firm study was replicated in a five-year time-series study within the food processing industry. In this replication, the PSI-3S was implemented in eight milk processing and delivery companies beginning in the first quarter of 1985. The eight firms were part of the same parent company. Each location

Table 14.1
Description and Reliability of PSI-3S Subscales

Scales	Descriptions
Honesty	Measures job applicants' attitudes toward theft and counterproductivity. People who score lower on this scale generally exhibit more rumination over theft activities, more projection of theft in others, greater rationalization of theft, less punitive attitudes toward thieves, and more inter-thief loyalty. Split-half reliability = .95. Examples of Honesty scale correlates include: theft apprehensions; admissions (self-report and polygraph exams); dollar value of thefts of cash, merchandise, and property; number of criminal acts committed; number of minutes of unauthorized work break extensions; convicted felon vs. job applicant status; prior criminal arrests; supervisor ratings for counterproductivity; cash drawer shortages; company shrinkage; terminations for theft; dysfunctional turnover; number of disciplinary actions for company cash mishandling; disregard for company rules in general; and low productivity.
Non-violence	Measures work applicants' tendencies toward on-the-job violent behavior and other related forms of counterproductivity, such as physical assault, vandalism of company property and merchandise, damage and waste of company materials, argumentativeness, and poor customer service. Split-half reliability = .87. Examples of Non-violence scale correlates include: number of violent acts committed; dollar amount of damaged company property and merchandise; physical assault of co-workers, supervisors, and/or customers; on-the-job waste of company materials and supplies; violence admissions

Table 14.1 (continued)

Scales	Descriptions
	(polygraph exams and self-reports); and poor customer service.
Drug-avoidance	Measures job applicants' tendencies toward illicit drug abuse in the workplace. Assesses risk of drug-related industrial accidents. Split-half reliability = .90. Examples of Drug-avoidance scale correlates include: weekly alcohol consumption rate; number of times intoxicated; coming to work hungover or intoxicated; number of on-the-job drug/alcohol use; self-reported on-the-job alcohol abuse; using and selling illegal drugs; industrial accidents; and unacceptable urinalysis results.
Safety-control	Measures a set of attitudes endorsed by applicants with a history of serious and costly accidents and injuries. Assesses if applicants feel responsible for and committed to accident prevention. Split-half reliability = .85. Examples of Safety Scale correlates include: injuries (minor, major); terminations due to unsafe behaviors; level of safety education; unsafe workplace; medical costs of workplace accidents; supervisors' ratings of safe performance; and driving safety.

employed approximately 35 to 40 employees. The employees within each company basically shared duties when it came to processing, packaging, and delivering milk and dairy products. From March 1985 through November 1986, the eight companies collectively processed over 200 PSI–3S's. They hired approximately 80 applicants who passed all of the PSI–3S subscales. Based on PSI–3S scores, these applicants were classified as being at low risk to have workplace accidents.

A single-factor repeated-measures research design was used. The single factor was the year in which the accidents were reported. Four years were studied: 1983, 1984, 1985, and 1986. Since the PSI–3S was implemented in the first quarter of 1985, it was predicted that a significant reduction in accidents would be observed in 1986. The dependent variable was the total frequency of worker compensation accidents recorded for each company during each of the four years studied. Accident frequency rates were obtained from computer databases maintained by the company's insurance agent.

The average accident rate for years 1983, 1984, 1985, and 1986 equaled 17.13 (SD = 11.04), 12.25 (SD = 9.22), 13.75 (SD = 4.86), and 6.5 (SD = 4.0), respectively. These between-year differences were statistically significant using a repeated-measures analysis of variance (F[3/21] = 6.01, p < .005). Post hoc analyses, using the Duncan multiple range test, revealed that the 1986 average was significantly lower than the 1985 (p < .05), the 1984 (p < .05), and the 1983 (p < .01) averages. No other accident reduction programs were introduced during this period. Therefore, since the results were in the predicted direction, they support the notion that the PSI–3S was a major contributing factor in the reduction of industrial accidents. These results are summarized in Figure 14.1.

The parent company was unwilling to provide exact figures on the costs of the worker compensation claims for the eight PSI–3S companies; however, they provided ballpark figures suggesting that total accident-related losses were approximately $1.3 million in 1983, $900,000 in 1984, $1.1 million in 1985, and only $300,000 in 1986. These findings are promising and might reflect the financial impact of the PSI–3S on the reduction of insurance losses.

The studies reviewed suggest that accident reduction through personnel selection is a promising new approach to corporate safety. Personnel selection systems like the PSI–3S can supplement the more traditional corporate safety programs. Yet the PSI–3S is a multidimensional selection system that has both industrial security and industrial safety applications. The safety inventory described in the next section was designed solely to control workplace accidents.

THE EMPLOYEE SAFETY INVENTORY

The Employee Safety Inventory (ESI) is a multiscaled predictor of on-the-job safety designed to help employers identify good safety attitudes in both job candidates and current employees.

The ESI is comprised of four diagnostic scales, one validity scale, and one overall Composite Safety Index. All ESI scales and the composite exhibit useful levels of reliability, often exceeding 0.80 (Boye, Slora & Jones, 1989). The ESI contains the following scales:

1. Safety Control: Differentiates individuals who take responsibility for maintaining a safe working environment from those who typically blame others or fate for their accidents.

Figure 14.1
Average Accident Rate, 1983–1986

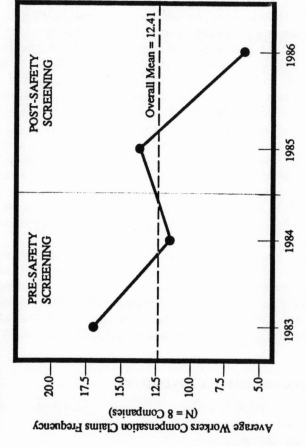

2. Risk Avoidance: Assesses tendencies to engage in high-risk, dangerous, and thrill-seeking behavior.

3. Stress Tolerance: Measures an individual's ongoing experience with stress and the ability to cope with it. Highly stressed individuals tend to have more accidents.

4. Driver Attitudes: A supplemental scale that assesses an individual's attitudes toward safe driving behavior.

5. Validity/Distortion: Indicates the extent to which an individual responds to the ESI in a socially desirable manner. Low scores indicate a tendency to exaggerate positive traits and minimize negative qualities.

The Composite Safety Index summarizes the results of each individual score to help evaluate the overall safety attitudes of an employee or applicant. Companies base all hiring, placement, and training decisions on the ESI composite Index.

A partial listing of ESI validity studies is provided in Table 14.2. Useful levels of validity were found across a wide variety of studies. Since the ESI is a relatively new personnel selection system, local validation studies are recommended. The ESI can be used by companies interested in hiring a safety-conscious work force.

CONCLUSION

This chapter has described two personnel selection systems that can be used to identify job applicants at highest risk for costly on-the-job accidents. High-accident-risk applicants could receive additional safety training or be selectively placed into safer jobs. Additional research on the contributions of personnel selection to industrial accident prevention is warranted.

REFERENCES

Behrens, G. M., Slora, K. B., & Jones, J. W. (1988). Construct validity of a standardized measure of risk avoidance. Technical Report ESI-S004. Park Ridge, IL: London House.

Boye, M. W., Slora, K. B., & Jones, J. W. (1989). Reliability of the Employee Safety Inventory. Technical Report ESI-S007. Park Ridge, IL: London House.

Huber, P. (1987). Injury litigation and liability insurance dynamics. *Science*, 238, 31–36.

Jones, J. W. (1980). Attitudinal correlates of employees' deviance: Theft, alcohol use, and non-prescribed drug use. *Psychological Reports*, 47, 71–77.

Jones, J. W., Britton, C. F., & Slora, K. B. (1988). The relationship of the Employee Safety Inventory to drug and alcohol use. Technical Report ESI-S002. Park Ridge, IL: London House.

Jones, J. W., & Slora, K. B. (1988). Predictive validation study of the Safety Control scale. Technical Report ESI-S001. Park Ridge, IL: London House.

Jones, J. W., Slora, K. B., & Boye, M. W. (1989). Relationship of Employee Safety Inventory scores to urinalysis results: A clinical case study. Technical Report ESI-S008. Park Ridge, IL: London House.

Table 14.2
Partial Summary of ESI Validation Research

Study	Sample	Design	Criteria	Findings
Jones & Slora (1988)	380 grocery store job applicants	3-month predictive validity using only the Safety Control scale	62 employees with record of on-the-job accident in personnel file versus 318 employees with no record	$t = 2.9, p < .01$
Jones, Britton & Slora (1988)	101 employed college students	Postdictive, criterion-related study with Risk Avoidance scale	Miscellaneous measures of self-reported illicit drug use	$r = .30, p < .001$ with frequency of on-the-job drug/alcohol use
Slora, Boye & Jones (1988)	63 employed students	Construct validity	Overall accident susceptibility scale derived from the MMPI. The scale measures distractability and social maladjustment.	Safety Control: $r = .57, p < .01$ Risk Avoidance: $r = .63, p < .001$ Stress Tolerance: $r = .65, p < .001$ Driver Attitudes: $r = .48, p < .001$ Composite Index: $r = .72, p < .001$
Behrens, Slora & Jones (1988)	482 retail applicants	Concurrent validity study with Risk Avoidance scale	Various valid measures of counterproductivity	$r = .57, p < .01$ with Honesty $r = .44, p < .01$ with Non-violence $r = .43, p < .01$ with Drug-avoidance
Rafilson & Rospenda (1988)	156 manufacturing employees	Postdictive, criterion-related study with Safety Control scale	On-the-job accident history	$r = .39, p < .001$

192

Study	Sample	Study Type	Criterion	Results
Slora, Boye & Jones (1989a)	83 publishing company employees and associates	Postdictive, criterion-related study with Driver Attitudes scale	21-item safe driving behavior checklist	$r = .24$, $p < .05$, speeding 25 mph over limit $r = .22$, $p < .05$, moving violation ticket $r = .24$, $p < .05$, a car accident with damage $r = .38$, $p < .01$, personal injury from car accident
Jones, Slora & Boye (1989)	13 manufacturing employees	Case study of illicit drug use	Urinalysis results of drugs in system (2 employees had positive urinalysis results)	$r = -.75$, $p < .05$
Slora, Boye & Jones (1989b)	90 drivers from a food processing company	Postdictive, criterion-related study with entire ESI battery	Comprehensive checklist of safe driving behavior	Safety Control: $r = .28$, $p < .01$ Risk Avoidance: $r = .33$, $p < .001$ Driver Attitudes: $r = .26$, $p < .01$ Composite Index: $r = .26$, $p < .01$

Jones, J. W., & Wuebker, L. J. (1985). Development and validation of the Safety Locus of Control Scale. *Perceptual and Motor Skills*, 61, 151–161.

Jones, J. W., & Wuebker, L. J. (1988). Accident prevention through personnel selection. *Journal of Business and Psychology*, 3(2), 187–198.

London House (1988). *The Personnel Selection Inventory: Form 3S*. Park Ridge, IL: London House Press.

Moretti, D. (1983). Employee counterproductivity: Attitudinal predictors of industrial damage and waste. Paper presented at the Annual Meeting of the Society of Police and Criminal Psychology, Atlanta, October.

National Safety Council (1983). *Accident facts—1983 Edition*. Chicago, IL: National Safety Council.

Rafilson, F. M., & Rospenda, K. M. (1988). Concurrent validation study of the Safety scale. Technical Report ESI-S005. Park Ridge, IL: London House.

Rotter, J. B. (1966). Generalized expectancies for internal versus external control of reinforcement. *Psychological Monographs* 80, 1, Whole No. 609.

Slora, K. B., Boye, M. W., & Jones, J. W. (1988). Construct validation study of the Employee Safety Inventory. Technical Report ESI-S003. Park Ridge, IL: London House.

Slora, K. B., Boye, M. W., & Jones, J. W. (1989a). The relation of the Employee Safety Inventory to safe driving behaviors among delivery drivers. Technical Report ESI-S009. Park Ridge, IL: London House.

Slora, K. B., Boye, M. W., & Jones, J. W. (1989b). The relation of the ESI Driver Attitudes scale to safe driving practices. Technical Report ESI-S006. Park Ridge, IL: London House.

Terris, W. (1985). *Employee theft: Research, theory, and applications*. Park Ridge, IL: London House Press.

Wuebker, L. J. (1987). The Safety Locus of Control scale: A construct validation study. Unpublished manuscript.

15

Reducing Turnover through Personnel Selection

DENNIS S. JOY

High rates of employee turnover have plagued many business organizations for years. Turnover leads to morale problems, disrupts team functioning, and results in high retraining costs. In 1980 the average monthly turnover rate for all companies was approximately 2 percent (Bureau of National Affairs, 1980), for an annual rate of approximately 24 percent. In an average company, turnover among newly recruited college graduates can be as high as 50 percent during the first five years of employment (*Fortune*, 1981). This is supported by more recent statistics that indicate the average tenure in current occupations for all ages and all occupations is 6.6 years (*Monthly Labor Review*, 1988). And, in high-turnover segments of the labor market (e.g., young entry-level sales and service workers, 16–24 year olds) the average tenure is only 1.7 years. The annual turnover rate among part-time clerks and cashiers in the convenience store industry can be as high as 134 percent (NACS, 1988).

COST OF TURNOVER

High rates of dysfunctional employee turnover can represent substantial and unacceptably high costs of doing business. Frequent consequences are administrative costs associated with recruitment, selection, training, and development (Cascio, 1982; Mowday, Porter & Steers, 1982). Cascio (1982) cites replacement costs for various insurance company personnel ranging from approximately $13,000 for a claims investigator to approximately $400,000 for an experienced sales manager. Some figures noted by Rosse (1990) indicate that replacement costs alone, as a percentage of annual salary, can range from 17 percent for hourly workers through 25 percent for salaried employees to 50 to 88 percent for department managers.

The rapidly increasing shortage of qualified entry-level workers may exacerbate the turnover problem in the foreseeable future (U.S. Department of Labor, 1988). This may be especially true in the retail and service sectors of the economy. A result of the aging population is a greater demand for goods and services. This increased demand could create 9 million new jobs in the next ten years (U.S. Department of Labor, 1988). New strategies for controlling turnover need to be explored.

THEORIES OF TURNOVER

Most research on the psychology of turnover has aimed at understanding the turnover decision process of job incumbents (e.g., Berte, Moretti, Jusko & Leonard, 1981; Cotton & Tuttle, 1986; Mobley, 1977; Steers & Mowday, 1981). While studying the attributes, beliefs, and intentions of job incumbents is important, recommendations stemming from this research (e.g., increased compensation in salary and nonwage benefits, reduced workloads, schedule changes) can often be costly or difficult to implement.

Recently personnel selection researchers (e.g., McEvoy & Cascio, 1985) have encouraged an examination of strategies that focus on job applicants rather than incumbents. They reason that preemployment approaches to reducing turnover can often be easier to implement and less costly. One possible strategy, preemployment selection using psychological testing, has been a cost-effective procedure in reducing other forms of employee counterproductivity for a number of years (cf. Jones & Terris, 1989; Jones & Wuebker, 1988; Joy, 1988, 1989; Werner & Jones, 1989). Therefore, some of the major theories of employee turnover were examined to see what implications they might have for the development of a standardized psychological inventory that assesses the attitudes and beliefs of job applicants that might predict their turnover risk.

Over the past three decades, several comprehensive research reviews and conceptual models of employee job turnover have appeared (March and Simon, 1958; Mobley, 1977; Mobley et al., 1979; Mowday, Porter & Steers, 1982; Porter & Steers, 1973; Price, 1977; Rosse, 1990; Steers & Mowday, 1981). The various conceptual models attempt to explain the processes that influence employees' decisions about whether to stay at or leave an organization. Ultimately, these models attempt to predict behavior (i.e., actual staying or leaving). Although there are differences among the models, they all indicate, in some form, significant relationships between levels of employee job dissatisfaction, counterproductive job attitudes, employee intentions to quit or stay, the evaluation of alternative job opportunities, work adaptation strategies, and eventual turnover.

The bulk of the literature points to three major psychological models of turnover: decision making, adaptation, and counterproductive attitudes models. The decision-making model (e.g., Mobley, 1977) views turnover as a rational and conscious decision-making process with affective and motivational components. The adaptation model (e.g., Rosse, 1990) postulates that the turnover process does not necessarily have to be conscious. This model views turnover as one of several alternative maladaptive attempts to cope with work life. Finally, with the "counterproductive attitudes" model (e.g., Joy & Jones, 1989), turnover, like other types of counterproductive work behaviors (e.g., theft, intentional damage of company property, poor work performance), is predominantly the result of associated counterproductive beliefs, values, and attitudes.

Decision-Making Model

This model is primarily a cognitive choice model, with most decisions to quit a job made for career advancement reasons. One model elucidated by Mobley (1977) is more complex than the others since its goal is to provide detailed intermediate linkages between attitudes and behaviors. Through these linkages, the model attempts to develop a better understanding of how job dissatisfaction leads (or does not lead) to job turnover.

In Mobley's model the sequential linkage for turnover proceeds in basically the following fashion: (1) an evaluation of one's existing job, (2) experienced job dissatisfaction, (3) thoughts of quitting, (4) evaluation of the expected utility of job search and the cost of quitting one's current job, (5) the intention to search for alternatives, (6) the search for alternatives, (7) the evaluation of alternatives, (8) the comparison of available alternatives to the current job, (9) the intention to quit, and (10) quitting. While much of this model involves the evaluation of alternative situations, there are critical choice points involving thinking of quitting and intention to search for a new job and to quit one's present job. While there are numerous intermediate linkages, intention to quit is the sole and last determinant of actual quitting. Therefore, intentions to quit should be more accurate and powerful predictors of turnover than is job dissatisfaction.

On the basis of a subsequent literature review, Mobley (1982) presented an expanded turnover model with intentions to stay or leave occupying a central position. These intentions were viewed as more important and direct determinants of turnover than was job dissatisfaction. Another feature of Mobley's model, albeit not as central, is that turnover is but one of several alternative forms of job withdrawal. Other ways of reacting to job dissatisfaction could be increased absenteeism and passive job behavior (i.e., poor performance), to name two. While Mobley allows for these alternative forms of employee withdrawal, they are not a formal part of his model.

Other major decision-making models (e.g., Steers & Mowday, 1981; Mowday, Porter & Steers, 1982) propose more direct connections between attitudes and behavior. These models, although they ignore many of the intermediate linkages in Mobley's model, also treat intentions to leave as the major immediate antecedent of an individual's leaving. Historically this direct link between intentions to leave and leaving has been shown consistently to be significant (Ajzen & Fishbein, 1972, 1977; Hom & Hulin, 1981; Hom, Katerberg & Hulin, 1979; Lee & Mowday, 1987; Michaels & Spector, 1982). One meta-analysis (Steel & Ovaile, 1984) indicated the average correlation between intention to quit and quitting to be r = .50. This link has been shown to be of such magnitude that in some cases intentions to search and intentions to quit have been treated as the criterion measures of actual turnover (cf. Berte et al., 1981).

A somewhat limiting factor, from the perspective of this review, is that the decision-making model is specific to job incumbents. However, there seems to be no logical reason that the model could not be expanded to include job applicants. An expanded model would place applicants in the position of evaluating prospective jobs along with available alternatives. If there are no available alternatives, applicants may accept a job even though they anticipate a fair degree of dissatisfaction. Conceivably this group of applicants would be at higher risk to quit a job as soon as another alternative becomes available, the turnover decision being formulated even before hiring.

Adaptation Model

Adaptation theory (Rosse, 1990) deals more fully with general classes of behaviors used to cope with work life. Rosse examines several classes of behavior: attempts to increase job outcomes (e.g., theft, moonlighting on the job), psychological job withdrawal (e.g., lowered work performance, use of drugs), specific change behaviors (e.g., transfer, unionization activity), and behavioral avoidance and withdrawal (e.g., absenteeism, tardiness, turnover). These last two classes include all behaviors that serve to increase the psychological or physical distance between employees and their work roles. Rosse treats these behavioral classes as habitual modes of adjustment or adaptation.

The several classes of behavior are subsumed under two general factors. The first factor represents positive "approach" or "commitment" behaviors, and the second represents a negative syndrome of "psychological and behavioral withdrawal." The implication of this model is that there are individual differences (i.e., personality and attitude) among employees and applicants as to their dominant mode of adjustment to work life (cf. Farrell, 1983).

Counterproductive Attitude Model

A counterproductive attitude model of turnover is an outgrowth of the Ajzen and Fishbein (1977) theory of attitude-behavior relationships. These researchers found that strong attitude-behavior relations are found only when there is high correspondence between the attitudinal qualities measured and the behavior being predicted. Hence, in order to predict a specific behavior with any reasonable degree of accuracy, one needs to measure the attitudes toward that act. This model has worked quite well when used to predict many forms of counterproductive work behavior such as theft (Jones, 1989; Joy, 1988; McDaniel & Jones, 1988), drug use on the job (Jones, 1980), intentional damage and destruction of company property (Moretti, 1986), and work-related accidents and injuries (Jones & Wuebker, 1988). Job applicants at greatest risk to turnover would tend to believe that this form of physical job withdrawal is common, acceptable, and a frequent way of coping at work.

What can be concluded from the review of the three models is that turnover is multidetermined and is not just a simple case of dissatisfied employees leaving or staying on a job. At a minimum, there are at least two types of turnover: career advancement turnover and counterproductive turnover. Career advancement turnover, a more rational type, typically occurs because an individual's dominant mode of thought is that it is normal and even desirable to leave a job as soon as a better alternative becomes available. This sort of individual is more likely to believe that the best way to advance one's career is to stay with one company for as short a period of time as necessary. Counterproductive turnover may occur when a person's dominant mode of adjustment to work life is to withdraw psychologically or physically from a stressful or burdensome situation. This mode of adjustment is supported by counterproductive attitudes, habits, values, and belief systems. Both of these modes should be measurable in a preemployment setting. All three models of turnover served as reference points when writing items for the Tenure scale.

TENURE SCALE DEVELOPMENT

The strategy adopted to generate experimental test items followed a prototype method of personality scale construction (Boughton, 1984). This method calls for achieving a close match between attitude items and criterion behaviors. With this approach, a group of experts on turnover generate test items and then rate them on the probability that they will predict actual turnover behavior. In this case, the experts were familiar with the three major theories of turnover.

Based on the reviewed theoretical and empirical work, several major themes were identified and used to generate prototypical items: (1) intentions to quit, (2) beliefs about the best way to advance one's career, (3) anticipated job satisfaction, (4) physical withdrawal as the dominant mode of adjusting to work life, (5) beliefs about what is common or normative behavior among workers, and (6) beliefs about the appropriateness of job change behaviors. Tenure scale items were developed to measure each of these dimensions of the turnover syndrome. The psychometric strategy of attempting a close match between attitude items and turnover behavior has been well described by Ajzen and Fishbein (1977) and was used to construct all items.

Based on this approach, 125 content-valid items, positively and negatively worded for both career advancement and counterproductive turnover, were developed. All items were then rated by a panel of 10 industrial psychologists and personnel experts with extensive experience in both turnover research and personnel selection test development. Each expert was asked to rate the extent to which each item was likely to predict turnover within an organization on a nine-point Likert-type scale ranging from "very unlikely" to predict turnover (rating = 1) to "very likely" to predict turnover (rating = 9). A final set of 22 items (half positively worded and half negatively worded), which were consistently rated as most likely to predict turnover, were selected for the research version of the scale.

A six-point Likert type scale ranging from "Agree Very Much" to "Disagree Very Much" was initially used for the response options for the items in the research version. Then item scores were weighted −1,0, or +1 based on a median split for each item. Item scores below the median in the negative direction were scored −1. Items scores above the median in the positive direction were scored +1. Items scores at the median were scored 0. When item scores were summed, a constant was added to the raw scale score to eliminate negative score values. Hence, the final raw score for the 22-item version could theoretically range from 1 to 45. Higher scores mean less turnover risk. When these raw scores are converted to standard scores, a mean of 50 and a standard deviation of 20 are used.

From these 22 items, two briefer scale versions (containing 12 and 18 items) were created. The 12-item set was based on the 12 items with the highest item–total score correlations. The 18-item set was based on the 18 items with the highest item–total score correlations. The result was one long version of the Tenure scale along with two shorter forms of it. These scales were designed to measure turnover risk and predict the likelihood an applicant, if hired, would remain with an organization.

STUDY 1

The purpose of this study was to begin to establish both the construct and criterion-related validity of the Tenure scale. Construct validity can be established by correlating Tenure scores with subjects' self-reported estimates of quitting their job and their self-reported commitment to their company. Criterion-related validity can be established by correlating Tenure scores with actual job search behaviors.

EMPLOYEE SAMPLE

Forty-one employees—17 professional and management personnel and 24 clerical and support personnel—from a midwestern publishing company participated in the initial validation study. Thirty-two were full time and 9 were part time. Sampling was nonrandom in that those employees available on a particular day were asked to participate.

PROCEDURE

All subjects anonymously completed the 22-item Tenure scale and a self-report questionnaire dealing with aspects of turnover and job commitment. The criterion checklist was divided into four sections:

1. *Job Tenure*: These dimensions assessed length of employment on each person's prior and current job, as well as future intended tenure on the current job. All variables were coded in months. Higher scores mean longer tenure.

2. *Likelihood of Quitting Present Job*: This assessment was rated on a five-point Likert-type scale ranging from "Very Low" to "Very High" during the course of the next 3, 6, 9, and 12 months. It was designed as a measure of intention to quit. Higher scores mean stronger intention to quit one's job.

3. *Job Search Behaviors*: These dimensions assessed job search behavior. The first set of items were self-reports of the frequency of actual search behaviors within the last year (e.g., looking in want ads for another job, talking to friends or relatives about getting another job, filling out applications for new jobs, missing scheduled work days to look for a new job, and interviewing for a new job). The second set assessed intended job search behaviors within the next year. Items in this latter section asked whether a person would engage in various search behaviors and were coded on a six-point Likert-type scale ranging from "Definitely No" to "Definitely Yes." Higher scores mean more frequent job search behaviors.

4. *Job Commitment Intentions*: This dimension assessed intentions to engage in future behaviors that would increase the probability that an individual will become more committed to the current company and stay on this job (e.g., making efforts to become promoted at their company, taking training classes to increase their chances of success in their company, becoming more involved at work by taking on more challenging work assignments). These were also coded on a six-point Likert-type scale ranging from "Definitely No" to "Definitely Yes." Higher scores mean stronger commitment.

RESULTS AND DISCUSSION

Reliability

Coefficient alpha reliability estimates were computed for each Tenure scale version. These reliability estimates, along with interscale correlations, are summarized in Table 15.1. Reliabilities ranged from .83 for the 18-item version to .87 for the 12-item version. These estimates are certainly above acceptable levels for a new test and indicate the items all tend to measure the same underlying construct. Since the 12-item version was based on items with the highest item–total score correlations, it yields slightly higher reliability. Descriptive statistics for each scale are summarized in Table 15.2.

Table 15.1
Interscale Correlation Matrix and Reliability Coefficients

	12	18	22
12	.87		
18	.97	.83	
22	.96	.99	.84

Reliabilities (alpha) are in main diagonal which is underlined.

Table 15.2
Raw Score Descriptive Statistics for the 12-, 18-, and 22-Item Tenure Scales

Tenure Scale (# Items)	N	Range	$\bar{X}$	S.D.
12	41	5 - 22	15.58	7.32
18	41	7 - 34	23.19	8.32
22	41	9 - 43	27.12	9.13

Validity

Preliminary validity results are divided into four sections, showing the relationship between the three Tenure scale versions and (1) job tenure (past, present, and intended tenure with current company), (2) estimated likelihood of quitting their job at various points within the next year, (3) job search activities (past behavior and future intentions), and (4) job commitment intentions.

Job Tenure. The relationships between Tenure scale scores and the four criterion measures of job tenure were analyzed. These measures, in months, were how long the subjects held their last job, how long subjects have been on their current job, and how long they intended to stay on that job. A fourth composite criterion was also constructed: the sum of the three tenure variables. The reliability (alpha) of this composite was .91. The descriptive statistics for the tenure criterion measures are shown in Table 15.3.

Table 15.4 shows the correlations between Tenure scale scores and each criterion measure of job tenure. Subjects who scored higher on each version of the Tenure scale also reported significantly longer tenure on their last job ($r = .31$ to $.32$; $p < .05$), as well as significantly longer tenure in their current job ($r = .40$ to $.43$; $p < .01$). Higher scorers also intended having longer continued tenure in their current job ($r = .46$ to $.50$; $p < .001$) and had a higher total tenure criterion composite ($r = .39$ to $.41$; $p < .01$).

Table 15.3
Descriptive Statistics for Job Tenure Criterion Variables

	Variable	N	Range	$\bar{X}$	S.D.
1.	Tenure Last Job (months)	41	2 - 120	33.40	31.26
2.	Tenure Present Job (months)	41	1 - 132	18.68	29.06
3.	Intended Tenure Present Job (months)	41	2 - 240	54.11	45.42
4.	Total Tenure Composite	41	5 - 261	84.30	68.50

Table 15.4
Correlations between Tenure Scales and Job Tenure Criterion

Tenure Scale	Tenure Past Job	Tenure Present Job	Intended Future Tenure	Total Tenure Composite
12	.32*	.43**	.46***	.40**
18	.31*	.40**	.46***	.39**
22	.32*	.40**	.50***	.41**

```
  * P < .05
 ** P < .01
*** P < .001
```

N = 41 in all cases

These findings represent important links with turnover theory. Length of service has been shown to be one of the better single predictors of turnover risk (e.g., Cotton & Tuttle, 1986; Mangione, 1973). That is, longer tenure means less risk. Also, since intentions have been shown to be the best predictor of actual turnover (e.g., Lee & Mowday, 1987), the scale's ability to measure or predict intended tenure of incumbents or applicants is critical.

Likelihood of Quitting Present Job. The four items assessing the subjects' estimates of the likelihood they would quit their job in the next 3, 6, 9, and 12 months were summed into one composite index of intent to quit. The reliability of this composite (alpha) was .95. Results of the correlational analysis are shown in Table 15.5.

Tenure scale scores from each version were significantly related to subjects'

Table 15.5
Correlations between Tenure Scales and Likelihood of Quitting Job within the Next Year

Tenure Scale	Likelihood of Quitting
12	− .35**
18	− .32**
22	− .30**

* P < .05
** P < .01

N = 41 in all cases

self-reports of their expected intent to quit their job at some time in the next year (r = -.30 to -.35; $p < .05$ to $p < .01$). Low scorers on the Tenure scale, who are at greater risk to turnover, reported a greater likelihood that they would quit their job within the next year. This finding, like those in the previous section, is important because it connects scores on the Tenure scale to intentions to leave.

Job Search Behaviors. Since the literature documents a link among actual search, intended search, and job turnover, the relationship between Tenure scale scores and measures of job search was examined. Two composite job search criterion variables were developed from the individual job search items. The first, actual job search, was based on eight self-report items assessing frequency of actual job search behaviors within the last year. The second, intended job search, was based on eight similar item scores on a Likert-type scale asking for the likelihood of engaging in search behaviors in the next year. The reliabilities (alpha) of those two composites were .76 and .66, respectively. Results of the correlational analyses are shown in Table 15.6.

Significant relationships were found between the 12- and 18-item versions of the Tenure scale and reported frequency of prior job search behaviors (r = − .34 and − .33; $p < .05$). While the correlation between the 22-item version and prior search just missed significance at the .05 level, it was in the expected direction. Thus, low scorers on the Tenure scale reported more frequent job search behaviors within the last year.

Significant relationships were also found between each version of the Tenure scale and intended future search behaviors (r = − .47 and − .50; $p < .001$). Low scorers on the Tenure scale reported a greater likelihood that they intended to search for a new job within the next year. These results further support the

Table 15.6
Correlations between Tenure Scales and Measures of Job Search

Tenure Scale	Prior Job Search Behaviors	Future Intentions To Search
12	– .34*	– .50***
18	– .33*	– .48***
22	– .31	– .47***

  * P < .05
 ** P < .01
*** P < .001

N = 41 in all cases

Table 15.7
Correlations between Tenure Scales and a Composite Measure of Intended Job Commitment ($N = 41$)

Tenure Scale	Job Commitment Intentions
12	.52***
18	.51***
22	.50***

  * P < .05
 ** P < .01
*** P < .001

N = 41 in all cases

validity of this scale since relationships with established measures of turnover risk, psychological and behavioral precursors of actual turnover, are documented.

Job Commitment Intentions. A single job commitment intentions composite was created from the three future job commitment items. The reliability of this composite (alpha) was .92. Results of the correlational analysis between this composite and the three versions of the Tenure scale are presented in Table 15.7. Significant relationships were found between each Tenure scale and intended job commitment (r = .50 to .52; p <.001). In each case high scorers on the Tenure scale indicated they were more likely to engage in job commitment behaviors in the upcoming year. Thus, another important link between the Tenure scale and turnover theory is established. Engaging in behaviors that reflect greater organizational commitment and strengthening one's position within the company could be considered the opposite of deciding one wants to leave an organization. Thus, intended job commitment represents lower turnover risk.

The results of study 1 provide initial support for the validity of the Tenure scale as a measure of turnover risk. Also, several links were established to criteria of importance in theories of job turnover behavior. High scorers on each version of the Tenure scale reported (1) longer tenure in their past and current job and longer intended tenure on their current job; (2) less likelihood that they will quit their job in the next year; (3) a lower frequency of past job search behaviors and less likelihood of search for a new job in the future; and (4) a greater likelihood of engaging in job commitment behaviors in the future. Conversely, low scorers on the Tenure scale reported (1) shorter tenure on their past and current job and shorter intended tenure on their current job; (2) a greater likelihood that they will quit their job in the future; (3) a higher frequency of past job search behaviors and a greater likelihood of searching for a new job in the future; and (4) less likelihood of engaging in future job commitment behaviors.

In a replication study, Joy, Werner, and Rospenda (1989) administered the Tenure scale and the same self-report criterion checklist used in study 1 to a sample of 58 employed college students. Statistically significant relationships were found between Tenure scale scores and expected tenure on their current job (r = .56; p < .01), likelihood of quitting current job in the next year (r = − .41; p < .01), and future job search intentions (r = − .61; p <.01). These results serve to cross-validate the findings in study 1 and suggest that future research on the Tenure scale is warranted.

STUDY 2

Study 1 demonstrated significant relationships between the Tenure scale and measures of tenure and turnover risk. Study 2 was conducted to expand these results and the results of the Joy et al. (1989) study by assessing the relationship between the Tenure scale and other measures of turnover risk.

Table 15.8 summarizes a conceptual model of job withdrawal (cf. Rosse, 1990). This model is comprised of two major factors: psychological withdrawal, ranging from inattention to job burnout, and behavioral withdrawal, ranging from tardiness to turnover. Turnover can be viewed as the final behavioral outcome, with the other elements comprising varying degrees of turnover risk. In this model, poor performance, like absenteeism and short tenure, is also viewed as one form of disengagement or job withdrawal (cf. McEvoy & Cascio, 1987; Mowday, Porter & Steers, 1982). Poor performers can be viewed as

Table 15.8
Conceptual Model of Job Withdrawal

I. Psychological Withdrawal

      A. Inattention
      B. Intoxication
      C. Feign Illness
      D. Feign Injury
      E. Exhaustion
      F. Apathy
      G. Job Burnout

II. Behavioral Withdrawal

      A. Poor Performance
      B. Work Slowdowns
      C. Tardiness
      D. Absenteeism
      E. Property Damage
      F. Turnover

Job withdrawal ranges from lack of attention to one's job duties to acts which slow down work to actual turnover.

moving away from job duties and responsibilities. This is similar in consequence to an employee's withdrawing from job demands due to chronic tardiness or excessive absenteeism. It was hypothesized that Tenure scale scores would be significantly lower for employees who were engaging in any form of job withdrawal behavior.

EMPLOYEE SAMPLE

One hundred and ninety-two hotel service personnel—53 males and 139 females from 21 geographically diverse properties—completed the 12-item version of the Tenure scale. Raw scores on the scale were then converted to normalized standard scores. These scores are based on a distribution with a mean of 50 and standard deviation of 20.

PROCEDURE

After testing was completed, supervisors were asked to provide performance evaluations, attendance records, and length of employment data for each employee in the study. Based on this information and for each criterion variable, employees were classified into three following categories: (1) top, middle, or bottom 33 percentile groups on an overall supervisory performance rating, (2) top, middle, or bottom 33 percentile groups on absences adjusted for the number of months employed, and (3) rankings for the number of months employed at

Table 15.9
Analysis of Variance (ANOVA) Results: Tenure Scale Standard Scores as a Function of Employee Turnover Risk Categories

Turnover-Risk Level	N	M	SD	F	p
(1) Highest Risk	21	40.81	16.90	2.93	< .01
(2) Moderately High Risk	19	39.00	16.87		
(3) Moderate Risk	30	44.87	17.79		
(4) Moderate Risk	23	51.69	15.97		
(5) Moderately Low Risk	14	44.07	16.21		
(6) Lowest Risk	19	55.32	14.20		
Total	126*	46.04	17.12		

*Total sample size reduced because of missing data.

the hotels (i.e., less than six months, six months to one year, one to two years, or greater than two years). Finally, composite criterion scores were created by summing the category scores obtained on some or all of the individual criterion variables. This procedure yielded the following job withdrawal or turnover risk composites: (1) performance and absenteeism per quarter plus length of employment, (2) performance and length of employment, (3) absenteeism per quarter plus length of employment, and (4) performance plus absenteeism per quarter.

RESULTS

For the primary analysis, employees were classified into six turnover risk groups based on the performance-absenteeism-tenure composite. Groups ranged from highest turnover risk ($N = 21$) (bottom percentile on performance, most absences per quarter, less than six months' tenure) to lowest turnover risk ($N = 19$) (top percentile on performance, least absences per quarter, over two years' tenure). Group sizes, means, and standard deviations for each group are shown in Table 15.9.

Results of an analysis of variance indicated significant differences among Tenure scale scores for the six groups of employees (F [5, 120] = 2.93; $p <$ .01). These results indicated that employees at greater risk to turnover scored significantly lower on the Tenure scale than did employees at lower risk to turnover.

Table 15.10
Comparison of Tenure Scale Standard Scores of High- and Low-Turnover-Risk Employees, by Performance and Length of Employment

Turnover Risk Category	N	Mean	SD	t	p
High Risk	25	43.36	14.96	3.16	< .01
Low Risk	32	55.06	12.96		

Table 15.11
Comparison of Tenure Scale Standard Scores of High- and Low-Turnover-Risk Employees, by Absenteeism and Length of Employment

Turnover Risk Category	N	Mean	SD	t	p
High Risk	29	39.48	17.06	2.63	< .01
Low Risk	21	52.43	17.37		

A series of secondary post hoc analyses examined differences in Tenure scale scores of the highest- and lowest-turnover-risk groups on each of the remaining three turnover risk composites. The first turnover risk classification was determined by performance appraisal scores and length of employment on the present job. Low-risk employees ($N = 32$) had performance reviews in the top percentile and had been employed for one year or more. High-risk employees ($N = 25$) had performance reviews in the bottom percentile and had been employed less than one year. Results of a t-test indicated low-turnover-risk employees scored significantly higher than high-turnover-risk employees ($t = 3.16$; $p < .01$; see Table 15.10).

The second turnover risk classification was determined by absenteeism per quarter and length of employment. Low-risk employees ($N = 21$) had absenteeism rates in the top percentile and had been employed for more than one year. High-risk employees ($N = 29$) had absenteeism rates in the bottom percentile and had been employed less than one year. Results of a t-test indicated low-turnover-risk employees scored significantly higher than high-turnover-risk employees on the Tenure scale ($t = 2.63$; $p < .01$; see Table 15.11).

The third turnover risk classification was determined by performance appraisal scores and absenteeism per quarter. Low-risk employees ($N = 23$) had performance reviews in the top percentile and absenteeism records in the top percentile. High-risk employees ($N = 22$) had performance reviews in the bottom percentile and absenteeism rates in the bottom percentile. Results of a t-test indicated low-turnover-risk employees scored significantly higher than high-turnover-risk em-

Table 15.12
Comparison of Tenure Scale Standard Scores of High- and Low-Turnover-Risk Employees, by Performance and Absenteeism

Turnover Risk Category	N	Mean	SD	t	p
High Risk	22	38.36	13.86	5.84	< .001
Low Risk	23	59.61	10.34		

Table 15.13
Comparison of Tenure Scale Raw Scores as a Function of Sex

Group	N	M	SD	t	p
Male	53	49.13	15.94	.06	N.S.
Female	139	49.13	15.77		
Total	192	49.15	15.85		

ployees on the Tenure scale ($t = 5.84$; $p < .001$; see Table 15.12). The results establish the initial validity of the Tenure scale.

EEOC Compliance

Average differences on scale scores for males ($N = 53$) and females ($N = 139$) were compared using a t-test. Results, summarized in Table 15.13, indicated no significant differences between these two groups on the Tenure scale ($t = .06$; $p > .05$). Race differences on average scale scores were compared using analysis of variance. Results, summarized in Table 15.14, indicated no significant differences among the four race groups ($F = 2.34$; $p > .05$). These preliminary analyses indicate the Tenure scale has no adverse impact against protected groups and should comply with Equal Employment Opportunity Commission (EEOC) guidelines for fair employment practices. Additional research is warranted.

STUDY 3

Based on the results of studies 1 and 2, the Tenure scale appears to be a valid predictor of tenure and turnover risk. Study 3 was conducted to assess the impact, fairness, and potential return on investment of a preemployment psychological screening battery, including a research version of the Tenure scale, on corporate turnover rates for a major hotel chain with more than 80,000 employees worldwide.

The London House Personnel Selection Inventory (PSI) was developed to

Table 15.14
Comparison of Tenure Scale Raw Scores as a Function of Race

Group	N	M	SD	F	p
White	105	46.31	15.77	2.34	N.S.
Black	31	53.06	15.91		
Asian	11	53.06	15.25		
Hispanic	35	53.23	15.60		
Total	185	49.09	15.79		

meet the needs of human resource directors and personnel managers to whom the responsibility of screening job applicants falls. The inventories in the PSI series have been designed for use as preemployment psychological measures useful for assessing the attitudes, values, and past job-related behavior of prospective employees. Scores on the PSI Employability Index and related subscales are used to predict the extent to which applicants will be honest, productive employees; avoid the use or sale of nonprescribed drugs or alcohol on the job; be more dependable; follow company policies regarding absenteeism and tardiness; respond appropriately to supervision; be less likely to have serious, costly on-the-job accidents; have better customer relations skills; and be at low risk to turnover. The PSI series has been validated as predictors of job-related behavior using self-report measures, contrasted groups (i.e., good versus poor employees), predictive and concurrent validation strategies, and quasi-experimental designs (e.g., time-series).

Several versions of the inventory are available with scales to measure the constructs described: These scales are Honesty, Drug-Avoidance, Non-Violence, Customer Relations, Supervision Attitudes, Work Values, Emotional Stability, Safety, and Tenure. The different versions of the PSI are comprised of various combinations of these scales with selection decisions based on the Composite Employability Index. Each PSI version includes a Validity (Distortion) scale, which assesses the degree to which a respondent is answering in a socially desirable manner. In addition, each PSI version includes a Validity (Accuracy) scale, which detects rare patterns of responses that are unlikely to occur when the applicant both comprehends the inventory and answers the questions in a careful manner.

PROCEDURE

The PSI was implemented for preemployment selection in six hotel properties from May 1988 until September 1989. Only applicants who scored above normal

Figure 15.1
Average Cumulative Turnover Percentage across Hotel Unit Locations

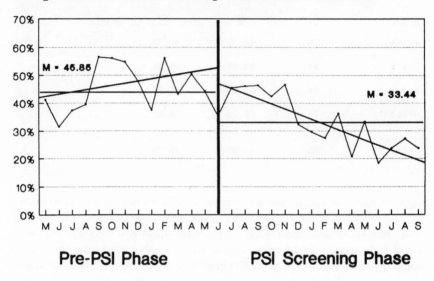

Pre-PSI Phase   **PSI Screening Phase**

recommended cutoff scores on the Employability Index were selected for employment. Over 7,100 applicants were tested during the implementation phase. The time-series design called for each property to supply periodic turnover rates for the one-year phase prior to implementation of the PSI (May 1987-May 1988) and for each reporting period following implementation of the PSI (May 1988-September 1989). This yielded 29 reporting periods (13 pretest and 16 posttest) for which turnover rates were available.

RESULTS

Statistical analyses compared the cumulative turnover percentage across all properties for the 13 pretest reporting periods to the cumulative turnover percentage across all properties for the 16 test-phase reporting periods. This analysis is presented in the time-series chart (Figure 15.1). The average cumulative turnover rate summed over all properties for each pretest period (Pre-PSI) was 45.85 percent. The average cumulative turnover rate summed over all properties for each test phase period was 33.44 percent. This represents a 27 percent reduction in turnover during the 16-month test phase as a result of implementation of the PSI.

The statistical significance of the difference between these averages was tested by means of a t-test. Results indicated that the test phase average was significantly lower than the pretest average (t [27] = 3.63; p < .001).

The analysis illustrated in Figure 15.1 also examines the trends in turnover during the pretest and test phases. The plots represent the results of linear regression analysis, showing the best-fitting line. There was an increasing trend in total turnover during the pretest phase. Although the trend was not statistically significant (r between time and turnover = .36; p > .05), it still represents a potentially problematic increasing trend. A similar regression analysis for the test phase shows a statistically significant decreasing trend in turnover (r between time and turnover = − .79; p < .001). This is a very meaningful finding: not only is there a significant difference in the level of turnover between the pretest and test phases but also implementation of the PSI has resulted in a reversal of the trend in turnover.

EEOC COMPLIANCE

A company-wide adverse impact study was completed using all 7,190 applicants to the hotel corporation completing the PSI during the course of the pilot study to ensure that the PSI is not adversely discriminating against any race or sex group. If the overall selection rate for any protected group is greater than 80 percent of the overall selection rate of the majority group (whites and males), this constitutes empirical evidence that the PSI does not have adverse impact and is a fair selection method. The results for race are summarized in Table 15.15 and those for sex in Table 15.16. In each case the selection rates for all minority groups were greater than the federally mandated four-fifths or 80 percent rate. These results indicate that the PSI complies with the EEOC Standards for Employee Selection Procedures (1978) and will facilitate fair selection practices.

RETURN ON INVESTMENT (ROI)

An ROI analysis is useful for documenting the financial impact of human resource programs. The analysis is based on the ratio between the benefits and the costs associated with the use of a particular personnel procedure. The total savings expected to result from the use of the procedure are compared to the costs required to implement the procedure. If, for example, no effective system is implemented to reduce some relevant business expense (e.g., the high costs associated with employee turnover), then the organization can anticipate significant expenditures in terms of recruiting, training, and replacing its work force with new employees. If, on the other hand, a valid procedure is used to prescreen applicants, these costs can be reduced substantially. The savings to the organization that result from the use of the procedure can be divided by the cost incurred in implementing the procedure. Then, as the name implies, the output of the ROI indicates the financial return managers can expect from their investment in the screening program.

Table 15.15
Adverse Impact Analysis for Race

Group	Sample Size	Number Passing	% Passing
Whites	2745	1765	64%
Hispanics	326	215	66%
Blacks	3381	2147	64%
Other*	159	100	63%
Unknown	579	410	71%
Totals	7190	4637	64%

* Includes Asians and American Indians

EEOC Compliance Ratios

Comparison	Ratio	Federal 4/5 Rule Met
1) Hispanics vs. Whites	.66/.64 = 1.03	Yes
2) Blacks vs. Whites	.64/.64 = 1.00	Yes
3) Other vs. Whites	.63/.64 = .98	Yes

Table 15.16
Adverse Impact Analysis for Sex

Sex Data

Group	Sample Size	Number Passing	% Passing
Males	3795	2243	59%
Females	3003	2112	70%
Unknown	392	282	72%
Totals	7190	4637	64%

EEOC Compliance Ratios

Comparison	Ratio	Federal 4/5 Rule Met
1) Females vs. Males	.70/.59 = 1.19	Yes

Table 15.17
Return on Investment Analysis: Annual Savings for Participating Hotels

Number of Employees:	5283
Baseline Annual Turnover Rate:	46%
Average Cost Per Hire:	$600
PSI Cost Per Applicant:	$6
PSI Passing Rate:	64%
Turnover Reduction:	20%

Hiring Costs

	With PSI	Without PSI
Number Screened:	2923	2430
Number Hired:	1871	2430
Hiring Cost:	$1,122,600	$1,458,000
PSI Cost:	$17,538	$0
Total Cost:	$1,140,138	$1,458,000

Return on Investment $= \dfrac{\text{Total Cost Savings}}{\text{PSI Costs}} = \dfrac{\$317,862}{\$17,538}$ 1812%

An ROI analysis was calculated as a function of the PSI's impact on reducing turnover for the hotel units that participated in the time-series study. The variables used to conduct this analysis were (1) number of employees for all units, (2) baseline annual turnover rate, (3) average cost per hiree (e.g., recruiting, training), (4) PSI cost per applicant screened, (5) PSI passing rate during the implementation phase, and (6) a 20 percent reduction in turnover.

The results of the ROI analysis (Table 15.17) revealed that the total annual savings in hiring costs due to the PSI's impact of reducing turnover by 20 percent was $317,860. This savings, divided by the PSI investment ($17,540), yielded a return of 1812 percent. That is, for every $1 investment in the PSI, the units saved an estimated $18.12 in hiring costs.

A projected return on investment for corporate-wide use of the PSI, based on 85,000 employees and an assumption of a 20 percent annual reduction of turnover, was also determined. This analysis revealed that the corporate return on investment would approximate $6.69 million annually in reduced turnover costs.

SUMMARY

The Tenure scale was constructed to be content valid. Studies 1 and 2 documented statistically significant relationships between Tenure scale scores and job-related criteria. High scorers on the Tenure scale were typically longer-tenure employees and above-average performers, with lower absenteeism rates. Low scorers were typically shorter-tenure employees and below-average performers, with higher absenteeism rates. Study 3 showed that psychological assessment programs, which incorporate the Tenure scale, can result in significant reductions in turnover when implemented for preemployment selection. Study 3 also showed that these assessment programs are fair to protected groups and capable of generating significant returns on investment.

The Tenure scale appears capable of predicting a variety of different employee withdrawal behaviors. Other researchers are starting to cross-validate these findings (e.g., Joy et al., 1989). For example, Behrens & Orban (1989) examined the relationship between Tenure scale scores and job stress using a sample of approximately 130 drugstore job applicants. He found that higher scorers on the Tenure scale (i.e., low turnover risk) reported significantly less job burnout ($r = -.65 \; p < .001$) and reliably more stress coping skills ($r = .55, p < .001$). It can be postulated that high scorers on the Tenure scale would therefore be less likely to quit a job since they are able to cope with stressful job demands. Behrens's results support the construct validity of the Tenure scale.

Nerad and Orban (1989a) administered the Tenure scale to 66 incumbent managers from a national restaurant chain. They found a statistically significant relationship between Tenure scale scores and actual job tenure ($r = .43, p < .05$). Loyal and committed managers who were employed the longest at the restaurant had attitudes that put them at low risk to quit their company. Nerad and Orban also found that Tenure scale scores correlated significantly with how interested managers were in their job ($r = .28, p < .05$) and how energized they were to complete their jobs in a prompt and consistent manner ($r = .28, p < .05$). These findings were replicated in another construct validity study (Nerad & Orban, 1989b) in which the Tenure scale was administered to a sample of 164 managers from a chain of home improvement stores. Significant results indicated that higher scorers on the Tenure scale also scored higher on a measure of job interest and motivation ($r = .17; p < .05$). These construct validity coefficients support the notion that high scorers on the Tenure scale are more committed to their jobs, as reflected in self-reports of high job interest and high enthusiasm and energy levels.

Further research is warranted with the Tenure scale. Predictive validity studies are especially needed since the Tenure scale has obvious relevance to personnel selection. Study 3 showed that the scale has no adverse impact against any sex or race groups and should therefore comply with EEOC guidelines. Standardized measures of turnover risk can conceivably provide corporations with information that will help them screen in applicants at lowest risk to quit a job prematurely.

REFERENCES

Ajzen, I., & Fishbein, M. (1972). Attitudes and normative beliefs as factors influencing behavioral intentions. *Journal of Personality and Social Psychology*, 27, 1–9.

Ajzen, I., & Fishbein, M. (1977). Attitude-behavior relations: A theoretical analysis and review of empirical research. *Psychological Bulletin*, 84, 888–918.

Behrens, G., & Orban, J. A. (1989). The prediction of retail pharmacists performance using the Pharmacist Applicant Inventory. Unpublished data.

Berte, D. L., Moretti, D. M., Jusko, R., & Leonard, J. (1981). An investigation of a combined withdrawal and counterproductive behavior decision process model. Paper presented at the Annual Conference of the American Academy of Management, San Diego.

Boughton, R. (1984). A prototype strategy for construction of personality scales. *Journal of Personality and Social Psychology* 47(6), 1334–1346.

Bureau of National Affairs (1980). *Job Absence and Turnover: 1979*. Washington, D.C.: Government Printing Office.

Cascio, W. F. (1982). *Costing human resources: The financial impact of behavior in organizations*. Boston: Kent Publishing Co.

Cotton, J. L., & Tuttle, J. A. (1986). Employee Turnover: A meta-analysis and review with implications for research. *Academy of Management Review*, 11, 55–70.

Farrell, D. (1983). Exit, voice, loyalty and neglect as responses to job dissatisfaction: A multidimensional scaling study. *Academy of Management Journal*, 26 (4), 596–607.

Fishbein, M. (1967). Attitude and the prediction of behavior. In M. Fishbein (ed.), *Readings in Attitude Theory and Measurement*. New York: Wiley.

Fortune (1981). College Grads who Leave. August, 48–50.

Hom, P., & Hulin, C. (1981). A comparative test of the prediction of reenlistment by several models. *Journal of Applied Psychology*, 66, 288–298.

Hom, P., Katerberg, R., & Hulin, C. (1979). A comparative examination of three approaches to the prediction of turnover. *Journal of Applied Psychology*, 64, 286–296.

Jones, J. W. (1980). Attitudinal correlates of employees' deviance: Theft, alcohol use, and nonprescribed drug abuse. *Psychological Reports*, 47, 71–77.

Jones, J. W. (1989). Attitude-behavior relations: A theoretical and empirical analysis of pre-employment integrity tests. Research study presented at the First Annual Convention of the American Psychological Society, Alexandria, Virginia, June.

Jones, J. W., & Terris, W. (1989). *Selection alternatives to pre-employment polygraph*. Park Ridge, IL: London House Press.

Jones, J. W., & Wuebker, L. J. (1988). Accident prevention through personnel selection. *Journal of Business and Psychology*, 3 (2), 187–198.

Joy, D. S. (1988). *Reliability and Validity of a Preemployment Honesty Test*. Manuscript submitted for publication.

Joy, D. S. (1989). Hiring: First line of defense against company crime. *Human Resources Professional* 1(2), 19–23.

Joy, D. S., & Jones, J. W. (1989). *The Human Resource Inventory: An assessment system for maximizing workforce potential*. Park Ridge, IL: London House Press.

Joy, D. S., Werner, S., & Rospenda, K. (1989). Predicting turnover risk with the Tenure scale: A replication. Manuscript.

Lee, T. W., & Mowday, R. T. (1987). Voluntarily leaving an organization: An empirical investigation of Steers and Mowday's model of turnover. *Academy of Management Journal*, 30(4), 721–743.

McDaniel, M. A., & Jones, J. W. (1988). Predicting employee theft: A quantitative review of the validity of a standardized measure of dishonesty. *Journal of Business and Psychology*, 2(4), 327–345.

McEvoy, G. M., & Cascio, W. F. (1985). Strategies for reducing employee turnover: A meta-analysis. *Journal of Applied Psychology*, 70, 242–253.

McEvoy, G. M., & Cascio, W. F. (1987). Do good or poor performers leave: A meta-analysis of the relationship between performance and turnover. *Academy of Management Journal*, 30(4), 744–762.

Mangione, T. W. (1973). Turnover: Some psychological and demographic correlations. In R. P. & T. W. Mangione (eds.), *The 1969–70 Survey of Working Conditions*. Ann Arbor: University of Michigan, Survey Research Center.

March, J. G., & Simon, H. A. (1958). *Organizations*. New York: Wiley.

Michaels, C. E., & Spector, P. E. (1982). Causes of employee turnover: A test of the Mobley, Griffith, Hand, and Meglino model. *Journal of Applied Psychology*, 67, 53–59.

Mobley, W. H. (1977). Intermediate linkages in the relationship between job satisfaction and employee turnover. *Journal of Applied Psychology*, 62, 237–240.

Mobley, W. H. (1982). *Employee turnover: Causes, consequences, and control*. Reading, MA: Addison-Wesley.

Mobley, W. H., Griffith, R. H., Hand, H. H., & Meglino, B. M. (1979). Review and conceptual analysis of the employee turnover process. *Psychological Bulletin*, 86, 493–522.

Monthly Labor Review (1988). Job tenure by occupation and age. 12, 13–16.

Moretti, D. M. (1986). The prediction of employee counter-productivity through attitude assessment. *Journal of Business and Psychology*, 1(2), 134–147.

Mowday, R. T., Porter, L. W., & Steers, R. M. (1982). *Employee-organization linkages: The psychology of commitment, absenteeism, and turnover*. New York: Academic Press.

Muchinsky, P. M., & Tuttle, M. L. (1979). Employee turnover: An empirical and methodological assessment. *Journal of Vocational Behavior*, 14, 43–77.

National Association of Convenience Stores (1988). *Annual state of the industry report*. New York: Arthur Andersen & Co. and Gerke Economics.

Nerad, A. J., & Orban, J. A. (1989a). *The prediction of restaurant manager performance using the retail management assessment inventory*. Park Ridge, IL: London House Press.

Nerad, A. J., & Orban, J. A. (1989b). *The selection of home improvement center department managers*. Park Ridge, IL: London House Press.

Porter, L. W., & Steers, R. M. (1973). Organizational, work, and personal factors in employee turnover and absenteeism. *Psychological Bulletin*, 80, 151–176.

Price, J. L. (1977). *The study of turnover*. Ames: Iowa State University Press.

Rosse, J. G. (1990). Understanding employee withdrawal from work. In J. Jones, B. Steffy, & D. Bray (eds.), *Applying Psychology in Business: The Manager's Handbook*. Lexington, MA: Lexington Books.

Steel, R., & Ovaile, N. (1984). A review and meta-analysis of research on the relationship between behavioral intentions and employee turnover. *Journal of Applied Psychology*, 69(4), 673–686.

Steers, R. M., & Mowday, R. (1981). Employee turnover and post-decision accommodation processes. In L. Cummings and B. Staw (eds.), *Research in Organizational Behavior* (Vol. 3). Greenwich, CT: JAI Press.

United States Department of Labor (1988). *Workforce 2000: Work and Workers for the 21st Century*. Washington, DC: Government Printing Office.

Wanous, J. P. (1977). Organizational entry: Newcomers moving from outside to inside. *Psychological Bulletin*, 84, 601–618.

Werner, S. H., & Jones, J. W. (1989). *Improving Corporate Profitability with Pre-employment Integrity Tests*. Unpublished manuscript. Park Ridge, IL: London House.

IV

IMPLEMENTING AN
INTEGRITY TESTING
PROGRAM

16

Incorporating an Integrity Assessment System into the Personnel Selection Process: Some Recommendations

STEVEN H. WERNER AND DENNIS S. JOY

Most companies use several selection methods when assessing the suitability of job applicants because no single screening procedure alone can perfectly determine overall employability potential and because each method has its particular benefits and limitations. Nevertheless, although a selection method is shown to have sufficient levels of reliability, validity, and utility, this does not guarantee that it will be an optimally effective screening instrument. For a selection tool to work effectively, the instrument also needs to be properly integrated into the company's overall hiring procedure. Lack of sufficient integration can cause a psychometrically sound selection device to be less than optimally effective at screening in the most desirable job applicants.

The purpose of this chapter is to provide a summary of recommendations that should be considered in order to facilitate the process of integrating an integrity testing system, like the London House Personnel Selection Inventory (PSI) (London House, 1988), into a company's total personnel selection program. It focuses on some procedures that should be followed in order to integrate the testing program successfully into the corporate policy regarding personnel selection and discusses those items that should be avoided if the program is to be integrated. In all, we strive to combine these lists of do's and don'ts into a basic prescription that will help to provide for an effective and efficient personnel selection program with the PSI as one of the major subcomponents in the process. London House psychologists are available to help companies integrate an integrity testing system into their overall hiring process.

The list of recommendations is a compilation of suggestions submitted by numerous personnel specialists and industrial psychologists, all of whom have worked with the PSI in varying capacities. Each individual is thoroughly aware of professional, legal, and ethical guidelines that are traditionally applied to psychological testing in industry.

Steps for Successful Implementation of an Integrity Inventory

1. *Make sure that the inventory fits into the system of existing selection procedures.* The inventory should become an integral part of the selection system and should not displace other procedures like application forms, interviews, or reference checks that are already in use. The inventory should add to the base of information that a company can gain about a prospective job applicant.

2. *Formulate a written policy statement on how the integrity inventory will be used in the selection process.* All inventory users and personnel administrators need to be made aware that the PSI will be part of the normal employment application procedure. Included in the policy statement should be a specification regarding the positions that require testing and documentation of the job relatedness. Finally, the company needs to document how any exceptions to inventory cutoffs or special applicant cases are to be handled. All exceptions to standard hiring procedures should comply with Equal Employment Opportunity Commission (EEOC) guidelines.

3. *Adequately train staff to administer, score, and interpret the inventory.* All procedures need to be explained and demonstrated fully and clearly to personnel and recruitment staff. The inventory should be used only for the purposes for which it is designed and specifically recommended by the test publisher. The way in which inventory scores will be used as part of the overall hiring decision needs to be explained and clarified to all inventory administrators.

4. *Inventory administrators should be instructed to avoid labeling low scorers as dishonest.* The PSI is not a pass-fail test; the scores must be considered in context with the person's total job qualifications. In addition, a standardized procedure for informing applicants of their (in)eligibility for hiring needs to be formulated. Administrators should be specifically instructed on how to inform applicants that they did not meet company standards.

5. *Familiarize users with basic statistical and testing concepts where appropriate.* Inventory developers should make an effort to explain basic statistical and testing concepts (the use of norms, reliability, validity, standard error of measurement, etc.) to individuals in a position to use such information when making assessments of the personnel screening program. The extent of the explanation of relevant measurement concepts should be at the level of detail appropriate for the intended audience.

6. *Standardize the point at which the inventory is used in the selection process.* The integrity inventory should be integrated into the overall selection procedure in a way that will make optimal use of the data that the inventory provides about an applicant. Exactly where to place the use of the inventory in the selection process is up to the individual company; however, London House professionals can make suggestions for placement of the inventory. Typically that PSI is administered after the applicant has completed both an application form and an initial screening interview. Hence,

it is part of a multiple-hurdle selection strategy. The key point, however, is to maintain consistency of administration across all applicants.

7. *Set up a system of inventory booklet and inventory results security.* The confidentiality of booklets and inventory scores must be maintained and regarded with the utmost respect.

8. *The inventory should be continually monitored for fairness and adverse impact data.* Like all other selection procedures, protected groups must not be discriminated against. In addition to monitoring for differential passing rates among protected groups, validation research should incorporate analyses to document the fairness of the integrity inventory. Sufficient sample sizes should be required for all adverse impact analyses.

9. *Inventory developers should provide timely and easily understood score reports.* Score sheets and analysis reports should describe inventory performance clearly and accurately. Test publishers should be consulted if there are any confusions.

10. *Realistic expectations about the effectiveness of the inventory should be defined and set.* Too often companies expect that all theft will stop once the inventory is in use—an unrealistic assumption. To compensate for this, staff should be trained on keeping shrinkage records and on spotting theft and potential areas at high risk for employee theft. Finally, inventory administrators need to be informed that some errors in prediction exist with all psychological tests and, for the most part, that all tests have been developed for use in the prediction of the behavior of groups. Overt integrity tests are the most valid predictors of employee theft.

11. *Set inventory cutoffs to meet the customer's staffing needs.* Inventory cutoffs need to be selected in order to maintain a reasonable acceptance rate and to control for classification errors. Inventory users need to specify, adhere to, and enforce any set of adopted cutoff scores. Finally, cutoff scores need to be adjusted in order to ensure that a company can hire ample applicants to staff the open jobs.

12. *Provide recruitment support for additional applicants.* Once the selection inventory is in use, the company should provide a mechanism with which to increase the size of the applicant pool since the use of the inventory will result in some applicant rejections. The company will have to provide additional advertising and/or recruitment efforts in order to maintain a sufficient pool of applicants. If this is not done, it is likely that the administrators will become disenchanted with the inventory since they will typically not have enough applicants to fill vacant job positions.

13. *Have knowledgeable professionals available for inventory score interpretation.* These professionals should be trained in inventory interpretation and should be able to explain the meaning, as well as the limitations, of reported scores. In addition, these individuals should be on guard for the possible misuse of inventory scores by companies. For example, purchasers of London House integrity assessment systems have access to London House professionals to aid in answering questions about the assessment procedure and results.

14. *Determine the reading grade level requirements of both the inventory and jobs for which it is intended to be used.* The inventory should be designed to be readable not only by applicants who actually take the inventory but also by the entire population of applicants who are eligible to apply for the position. The inventory developer

should ensure that the inventory is readable by the applicant who possesses only the minimum educational qualifications for a particular job.

15. *Obtain support from key decision makers in top management*. Like all other programs that affect a significant part of the total organization, it is crucial that the parties involved be informed not only of the worthiness of the integrity inventory but also of the procedures that will be followed when the testing system becomes a standard part of the selection process. It would also be useful for the inventory publisher to demonstrate periodically the increased dollar savings gained by use of tests like the PSI by conducting utility analyses or shrinkage reduction studies, for example. This would help in gaining support from upper management by demonstrating both the need for integrity testing and its beneficial effect on the organization.

16. *Keep track of the effectiveness of the program*. It is important for the test user to develop methods to document the beneficial impact of the integrity testing program. These methods would include cost-effectiveness studies and utility analyses. Finally, personnel administrators should periodically interview their staff to assess the effectiveness of the PSI program.

This list represents recommendations made by a group of professionals who have had much experience with integrity testing programs in a host of industrial settings. In general, the key to successful implementation of tests like the PSI can be found in the planning stages. Once managerial support is obtained, it is crucial that the users of the PSI (the inventory administrators and personnel department staff) become thoroughly trained on how to use the inventory correctly. Only after they understand, recognize the need for, and feel comfortable with the new procedures in the selection process will they begin to accept them.

The group of psychologists and personnel specialists also provided a list of items that should be specifically avoided throughout the personnel selection process when an integrity inventory is used. In general, integrity test developers should be on guard for and constantly control the potential misuse of the inventory. This is especially likely to occur when the inventory user is not trained in the proper administration procedures, is not consistent in the application of the testing program, or is not made aware of the limitations of the inventory. (These cautionary notes are relevant to all types of employee selection programs, not just integrity testing.)

Controlling Possible Misuse of the Integrity Inventory

1. *Do not use the inventory without discussing and developing proper guidelines for its use*. The inventory developer needs to educate clients adequately in order to ensure that they understand the characteristics, usefulness, and limitations of the inventory. London House provides written, audiovisual, on-site, and telephone support for this purpose.

2. *The use of the inventory must be consistent across inventory administrators, organizational departments, and applicants*. Any lack of consistency in the application of the integrity inventory could serve to undermine its effectiveness seriously. In fairness

to all applicants, the procedures for using the inventory must be standardized across the population for which it is intended.

3. *Do not allow uninformed and untrained staff to administer and interpret the inventory.* All inventory administrators can consult with the professional staff of the publisher for interpretive support.

4. *Do not rely exclusively on the integrity inventory as the sole piece of information to be used in the hiring decision.* The information gleaned from the PSI should be regarded as supplemental information that needs to be considered in addition to the individual's job qualifications. Companies should never become completely dependent on an integrity test and forgo the use of other screening procedures that the PSI is intended to complement (e.g., application forms, interviews, work samples).

5. *Do not indicate the inventory is perfect.* The client must be made aware that no psychological inventory is able to discriminate among the counterproductive and non-counterproductive employees 100 percent of the time. However, tests like the PSI have relatively high levels of validity and improve companies' hiring success rates substantially. Because of their higher levels of validity, integrity tests nearly always yield fewer classification errors than alternative procedures (e.g., interviews, application forms, biographical questionnaires, random selection).

6. *Do not set cutoffs and standards so high that too many people are rejected by the inventory.* Extremely stringent cutoffs may result not only in large reduction in the number of "qualified" applicants but also in general disenchantment with the inventory. Inventory administrators will be forced to screen many more applicants in order to meet their staffing needs, and screening costs may become prohibitive. This can cause users to question the effectiveness of the inventory.

7. *Inform inventory administrators not to deemphasize the importance of the inventory.* It is crucial that inventory administrators not tell applicants that they intend to hire them regardless of their PSI score. PSI results are a valuable piece of information that will contribute to the overall quality of the hiring decision.

8. *Do not overreact to applicants who may feel offended when asked to take the integrity test.* Companies have both a right and a need to protect their assets from potentially dishonest and counterproductive employees. Research shows that the majority of applicants (typically 90 percent or more) are not offended at having to take an integrity test. Moreover, research shows that the applicants who are offended are more likely to have a history of theft than the applicants who are not offended. Hence, the expression of dissatisfaction at having to take the test might be a defensive reaction and should not be overinterpreted.

These lists address the role of inventory developers and inventory users alike. Each party needs to be responsive to the needs of the other while adhering to company-specified guidelines, policies, and ethics related to personnel testing and evaluation.

There are two main areas of responsibility with which the inventory developer needs to be concerned. The primary area of responsibility for the inventory developer is that of providing a scientifically developed instrument that has been shown to be job related, constructed in accordance with professional and legal standards for psychological tests and the regulations of local and federal government, reliable, valid, and fair. A secondary area of responsibility is the instruction and training of the users of the inventory. It is imperative that inventory developers train the companies that purchase their tests in administration, the accurate use of inventory scores for selection, and ensuring confidentiality while avoiding labeling.

There are other important areas of responsibility with which the inventory user should be concerned. It is important that inventory users take the steps necessary to ensure that they understand and are comfortable with the intended purpose and indications of the inventory, the testing procedures, particular aspects of score interpretation, the role that the results are to play as part of the hiring decision, and the fit of the inventory into the overall selection process.

If all of these suggestions are taken into consideration when an integrity inventory (or any other selection device, for that matter) is incorporated into a personnel selection program, the integration process is more likely to be smooth. Obviously, the integration process is not one that can be accomplished overnight: however, it can be made easier if the basic suggestions are regarded as sound advice from those who have experienced both success and failure.

REFERENCE

London House (1988). *The Personnel Selection Inventory*. Park Ridge, IL: London House Press.

17

Protecting Job Applicants' Privacy Rights When Using Preemployment Honesty Tests

John W. Jones, Philip Ash, Catalina Soto, and William Terris

The estimates of employees who steal range from approximately 20 percent to 40 percent, depending on the industry, survey methods, and the theft criteria (cf. Hefter, 1986; Hollinger & Clark, 1983; Jones & Joy, 1989a). While researchers are still attempting to quantify both the total frequency and cost of employee theft, the existence of meaningful amounts of theft by employees is widely accepted.

Jones and Terris (1989) reviewed personnel selection programs employers can use to increase their odds of selecting applicants at lowest risk to steal. Most of the programs reviewed were used in place of preemployment polygraphs, which are now restricted in most contexts under the Employee Polygraph Protection Act of 1988. Selection programs differ on a number of dimensions, including validity and usefulness (Table 17.1).

In recent years, the potential of paper-and-pencil honesty tests on job applicants' privacy right has been explored (Lehr & Middlebrooks, 1985). Since preemployment polygraphs were often viewed as invasive (Frierson, 1988), the concern exists as to whether paper-and-pencil honesty tests are invasive too. This chapter briefly reviews the concept of the right to workplace privacy. In addition, practical steps that companies can take to ensure that their honesty testing program does not infringe upon job applicants' privacy rights are described.

Table 17.1
Preemployment Integrity Screening Methods Available to Business and Industry

Screening Method	Convenience Issues	Main Problems	Main Advantages
Honesty tests	Can easily be made part of the usual screening procedure	Company representative(s) must be trained to use test scores Not all integrity tests are thoroughly validated	More validity evidence than other selection methods Not offensive No adverse impact (meets EEOC guidelines) May discourage dishonest applicants from even applying
Selection interview	Usually part of hiring procedure	No evidence of validity with theft criteria Difficult to determine applicant's truthfulness in discussing theft and counterproductivity	Inexpensive (already part of hiring procedures) Structured interviews show more promise than traditional interviews
Reference checks	Often time-consuming	Little evidence of validity Most misconduct is undetected Company reluctant to give negative information	May increase truthfulness of applicants Verifies information provided on application form and resumes
Criminal background checks	Typically provided by vendors, yet lengthy turnaround of results occurs	Not all criminals are on record Information obtained must be job relevant	Complete and verifiable data can be obtained if available
Credit checks	Quick but somewhat costly	Relevance to theft not clear May not meet EEOC guidelines	Obtains information relevant to financial need and fiscal responsibility
Graphology	Faddish Complicated scoring procedures exist	No evidence of validity against theft or any criteria when controlling for content Difficult to standardize	None identified

THE RIGHT TO PRIVACY

There are three major sources of workplace privacy rights: common law torts, the U.S. Constitution and federal statutes, and state constitutions and laws. The main task confronting employers is to determine which privacy rights have been recognized and protected and how they apply to honesty testing in the workplace (cf. Shepard & Dutson, 1987; Decker, 1987, 1989). Common law torts serve to protect applicants against unreasonably intrusive selection programs and any adverse publicity that could place an applicant in a false light before the public. Honesty testing programs should clearly be job relevant, and procedures for ensuring the confidentiality of applicants' completed test booklets and score reports should be implemented.

Although the U.S. Constitution does not have specific language providing a right to privacy, the courts have added such a right, primarily from the First, Fourth, Fifth, Ninth, and Fourteenth amendments. For example, the Fourth Amendment offers protection against unreasonable searches and seizures. Asking job applicants to complete a professionally developed paper-and-pencil honesty test does not appear to be a ''search and seizure'' in the same way that searching a person's locker or taking a urine or blood sample for a drug test is construed as a search. The Fifth Amendment's self-incrimination clause, relating primarily to criminal cases, protects a person accused of a crime from being forced to be a witness against self. This clause is not applicable to private sector preemployment testing programs that determine worker suitability for employment.

Finally, state constitutions and laws provide additional rights and protections against intrusions into personal privacy. One state, Massachusetts, has a law prohibiting the use of any measure of honesty (O'Bannon, Goldinger, & Appleby, 1989). Companies in Massachusetts concerned about controlling employee theft must substitute tests that measure ''dependability'' for tests that clearly assess an applicant's risk for theft. Unfortunately, research to date suggests that measures of dependability do not predict theft as accurately as clear-purpose measures of honesty (Rafilson & Frost, 1989).

The remainder of this chapter describes how companies should select and use preemployment honesty tests so that they do not infringe on job applicants' privacy rights. Current or prospective users of honesty tests should consult with personnel psychologists if they are confused about any of the testing concepts and practices.

INSTRUMENT SELECTION

Four privacy issues are covered in this section. They are concerned primarily with the job relevancy and professional quality of preemployment honesty tests.

Job Relevance

Tests that measure attitudes toward job-related behaviors (e.g., attitudes toward theft) are less likely to be perceived as invasive compared to tests that ask questions about issues that are unrelated to the workplace (e.g., attitudes toward one's family). Honesty tests should be purchased primarily by organizations (e.g., retail stores, banks) that have a significant exposure to employee theft and other counterproductivity. Following are some major types of on-the-job theft and counterproductivity:

Theft of cash, merchandise, and property.

Misuse of discount privileges.

Damaging merchandise to buy it on discount.

Turnover for cause.

Using sick leave when not sick.

On-the-job illicit drug use.

Selling illicit drugs at work.

Chronic rule breaking.

Intentional damage and waste.

Vandalism.

Physical or verbal assault.

Standards for Honesty Testing

Professionally developed honesty tests should comply with the *Standards for Educational and Psychological Testing* (AERA, APA, NCME, 1985) and the *Principles for the Validation and Use of Personnel Selection Procedures* (Division of Industrial Organizational Psychology, 1980). These professional guidelines ensure that an employment test is job relevant, valid, fair to protected minorities, and effective.

The Association of Personnel Test Publishers (1990) has published a set of standards that apply directly to preemployment honesty tests: *Professional and Ethical Guidelines for Preemployment Integrity Testing Programs*. The guidelines are designed to help those in charge of selecting, administering, and basing personnel decisions on honesty tests. These guidelines can be followed to ensure that both test publishers and test users adhere to effective and ethical testing practices in test development and selection, test administration, scoring, interpretation, and accuracy, test fairness and confidentiality, and public statements and test marketing practices.

Impermissible Questions

Companies should ensure that only legally permissible questions are included in any preemployment honesty test they choose (Ash, 1987). The questions typically asked in honesty tests are job related and assess applicants' attitudes toward on-the-job theft and/or counterproductivity.

Selection Alternatives

To date, preemployment honesty tests appear to be one of the most reliable, valid, and fair assessment instruments for selecting employees at lowest risk to steal (cf. Jones & Terris, 1989). This claim is based in part on recent reviews of both published and unpublished research (e.g., McDaniel & Jones, 1988; Sackett & Harris, 1985; Sackett, Burris & Callahan, 1989). Companies should closely scrutinize the validation research for any selection procedure they intend to use.

ADMINISTRATIVE PROCEDURES

Six privacy issues are examined here that primarily deal with test administration practices and perceived offensiveness of honesty tests.

Test Administration Guidelines

Only properly trained and supervised company representatives should administer and use preemployment honesty tests. Personnel psychologists can be consulted to help establish procedures for proper test use.

Offensiveness

A number of independent research studies reveal that the vast majority of people are not offended at having to take a preemployment honesty test, nor do they feel that the test is an invasion of privacy (cf. Jones & Joy, 1989b; Ryan & Sackett, 1987). Applicants should reasonably expect that companies with theft exposures have a responsibility to establish a highly reliable work force at lowest risk to steal.

Informed Consent

Applicants should be required to sign an informed consent form acknowledging that they have carefully read the instructions and authorize the test publisher and/or employer to review and evaluate their answers and make these answers known to appropriate parties. Applicants should be informed that the preemployment honesty test is merely one part of an overall personnel selection program.

Random and Unannounced Testing

All applicants for a particular job should be required to undergo the same screening procedures. Random and inconsistent preemployment testing practices should always be avoided.

Inappropriate Search and Seizure

Paper-and-pencil honesty tests are not to be confused with any assessment procedure that involves a search-and-seizure process (e.g., urinalysis and blood testing). Honesty tests are paper-and-pencil inventories used for assessing job applicants' propensity for on-the-job theft and other counterproductivity.

Harassment of Applicants

Test administrators should be trained to administer honesty tests in a quiet and comfortable test-taking environment. All applicants should be treated with utmost respect. Only properly trained and qualified staff should administer and use the test.

ACCURACY OF RESULTS

The four privacy issues here deal with overall accuracy of the test and the impact of the testing program on theft-related losses.

Accuracy of Results

Job applicants who share information with prospective employers have a right to expect that their test answers are accurately collected, entered into a scoring service, interpreted, and scored. Honesty tests typically are computer-scored tests, ensuring a high degree of scoring accuracy (cf. Werner, 1989). Test publishers usually assume the responsibility of accurately scoring the honesty tests.

Classification Errors

The most valid honesty tests should be used so that the very lowest level of classification errors occurs. Company personnel need to be taught that some classification errors exist with any personnel selection procedure (e.g., application forms, interviews, background checks, work simulations), and therefore applicants should never be labeled as being ''dishonest'' or ''counterproductive'' if they score below standards. Martin (1989) found that classification errors for honesty tests were substantially lower than the errors estimated for the traditional employment interview, the biographical data blank, and random selection (i.e., no formal screening procedure used). All else being equal, classification errors are always lower with the most valid selection procedure, and research to date indicates that honesty tests are the most accurate predictor of employee theft potential.

Confirmation Testing

When screening for honesty, companies should be encouraged to use honesty tests as only one part of their overall personnel selection process. They can assess applicants' integrity using honesty tests, structured interviews, and reference or criminal background checks. Any discrepancies in information obtained can then be closely analyzed, and additional information can be obtained. Overreliance on honesty test results should be discouraged.

Document Impact on Losses

If a professionally developed honesty test is implemented, theft-related losses should go down or at least be lower than at a comparable location or store that does not use the tests. If a company can provide evidence that an honesty testing program is effective, challenging the business necessity of the program is difficult (cf. Werner, Joy & Jones, 1989).

CONFIDENTIALITY AND SECURITY

The three privacy issues examined are primarily related to ensuring confidentiality of applicants' scores and security of test booklets and scoring keys.

Access to Test Scores

Test booklets and test scores should always be treated as confidential information. Designated company representatives should have access to an applicant's test scores only on a need-to-know basis. The scores should never be made public. Used test booklets, answer sheets, and test reports should be secured with other sensitive personnel information.

Public Disclosure of Test Scores

Employers administering honesty tests should not share test results with any of the applicants' past employers, or with any other company where the applicants are, or will be, applying for work. An employer who divulges information about an applicant (e.g., "Mr. X failed our honesty test") to another company, for example, could be exposed to a defamation suit (libel or slander).

Test and Scoring Key Security

Companies using honesty testing programs should keep the unused test booklets and the test scoring software or templates locked up at all times to prevent applicants from unfairly having access to the test before taking it. Many honesty test publishers have a proprietary scoring key in order to ensure the security of the scoring system and to assume the professional responsibilities involved with scoring and interpreting a psychological test.

GROUPS WITH SPECIAL CONCERNS

This final section addresses the privacy issues of four special interest groups.

Negligent Hiring

Employers may be held liable for negligently hiring employees who prove to be dangerous or dishonest workers. The tort of negligent hiring addresses the risk created by exposing both members of the public and other employees to a potentially dangerous or counterproductive individual. Many companies use honesty tests to reduce their exposure to negligent hiring claims.

Disparate Impact on Minorities

Based on the Equal Employment Opportunity Commission's guidelines (1978), honesty tests have consistently shown no adverse impact against any protected minority group. Published research supports this claim (e.g., Terris & Jones, 1982; Sackett, Burris & Callahan, 1989). Companies typically conduct ongoing adverse impact studies to document the fairness of the honesty testing program to all protected minority groups.

Discharging Dishonest Employees

This is not an issue for preemployment honesty tests since they are used only with job applicants. Wrongful discharge lawsuits are not relevant with preemployment selection instruments.

Unions

Preemployment honesty tests are administered to job applicants, not to current employees. Hence, in most industries, the majority of applicants are not members of a union before hiring. Whenever appropriate, however, companies using preemployment honesty tests should seek union officials' opinions on how best to implement the testing program. Unions also want to ensure that the work force is not endangered or distressed by the hiring of dishonest or counterproductive employees.

SUMMARY

Professionally developed preemployment honesty tests do not appear to infringe on the privacy rights of job applicants. Twenty-one privacy issues were reviewed, and strategies for ensuring that honesty testing is an acceptable loss control procedure were furnished. Honesty tests are one of many loss control programs that can help companies control their theft-related losses and better avoid negligent hiring lawsuits. Honesty tests need to be job relevant, appropriately administered, valid, and fair. They should comply with all relevant legal and professional standards for psychological tests. Finally, many workplace privacy issues (e.g., inappropriate search and seizure, wrongful discharge, random and unannounced testing) are not relevant to preemployment honesty tests.

Companies should make sure they use professionally developed and validated honesty tests and not "overnight" tests that might have been developed by companies trying to capitalize on the demise of the polygraph. The paper-and-pencil honesty testing industry spans more than 40 years (Ash, 1988), and there are a number of psychological test publishers that market professionally developed, scientifically sound honesty tests. In an age where companies must control theft-related losses while avoiding privacy-related lawsuits, preemployment honesty testing programs appear to be an acceptable strategy on both fronts.

REFERENCES

American Educational Research Association, American Psychological Association, & National Council on Measurement in Education (1985). *Standards for educational and psychological testing*. Washington, DC: American Psychological Association.

Ash, P. (1987). *The legality of preemployment inquiries*. Park Ridge, IL: London House.

Ash, P. (1988). A history of honesty testing. Paper presented at the 96th Annual Convention of the American Psychological Association, Atlanta.

Association of Personnel Test Publishers (1990). *Model guidelines for preemployment integrity testing programs*. Washington, DC: APTP.

Decker, K. H. (1987). *Employee privacy law and practice*. New York: Wiley.

Decker, K. H. (1989). *Employee privacy law and practice* (1989 Supplement). New York: Wiley.

Division of Industrial-Organizational Psychology (1980). *Principles for the validation and use of personnel selection procedures*. 2d ed. Berkeley, CA: American Psychological Association.

Employee Polygraph Protection Act of 1988 (1988). Public Law 100–347.

Equal Employment Opportunity Commission (1978). Adoption of four agencies of uniform guidelines on employee selection procedures. *Federal Register*, 43, 38290–38315.

Frierson, J. G. (1988). The new federal polygraph law's impact on business. *Commerce* (Fall), 70–71.

Hefter, R. (1986). The crippling crime. *Security World*, 23, 36–38.

Hollinger, R., & Clark, J. (1983). *Theft by employees*. Lexington, MA: Lexington Books.

Jones, J. W., & Joy, D. S. (1989a). Employee deviance base rates: A summary of empirical research. Technical report. Park Ridge, IL: London House Press.

Jones, J. W., & Joy, D. S. (1989b). Empirical investigation of job applicants' reactions to taking a preemployment honesty test. Paper presented at the Annual Conference of the American Psychological Association, New Orleans.

Jones, J. W., & Terris, W. (189). After the polygraph ban: Selection alternatives to preemployment polygraph. *Recruitment Today*, May-June, 25–31.

Lehr, R. L., & Middlebrooks, D. J. (1985). Workplace privacy issues and employer screening policies. *Employee Relations Law Journal*, 11, 407–421.

McDaniel, M. A., & Jones, J. W. (1988). Predicting employee theft: A quantitative review of a standardized measure of honesty. *Journal of Business and Psychology*, 2, 327–345.

Martin, S. L. (1989). Estimating the false positive rate for alternative measures of integrity. Technical report. Park Ridge, IL: London House.

O'Bannon, R. M., Goldinger, L. A., & Appleby, G. S. (1989). *Honesty and integrity testing: A practical guide*. Atlanta: Applied Information Resources.

Rafilson, F. M., & Frost, A. G. (1989). Overt integrity tests versus personality-based measures of delinquency: An empirical comparison. *Journal of Business and Psychology*, 3(3), 269–277.

Ryan, A. M., & Sackett, P. R. (1987). Preemployment honesty testing: Fakability, reactions of test takers, and company image. *Journal of Business and Psychology*, 1, 248–256.

Sackett, P. R. & Harris, M. E. (1985). Honesty testing for personnel selection: A review and critique. In H. John Bernardin and David A. Bownas, eds., *Personality Assessment in Organizations*. New York: NY: Praeger.

Sackett, P. R., Burris, L. R. & Callahan, C. (1989). Integrity testing for personnel selection: An update. *Personnel Psychology*, 41, 421–429.

Shepard, I. M., & Dutson, R. L. (1987). *Workplace privacy: Employee testing, surveillance, wrongful discharge, and other areas of vulnerability*. Washington, D.C.: Bureau of National Affairs.

Terris, W., & Jones, J. W. (1982). Psychological factors related to employee theft in the convenience store industry. *Psychological Reports*, 51, 1219–1238.

Werner, S. (1989). *Reliability of the London House, Inc., Immediate Test Analysis by Computer (ITAC) Data Entry System*. Technical Report. Park Ridge, IL: London House Press.

Werner, S., Joy, D. J., & Jones, J. W. (1989). *Improving corporate profitability with preemployment integrity tests*. Technical Report. Park Ridge, IL: London House, Inc.

18

Model Guidelines for Preemployment Integrity Testing: An Overview

JOHN W. JONES, DAVID ARNOLD, AND WILLIAM G. HARRIS

Companies use preemployment integrity tests to screen out potentially theft-prone job applicants, while selecting in the most dependable and productive applicants. Several recent independent reviews of paper-and-pencil integrity tests by personnel psychologists (O'Bannon, Goldinger & Appleby, 1989; Sackett, Burris & Callahan, 1989) indicate that professionally developed integrity tests are job relevant, yield useful levels of validity, and are fair to protected minority groups.

To ensure proper use of integrity testing programs, the Association of Personnel Test Publishers (APTP) published the *Model Guidelines for Preemployment Integrity Testing Programs* (APTP, 1990), developed by some of the leading experts in the field of psychological testing and personnel law. Industrial psychologists, lawyers, and human resource professionals contributed to these guidelines, along with representatives from psychological test publishers, test user groups, and leading universities. Over 90 percent of the 20-person APTP task force on integrity testing practices are also members of the American Psychological Association.

The *Model Guidelines* are to be used in conjunction with other legal and professional standards governing employment testing in American businesses.

Companies may request a copy of the Association of Personnel Test Publisher's *Model Guidelines for Preemployment Integrity Testing Programs* by writing *Model Guidelines*, APTP, 655 Fifteenth Street, N.W., Suite 320, Washington, D.C. 20005

For example, the guidelines are to be used as a companion document to both the *Standards for Educational and Psychological Testing* (AERA, APA & NCME, 1985) and the *Principles for the Validation and Use of Personnel Selection Procedures* (SIOP, 1987). The guidelines are also consistent with the 1978 Equal Employment Opportunity Commission's *Uniform Guidelines on Employee Selection Procedures*.

The focus of the *Model Guidelines* is on the mutual responsibilities of both integrity test publishers and their clients in the appropriate use of these tests. Publishers develop and market preemployment integrity tests, as well as establish procedures for implementing a particular personnel selection program. Users select and administer integrity tests and make personnel decisions on the basis of test scores. Test users might also commission test development services, like predictive validation studies. Both publishers and users play a vital role in ensuring the quality and fairness of preemployment integrity testing practices. While the guidelines are specifically designed to govern integrity test use, many of its recommendations can profitably be applied to any selection technique in order to ensure fair and accurate applicant screening.

THE *MODEL GUIDELINES*: AN OVERVIEW

In developing the *Model Guidelines*, the APTP addressed five major issues: (1) test development and selection; (2) test administration; (3) scoring, interpretation, and accuracy; (4) test fairness and confidentiality; and (5) public statements and test marketing practices. Throughout, the format presents the responsibilities of both test publishers and test users.

Test Development and Selection

Test publishers should provide accurate information to guide test users in selecting the appropriate test. They should provide a specimen test, directions, answer sheets, manuals, administration guides, sample score reports, and procedures for proper test use.

Test publishers should describe what the test purports to measure, the test populations (e.g., bank tellers, accountants, retail clerks, managers) for which the test is appropriate, and scientific evidence documenting that the test is valid for its intended purpose. Types of scientific evidence typically include technical reports and journal publications that accurately represent research on the test's reliability, validity, fairness, and expected return on investments.

Test publishers should inform test users that no employment test is a perfect predictor of any on-the-job behavior. In fact, they should inform users of the strengths and limitations of all assessment procedures available to select honest and dependable employees, including integrity tests, interviews, reference checks, credit checks, criminal background checks, and application forms.

Test users also have some overlapping and distinct responsibilities in test development and selection. They must document the business necessity of the integrity testing program and identify the population of job applicants to be tested. In addition, they should select a test that has been normed and validated on a group of comparable job applicants.

Test users should strive to select and implement an integrity testing program that is professionally developed and validated and meets all state and federal guidelines. This means that test users must read and critically evaluate all support materials provided by test publishers, including test specimens, validation studies, and legal analyses. Users should avoid using integrity tests for which incomplete information is provided. A list of relevant support materials that should be available from reputable integrity test publishers follows:

Test booklet

Description of test scales

Description of norms

Scoring procedures

Administration guide

Reading level documentation

Sample test reports

Validation studies

Examiner's manual

Test reviews

Adverse impact studies

Legal analyses

Test user training program

Ongoing professional support services

Test publisher's staff credentials

References

Test Administration

Test publishers should provide the levels of training, support, and supervision required to ensure that clients are properly qualified. Training should include a description of the test scales, the relationship of test scores to job performance, restrictions on how test data are to be used, how to give feedback to applicants, and how to maintain confidentiality of scores and answers.

Publishers should train users on how to administer integrity tests and how to use the publisher's scoring services properly. They should provide a standard set of instructions for administering the test, along with information on the test's reading level.

Test users should establish, implement, and enforce a policy on the proper use of the testing program. Only trained, qualified, and supervised staff should administer integrity tests, receive test results, and use these results to make personnel decisions. Integrity tests should be used only for the purposes for which they were designed, developed, and validated. A training checklist for test users is summarized below.

Importance of consistency in integrity testing process

Need to ensure confidentiality of test results

What the integrity test measures

How test results are used in overall selection process

Understanding of test manual and/or administration guide

Importance of quiet, well-lighted, and comfortable testing environments

What to say and not say to job applicants

How to avoid labeling job applicants

How to encourage candor and thoroughness by applicants

How to answer applicant questions

Proper use of scoring service, including accurate transmission of test responses

Importance of scoring accuracy

Where to go with questions and for supervision

How to use test scores properly and consistently

How to provide feedback to applicants

How to detect language and/or reading problems

How to establish a facilitative testing climate

Record-keeping and test retention and security practices

Procedure for retesting applicants

Test users should inform applicants that the test is only one part of the overall selection process. Applicants should be presented with a standard set of test instructions. When appropriate, applicants should sign an informed consent agreement acknowledging that they have carefully read the instructions, authorize the employer and/or test publisher to review and evaluate their answers, and disseminate these answers to appropriate employer representatives on a need-to-know basis.

Test users should never minimize the importance and sensitivity of the integrity testing program or coach applicants on how to answer a test to achieve a desired score. Most important, users should avoid labeling low scorers as dishonest, undependable, or irresponsible. Instead, users should standardize a procedure for informing applicants of their results on specific components of the overall screening process, such as their results on the integrity test.

Scoring, Interpretation, and Accuracy

Test publishers should have professional staff (e.g., psychologists, personnel specialists) available to help test users with the scoring of tests and interpretation of their results. Publishers should ensure accurate scoring, train test users to interpret scores accurately, and provide them with relevant norm groups. Most important, publishers should warn clients to avoid using integrity tests in ways not supported by validation research.

Publishers should help test users integrate the test into the company's entire selection program. Users should be encouraged not to replace other useful selection procedures with the integrity test but instead to add the test to the overall selection battery as an additional source of job-relevant information.

Test publishers should assist users in establishing cut scores and selection rules that minimize classification errors, maximize fairness to protected groups, and meet the company's staffing requirements. This allows companies to establish a dependable work force even in tight labor markets (research exists that warns companies against lowering or dropping their hiring standards in an attempt to cope with labor shortages [Jones & Orban, 1990]).

Test users should refrain from using integrity tests for any purposes not specifically recommended by the test publisher and avoid using tests that are based on clearly inappropriate norm groups. Users should request a local validation study from the test publisher or a consultant if insufficient or inappropriate evidence of validity exists.

Test users should not replace other useful selection procedures with an integrity test but should instead use test information in conjunction with other relevant screening results. Users should ensure that job applicants correctly mark their answers and that they respond to all questions. Finally, users should ensure that applicants' responses are accurately transmitted to, and received from, the scoring service provided by the test publisher.

Test Fairness and Confidentiality

Test publishers should develop and market selection tests that are fair to all protected minority groups, including but not limited to racial minorities, women, and people 40 or older. Publishers should provide actual research studies that document the level of fairness.

Tests and related material should avoid content or language that may disparage protected groups. In general, publishers should avoid test items that are overly invasive or offensive. Publishers should offer foreign-language test versions to organizations that screen job applicants whose primary language is not English.

Test publishers should require that test users have an established procedure for ensuring the confidentiality of all test data, including, for example, an applicant's answers to individual items and an applicant's test scores. Integrity test scores should never be released to unauthorized individuals. They should be released only to appropriate company representatives on a need-to-know basis.

Test users should select integrity tests that are fair to protected minority groups. Records should be maintained so that adverse impact analyses can be conducted when necessary. Ideally, testing programs should be continually monitored for fairness.

Test users should provide guidelines on all matters related to test security. Users should never share test scores or data with inappropriate parties, including the organization currently employing the applicant, organizations where the applicant might be applying for work, and general business databases. Users should establish a secure system of inventory control for both used and unused test materials and should secure all scoring system material (e.g., scoring templates and software disks). Finally, both test publishers and test users should ensure the confidentiality of an applicant's completed test booklet, answer sheet, and test report.

Public Statements and Test Marketing Practices

Test publishers should strive to maintain the highest standards of ethical test marketing practices in the creation and dissemination of advertisements in the professional, commercial, and lay press; the preparation and distribution of marketing brochures; the presentation of test products at trade shows, conferences, and other public forums; and direct sales approaches to prospects and clients. For example, in mass media advertising and direct marketing efforts to publicize the availability of integrity tests, publishers should give a clear statement of the test's purpose and a clear description of the strengths and limitations of the testing instrument. Test publishers should ensure that their sales and marketing representatives promote the integrity test(s) fairly and accurately, avoiding misrepresentation, exaggeration, sensationalism, and superficiality.

Publishers' public statements should be based on clear and accurate use of technical terms, including but not limited to correlation, reliability, validity, freedom from adverse impact, and utility. All public statements about a test's technical properties should be based on actual research. Test publishers should refrain from using "satisfied customer" testimonials as a replacement for research that documents a test's reliability, validity, impact on losses, fairness, and return on investment. Finally, test publishers should accurately and without exaggeration present the qualifications of professionals participating in the publisher's research and development program.

Test users should carefully read and listen to all sales, marketing, and other promotional material. When in doubt or skeptical about claims made by sales representatives, users should consult with an independent professional psychologist and attorney, preferably those specializing in psychometrics, personnel selection practices, and employment law. Reputable test publishers will frankly admit the limitations of their instruments.

Finally, test users should recognize the inherent limitations of predicting human behavior. Classification errors, in which a few good applicants are rejected and a few bad applicants are accepted, are an unfortunate but inevitable part of all personnel decision-making systems. Test users should avoid evaluating a selection instrument against an absolute standard of perfection or perfect accuracy. Instead, they should compare the cost, potential error rate, and expected return on investment of the test against the cost, potential error rate, and expected return on investment of alternative screening approaches or against the use of no formal selection approaches.

SUMMARY

The *Model Guidelines* are designed to benefit test publishers, user companies, and job applicants. They should be used in conjunction with other legal and professional guidelines on the proper use of personnel selection tests. A personnel selection program designed to control employee theft should ideally be used in conjunction with other loss control programs, such as training sessions to teach current employees how to exhibit the highest level of integrity while coping with various workplace pressures (e.g., peer pressure to steal) and temptations (e.g., unsupervised access to cash and valuable merchandise). American companies need to control employee theft and related counterproductivity and should benefit from using the *Model Guidelines* to help them select and use preemployment integrity tests.

REFERENCES

American Educational Research Association, American Psychological Association, & National Council on Measurement in Education (1985). *Standards for educational and psychological testing*. Washington, DC: American Psychological Association.

Association of Personnel Test Publishers (APTP) (1990). *Model guidelines for preemployment integrity testing programs*. Washington, DC: APTP.

Equal Employment Opportunity Commission, Civil Service Commission, Department of Labor, & Department of Justice (1978). Adoption of four agencies of uniform guidelines on professional selection procedures. *Federal Register*, 3(166), 38290–38313.

Jones, J. W., & Orban, J. A. (1990). Personnel testing in service stations and convenience stores. Paper presented at the 1990 Petroleum Marketing Education Foundation Conference, Vail, Colorado.

Jones, J. W., & Terris, W. (1989). Selection alternatives to preemployment polygraph. *Recruitment Today*, May-June, 24–31.

O'Bannon, R. M., Goldinger, L. A., & Appleby, G. S. (1989). *Honesty and integrity testing: A practical guide*. Atlanta: Applied Information Resources.

Sackett, P. R., Burris, L. R., & Callahan, C. (1989). Integrity testing for personnel selection: An update. *Personnel Psychology*, 42, 491–529.

Society for Industrial and Organizational Psychology, Inc., American Psychological Association (1987). *Principles for the validation and use of personnel selection procedures*. 3d ed. College Park, MD: Author.

Author Index

Subject Index